THE EVERYTHING®
GUIDE TO
WORKING WITH
ANIMALS

Dear Reader,

One of the best compliments I ever received was from a friend who said, "If there is such as thing as reincarnation, I would want to come back as one of your cats." I do treat my animals well, and I get so much love in return. Those of you who have similar connections with animals understand.

The people I interviewed for this book have a genuine love of animals—big and small, feathered and furry. As varied as their professional choices range—from animal trainer to zoologist—they all share a deep concern for the welfare of animals.

They also like the fact that each day can be unpredictable. Animals have different temperaments—just like people. So, work can be filled with fun surprises and lots of challenges too.

Whether you are interested in a career on a movie set supervising the humane treatment of the animal actors, working as a veterinarian in private practice, or training puppies to be on their best behavior, the opportunities are broad. In fact, as we continue to dote on our pets and care about the treatment of all animals and our environment, the variety of careers in the field of working with animals continues to grow.

Michele C. Hollow

THE

EVERYTHING®
Series

These handy, accessible books give you all you need to tackle a difficult project, gain a new hobby, or even brush up on something you learned back in school but have since forgotten. You can choose to read from cover to cover or just pick out information from our four useful boxes.

 Alerts: Urgent warnings

 Essentials: Quick handy tips

 Facts: Important snippets of information

 Questions: Answers to common questions

When you're done reading, you can finally say you know **EVERYTHING**®!

PUBLISHER Karen Cooper

DIRECTOR OF ACQUISITIONS AND INNOVATION Paula Munier

MANAGING EDITOR, EVERYTHING SERIES Lisa Laing

COPY CHIEF Casey Ebert

ACQUISITIONS EDITOR Lisa Laing

DEVELOPMENT EDITOR Brett Palana-Shanahan

EDITORIAL ASSISTANT Hillary Thompson

THE
EVERYTHING®
GUIDE TO
WORKING WITH
ANIMALS

From dog groomer to wildlife rescuer—
tons of great jobs for animal lovers

Michele C. Hollow and William P. Rives, VMD

Avon, Massachusetts

Dedication
To my family for their support and love, and to all
of you who truly care about animals.

An Everything® Series Book.
Everything® and everything.com® are registered
trademarks of F+W Media, Inc.

Published by Adams Media, a division of F+W Media, Inc.
57 Littlefield Street, Avon, MA 02322 U.S.A.
www.adamsmedia.com

ISBN 10: 1-59869-786-2
ISBN 13: 978-1-59869-786-5

Printed in Canada.

J   I   H   G   F   E   D   C   B   A

Library of Congress Cataloging-in-Publication Data
is available from the publisher.

This publication is designed to provide accurate and authoritative information with regard to the subject matter covered. It is sold with the understanding that the publisher is not engaged in rendering legal, accounting, or other professional advice. If legal advice or other expert assistance is required, the services of a competent professional person should be sought.
　　　—From a *Declaration of Principles* jointly adopted by a Committee of the American Bar Association and a Committee of Publishers and Associations

Many of the designations used by manufacturers and sellers to distinguish their products are claimed as trademarks. Where those designations appear in this book and Adams Media was aware of a trademark claim, the designations have been printed with initial capital letters.

This book is available at quantity discounts for bulk purchases.
For information, please call 1-800-289-0963.

Contents

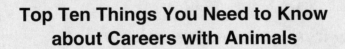

Top Ten Things You Need to Know about Careers with Animals

1. People who work with animals must be compassionate.
2. Working with animals requires good people skills.
3. Career opportunities with animals continue to grow and expand, even during hard economic times.
4. Switching from the corporate world to a career with animals is not unusual.
5. The majority of careers require continuing education courses.
6. While opportunities abound throughout the country, animal care workers are sharply needed in rural areas.
7. Many careers with animals have similar requirements and can lead to other jobs in the field.
8. While the animal care industry continues to grow, more women enter the profession than men.
9. Animal care workers can earn a comfortable living.
10. The emotional rewards are rich.

Introduction

It is impossible to say who the first veterinarian was because the profession goes as far back as Roman times and possibly further back than that. The word "veterinarian" was not in use. Instead, people who treated animals were called "horse doctors" or "animal doctors." Doctors who cared for humans would often care for sick or injured animals.

Often these were working animals that lived on farms or served in the military. These working animals were used for food, protection, and transportation. The doctors who cared for these animals had basic skills. Much like human medicine, caring for animals involved more guessing than science. Animal disease, like human illness, was surrounded by mystery and superstition.

One of the first veterinary schools opened in Lyon, France, in 1762. The profession changed dramatically at that time, and today it continues to morph and grow. The transformation of the industry is due to our love of animals. According to a survey from the American Pet Products Association, there are 73 million owned dogs and 90 million owned cats in the United States. Dog and cat owners spend an average of $200 on veterinary visits annually.

People also own birds, rabbits, ferrets, guinea pigs, hamsters, gerbils, fish, turtles, snakes, lizards, and other reptiles. It doesn't seem to matter what type of animal you own. One thing for certain is that people love and care deeply about their animals. Often animals are treated as members of the family. With that, the pet industry has seen so many new professional opportunities arise. Just five years ago, doggie daycare centers didn't exist. If you inquired about boarding your pet in a pet hotel, you probably got a roll of the eyes or a blank stare. Today, these industries are a growing business.

Animal actors have been around since the beginning of the movies. However, today there is an entire industry devoted to making sure that animal actors are treated fairly and safely on movie sets.

CSI (crime scene investigation) units now are available to study animal abuse. Take the Michael Vick dog fighting case. Crime scene investigators looked at evidence to see how the dogs in this case were abused. Units such as this one didn't exist a handful of years ago. Today, they are part of a growing industry.

As our love of animals grows, career opportunities expand. That is why the industry changes so often. New technologies and branches in veterinary medicine, new positions at zoos, our interest in the environment, and more services for our pets have fueled the expansion of the animal care industry.

Several studies have shown the positive effects that pets have on the mental and physical health of humans. In turn, people want to work with animals. The benefits are enormous, and there really is no typical day. The surprises that come from working closely with animals attract many people to the industry and its varied careers.

The people interviewed in this book share personal stories about why they chose to work with animals, and how each day is different. They talk about the challenges of the job and how they got into their chosen professions. Some were bankers and corporate executives who wanted to change careers. Others always knew that they wanted to work with animals. They took a direct path, starting by volunteering at their local veterinarian's office or zoo after junior high or high school, studied hard in school, went to the appropriate universities, and got their degrees. Career paths vary depending on the position.

Positions range from entry to executive level. Some people work with large animals; others with dogs and cats. Training, schooling, and temperament also vary from job to job. Some positions require high school diplomas; other jobs require several years of education. Careers are available in every state and at various income levels. This is not a one-size-fits-all field. It is, however, a field with lots of benefits and many growth opportunities.

CHAPTER 1

Do You Have What It Takes to Work with Animals?

Being passionate about animals certainly is the major requirement for working with them. However, a flexible attitude and good sense of humor also are mandatory. Animals, just like humans, have good days and bad. Being able to laugh at a situation, solve problems, and handle a lot of responsibility are essential attributes that you must have if you want to work with animals. A background in basic psychology is also helpful. When working with animals and people, it is important to understand different behaviors.

Do You Have the Right Temperament?

The majority of people who work with animals—in all capacities—share one thing in common: they all are passionate about animals. "We don't go into this profession for the money," says Kimberly May, DVM, MS, DACVS (Diplomate of American College of Veterinary Surgeons), and assistant director of the Communications Division of the American Veterinary Medical Association. "While the financial rewards can be high, the work itself is rewarding. Healing an animal just makes you feel so good. We get a different kind of positive feedback. The animals don't tell us in words, but seeing how much better they are is an overwhelmingly good feeling. Pet owners are the ones who express their joy when they see that we are helping their pets. People consider their pets a part of the family. They dote on their pets."

Helping animals can be a definite high. It can also be sad when an animal dies. "It is important to not take work home with you," says Dr. May. "It's hard not to when emotions are involved. You do think about your patients and their owners. This is a caring profession. However, we don't usually bring work home with us, like others do in the corporate world. We can think about our patients. We can also put in long hours. It depends on the job. Some people have flexible schedules. Overall, the positives in this business outweigh the negatives."

 Fact

According to the American Veterinary Medical Association, more women than men are entering veterinary schools. In the 1960s women made up 5 percent of the student body. Today, 79 percent of the students at the nation's twenty-eight veterinary schools are female. At some schools, such as Tufts, the ratio is even higher. Last year women composed 89 percent of the first-year class at Tufts.

"One sure thing is that people who go into this business must be adaptable to change," Dr. May says. "It takes a lot of creativity and flexibility too. You must be a well-rounded person with good business sense too."

People don't always think about the business side of working with animals. "It's an important element that shouldn't be overlooked," says Dr. May. "Many people who work with animals go into private practice, and they should know how to set up and run an office. If you run a small practice, you will have many jobs—from bookkeeper to publicist to animal worker. You will most likely hire a staff, and you need good business sense to know how to hire and train the people who work for you."

Bedside Manner

It's a major misconception that working with animals means having no contact with people. In fact, you will need top-notch people skills. Medical doctors can sometimes be brusque. Veterinarians, zookeepers, animal trainers, pet groomers, dog show judges, and animal welfare workers work with people. Even researchers work with other scientists. So the bottom line is that you need to be able to work with people. Whether it's asking the pet owner about the behavior of his golden retriever, supervising an obedience training session in a client's home, or working to change animal welfare laws to improve the lives of animal actors, people are always involved. "This is a people profession," says Jim Burwell, a dog trainer and owner of Petiquette, a dog-training franchise based out of Houston, Texas. Nicknamed "Houston's dog whisperer," Burwell explains, "I spend a lot of time with people, often in their homes. You have to know how to deal with people as a dog trainer. I don't only observe the dog, I observe the family. Some of the issues the dog has can stem from its environment. It's a total package."

E *ssential*

Many of the national associations can assist you with the business side of running an office, hiring workers, and publicizing your business. If you join a professional association, you can take advantage of the many workshops that teach business-building skills.

"The dog you are training is a key member of the family," he adds. "These people invested time and money on their dog. You go to people's homes and see photos of their children and their pets. You know how important this animal is to them. That's why a good bedside manner is needed in this business."

Dealing with Pet Owners

Pet owners can be very emotional when dealing with their pets. They want trainers, veterinarians, and others who care for their pets to be reliable, good at what they do, and to be caring. "I remember when my twenty-year-old cat got ill," says Rachel Cohn. "I called my vet, who happened to be in his office on a Saturday evening. He told me to bring her right over. He gave me some medication for her, but told me that I needed to make a decision about putting her down. She lived a long and good life.

 Fact

According to an article in *Pet Product News*, dog training is the fastest-growing segment of the pet industry. It grew 10.5 percent annually between 2001 and 2005, from $595 million to $887 million in gross revenue. This includes dog training franchises in addition to the lone dog trainer. With an increase in dog ownership, services in the pet industry are expected to grow 6.8 percent over the next five years.

"He told me to take my cat home and to think about it overnight. He would be in his office on Sunday, and he would euthanize her. That night she made the decision for us. She died in my arms. I brought her to my vet the next morning and he made arrangements to have her body cremated. He was so caring."

A year later, Cohn got another cat, which she takes to the same vet for annual checkups. "I wouldn't think of going to another veterinarian," she says. "He was there for me when I needed him. It's amazing that we often get abrupt service from our personal physicians, and we don't complain. However, when it comes to our pets, we expect veterinarians, the assistants, technicians, and office workers in the vet's office to be caring and nice. Medical schools are implementing good bedside manner courses for doctors. Veterinarians and others who work with animals usually have great people skills. I think that is why they go into this profession—because they are nurturing individuals."

Loyalty, emotions, and the bonds of friendship are part of the patient/animal worker relationship. "Pet owners can easily get emotional," says Dr. May. "The bonds we form with our pets are tight, and that is a good thing. It's important that we are kind and caring when we deal with pet owners."

Susan Briggs, owner of Urban Tails, a pet daycare and overnight hotel in Houston, Texas, agrees. "When pet owners drop off their pets, they want to make sure that their pets are well treated. Actually, before they bring in their dogs or cats, they come in first to check out the place. They want to make sure that their dog or cat is not confined in a small cage all day long. Thankfully, that is a thing of the past. We have luxury suites here with daybeds and televisions. We also have open spaces in our fenced-in yard for doggie runs.

"The clients are a big part of the business, and my staff knows that they must have strong people skills. They trust us and we must prove that we are caring and responsible. While we have their pets' best interests in mind, we also have to be able to talk to and communicate with the pet owners; otherwise, we would be out of business."

Combining Caring with Science

It's a blessing when you have found your calling and know exactly what you want to do. It's even more exciting when you get the opportunity to practice your craft day in and day out. Most people who go into this field knew at a very young age that they wanted to work with animals. They started out with a passion for animals, and that passion grew as they learned more about animals. For the majority of people in this industry, the science of it has become equally as important as the concern for animals. Combing science with care makes perfect sense.

Animal caretakers often possess certain personality traits. They must be adaptable to different situations. They must be friendly and patient, and have a good sense of humor. Being able to laugh at certain situations not only makes the job more fun, it lessens the stress that can sometimes come with the job.

There also is a lot of excitement in this field. It's thrilling to be on the cutting edge of research or to connect with an animal. "Scientific discoveries are being made all the time, and finding ways to use the new techniques will provide an opportunity for someone," says Ronda Hamm, an entomology student at Cornell University. "For example, you can learn a lot about an animal based on genetics. It might be something in the genetics that can be used to help a species or eliminate a problem they face. Think about using genetic resistance to a disease that might be driving populations to extinction."

 Fact

A large number of animal-related careers require a broad knowledge of animal science, but more important, you must also possess empathy. Caring about the animals you work with, the pet owners, and employers is part of the job. People in this profession must also be excellent listeners. In many cases, you will be working with people (pet owners) who want to share their concerns and observations. Being a good listener and a good communicator are essential traits in this field.

Solving problems by using scientific methods is all about caring. Entomologists and other animal scientists like finding solutions to troubling mysteries. The bottom line for people in this field is to help animals and people.

A Typical Day

What most animal care workers love about their jobs is that there is no such thing as a typical day. Animals are a lot like small children. We can interact with them, but communicating clearly takes a bit of work. Animals, like people, can have good moods and bad moods. They can be caring and mischievous. "Each animal has a different personality," says Dr. Mary Burch, a certified animal behaviorist who holds the title of Canine Good Citizen Director at the American Kennel Club. "Even different breeds of dogs exhibit different behaviors. When you are training a dog or judging, you know that each dog is different. You have to approach the dogs differently. For instance, when handling a Chinese Shar-Pei, they don't like it when you reach down and approach them from above the head because they can't see. You have to learn all the nuances of each breed."

Even for Susan Smith, who doesn't work directly with animals, each day is different. She handles public relations and development (grant writing) for the Palisades Park Conservancy. Her office is located in Bear Mountain, a state park in New York. "I write grants and press information alerting the media about upcoming events such as nature talks and environmental issues," she says. "I have a lot of contact with the park rangers and animal care experts."

She recently promoted a talk on raptors and another one on reptiles, including an albino Burmese python. While her job isn't hands-on with animals, she does come into contact with them. "What's great about this job is that I love interacting with the people who bring awareness about animals to the public," she says. "Also, the scenery here (in the woods) is breathtaking. If I'm having a bad day, all I have to do is take a walk.

"Everyone here cares about animals and the environment," she continues. "The issues and programs we promote constantly evolve, and that makes this a very interesting job."

Jim Burwell used to have a lot of typical days. As a former bank executive, he remembers arriving at work at 7 A.M. and leaving after-hours. "It wasn't exciting, and the days were predictable," he says.

His life changed when he attended an auction for a local charity several years ago. He bid on and won a golden retriever named Charlie. "Charlie was an unruly puppy," he says. "He was so hard to control. I decided that if I wanted to keep him that I would have to take him to an animal obedience trainer. I was amazed at the outcome."

E ssential

According to the Centers for Disease Control, owning a pet is beneficial to your health. Pets can lower your blood pressure and cholesterol levels. They also decrease feelings of loneliness and isolation. Dog owners have better overall physical health due to walking their dogs and exercising with them.

He was so pleased with the training that he decided to go into the profession. "What I have found is that each day is truly different from the next," he says. "It's liberating. I make my own hours, and thanks to the different personalities of the dogs and the pet owners, I get to interact with a wide range of pets and people. When I started, I did work a lot of nights and weekends. However, it's different today. We have a lot of stay-at-home moms, and others who work at home offices. So, I work during the day. My schedule is very flexible. I feel like I got my life back. It's nice being in control of your schedule. And more importantly, it's nice being surprised by your clients and the personalities of the dogs I interact with. Those surprises—seeing people change their behaviors to work with their dogs, and seeing the dogs' behaviors change for the better makes each day fun."

Talking to Animals

The fictional character Dr. Doolittle talked to the animals. What a world it would be if everyone could communicate in the same manner as Dr. Doolittle. Animal workers actually do. Well, they don't speak horse, snake, or chimpanzee, but they do understand body language, moods, and mannerisms. All animal care workers have an ability to "talk" to the animals. It's a skill that can be innate or learned.

"When you work with different breeds of dogs," says Susan Briggs, "you get a better understanding of the breeds." "For instance, Border collies are working dogs. Most of the bloodlines were bred for their herding abilities. [In New Zealand and Australia, they are used to herd sheep.] They need space to run. Golden retrievers are social dogs; they need to be around people and other dogs. Golden retrievers like to play wrestle. Yorkshire terriers, on the other hand, don't like rough play like a golden retriever. We can't put a Yorkshire terrier together with a large dog like a golden retriever in our doggie daycare center.

"When you work with animals, you get to know the breed," says Briggs. "Those mannerisms tell a lot. You can read about and study different animals, and if you are going to work in this profession, you need to. However, you can also learn a lot on the job."

American Kennel Club judges actually study one breed at a time. They specialize in a handful of breeds. "Since so many dogs are different, we focus on one breed at a time in order to better communicate with them," says Dr. Burch.

 **Question**

How many jobs are available for dogs?
The jobs are too numerous to count. Dogs work as assistance dogs, guard dogs, herding dogs, and animal actors. The jobs for dogs and the people who work with them are quite broad.

Understanding biology and science also factors into reading what an animal is trying to tell us. Veterinarians, zookeepers, and even pet owners know when an animal isn't feeling well. "Science comes into play a lot when trying to figure out why an animal isn't feeling well," says Dr. May.

Before taking a position with the American Veterinary Medical Association, Dr. May worked as a board-certified equine/large animal surgeon. "You could easily tell if an animal wasn't feeling well," she says. "By understanding veterinary medicine and horses, in my case, I knew what was wrong. It's a lot of science and you also use your intuition too." That's how it is possible to talk to animals.

Furry or Feathered, Large or Small

Most animal care workers go into the profession thinking they are going to work with cats and dogs. "For me it was horses," says Dr. May. "I always knew that I would work with horses. I grew up around them, and have a deep love of horses. I made my choice based on what I was familiar with, which is what most of us do."

 Fact

> The American Humane Association (also simply called American Humane) has sent animal welfare workers onto the sets of movies, commercials, and television series to make sure that animal actors are safe while portraying heroes, bad guys, and companions. The American Humane Association's Film & Television Unit works under the direction of the Screen Actors Guild.

Dog trainers often take an obedience class with their dog and become hooked. That's what happened to Jim Burwell. "I imagined what it would be like to take my dog to work with me," he says. "I also thought in this profession, I could be around dogs all day."

Kenneth Gold, PhD, an animal welfare specialist, chose to work with primates. "My sister says it's because I grew up reading 'Curious George' books," he laughs. He studied psychology, biology, and zoology, and worked at zoos in the United States and abroad. His background and broad experience have led him to a position as an animal welfare specialist and field representative for the American Humane Association's Film & TV Unit.

Dr. Gold spends his days on movie and television sets making sure the animal actors are safe and treated well. "As a member of the American Humane Association, I am not working for the studios," he explains. "I'm not beholden to the director or producer. My job is to make sure the animals are properly treated and that they avoid dangerous situations."

He has safeguarded both large and small animals. "There are a lot of different types of animal actors," he says. "I've worked with primates and household pets."

E ssential

According to the American Veterinary Medical Association, the majority of veterinary technicians are employed in private practice. However, there is a demand for technicians in biomedical research, colleges and universities, humane societies, zoos and wildlife facilities, and the military.

The diversity in this business is vast. It is possible to work as a veterinarian at a zoo and be around chimpanzees. You can work on a farm and take care of sheep and goats. Zookeepers interact with many different types of animals. Oceanographers and marine biologists work underwater with creatures from the sea. The animal population under the sea is as varied as on land.

"It's possible to specialize or be a generalist," says Dr. May. "The work is out there, and the possibilities are truly endless. Whether you are working as a veterinarian on a farm or running a private practice taking care of dogs and cats, there are plenty of opportunities. It's just not the traditional places to work either. You can work at a wildlife center rescuing injured birds or as a police officer training dogs or horses."

"Once you start investigating the different options, more doors open up," says Dr. May. "Then you have to narrow down your choices. Animal workers can work with large or small, finned, feathered, or furry creatures. And you can specialize and work with multiple kinds of animals."

Coping with Life and Death

The one downside of the job is losing a patient. It's hard not to form attachments. Caring while also keeping a safe distance doesn't always work. However, professionals do learn how to keep emotionally detached while showing compassion. "Over time healthcare workers learn that it's normal to deal with sadness," says Ulla Anneli, RN, RYT (registered yoga teacher).

E ssential

The best way to deal with losing a patient is to talk about it. Keeping emotions bottled up inside causes stress, and it is known that stress can lead to illness. It is important to tell a friend, supervisor, or therapist about the loss you are feeling. Chances are that colleagues at work—especially those who have been there longer than you—have experienced similar emotions. By expressing your emotions, you are starting to let go of them and heal.

"Everyone deals with loss differently," says Anneli. "People who go into this business are natural nurturers. If they are part of a large group—like a zoo or veterinary hospital—they should have a support group. If they are self-employed workers, they should get support from friends or even professional help. It's normal to mourn and grieve, and essential for your health to talk about the loss."

"Don't bring the stress home to your spouse or family," says Anneli. "Yes, your spouse cares about you, and you can even share your feelings about how sad you feel. Just don't dwell on it over and over again with a loved one. If it gets to that level, then you need to talk to a professional therapist to learn how to deal with your emotions."

CHAPTER 2

Growing Opportunities

The need for animal care and animal service workers is expected to grow faster than other occupations, according to the U.S. Department of Labor's Bureau of Labor Statistics. The Department of Labor cites that the number of job openings will increase by 18 to 26 percent by 2014. The jobs will be found in kennels, doggie daycare centers, pet hotels, grooming shops, animal shelters, veterinary private practices, veterinary clinics, veterinary hospitals, government, and other service industries. Fueling this growth is people's obsession with their pets.

Occupations Most in Demand

When most people think of veterinarians, they tend to think of the animal doctor who works in private practice taking care of dogs and cats. Today's veterinarians work in a wide array of professional fields. The opportunities are plentiful in traditional small animal private practice and at animal hospitals. Other growth areas include working in labs for the government helping with the safety of food processing plants or water supplies, working on farms to prevent disease in livestock, and teaching others to become veterinarians. Veterinary specialties that expect growth spurts in the future include surgery, ophthalmology, dentistry, and dermatology.

A veterinarian, veterinary technician, or assistant can easily find employment almost everywhere in the country. However, there is a greater need for all animal healthcare workers on farms and in rural areas.

Currently there is a scarcity of veterinary professionals in rural areas. The low numbers of animal husbandry workers in rural areas leads to a higher demand and often to a longer workday. When Dr. Kimberly May worked as a board-certified equine/large animal surgeon, she worked long days and night shifts. While she loved being around horses, the long hours got to her. So she switched careers and is now employed as the assistant director of the Communications Division of the American Veterinary Medical Association. "I wanted to work to live, not live to work," she says. Her job allows her to spend time with her family and friends. "This worked out perfectly for me," she says. "I get to write and inform the public about animals, animal welfare issues, animal care, and careers working with animals."

Alert

Shortages of veterinarians at universities, in public health, and other areas of the profession where hands-on doctor-patient practice doesn't occur is a major concern. To reverse this trend, universities such as Texas A&M University College of Veterinary Medicine & Biomedical Sciences are trying to fill the gap by offering alternative career options to fourth-year veterinary students by designing nonclinical programs.

Burnout is a factor that many animal care workers face. A high incidence is found among animal caretakers who work in shelters. Most of these jobs require little training and only a high school diploma. The jobs entail a lot of grunt work such as cleaning cages and making sure shelter animals are fed and exercised. These jobs attract part-time workers and a lot of students who want experience working with animals. Some shelters euthanize stray dogs and cats. This grunt work can take a toll on the workers, causing depression and burnout. Burnout results in a high turnover of jobs, making opportunities constantly available.

On the positive side, shelters are becoming more humane. Many residents take an active role in their local animal shelter by hosting fundraisers and by volunteering to walk dogs and play with the sheltered dogs and cats. The potential to earn a good living by working at a shelter is tough. Shelter workers often earn minimum wage. Most people are students who want experience working with animals, or neighborhood volunteers who want the companionship of dogs and cats without a lot of the responsibilities. If you are interested in a career with animals, it is a good idea to take a part-time job or volunteer at a local shelter. Shelters are a good starting place for people who want to work with animals. Many veterinarians, scientists, and educators got their first experience working with animals at shelters as volunteers or interns while attending high school or college.

 Fact

The Kahun Papyrus, an ancient medical text dating back 4,000 years, is one of the earliest records that discuss animal diseases and treatments. It was discovered in 1889 by Flinders Petrie, an English Egyptologist. Today fragments of the Kahun Papyrus are kept at University College, London.

Running a shelter is a different story. Shelters are nonprofit businesses. It is possible to earn a decent living, but it will not make you rich. People don't work at a shelter to make a lot of money. They do it to be around animals, and to help raise awareness about the importance of animal welfare.

According to the Bureau of Labor Statistics, another key reason behind the steady growth in the need for animal care workers and for the ongoing improvements at animal shelters is the connection between animal abuse and abuse toward humans. "There have been several studies showing us that there is a direct link between the two," says Dr. May. "There are those of us who grew up with a pet. We have a close regard for animals. Even those who never had a pet in their lives get shocked when they hear about animal abuse. The bottom line is that animal abuse is wrong, and thankfully, even people who don't have pets care enough to feel sad and outraged when they hear about animals being harmed."

 Fact

When the media focuses attention on animal abuse, the heightened awareness of the plight of animals causes individuals to donate private funds to animal shelters. Private donations enables shelter owners to make often much needed improvements. Shelter owners and workers expect that improved conditions will make working at shelters a less stressful environment for all.

Another growth field is obedience dog training. The trainers often are self-employed entrepreneurs. Jim Burwell, a Houston-based owner of Petiquette, a dog-training franchise, believes that dog training is the fastest-growing segment of the pet industry. "Services in the pet industry are expected to grow more than 6 percent over the next five years," he says. "Being a dog trainer is a field with multiple opportunities and plenty of growth."

Other jobs are more limited in scope. It may sound cool being a zoo director or an animal trainer on a movie set. However, those jobs are few and far between. That is not to say that it is impossible to get a job in these fields. Depending on the position and the amount of schooling involved, you may have to start in an entry-level position and work your way up.

From Animal Trainer to Zoologist: Myriad Careers

When considering a career in working with animals, most people immediately think "veterinarian." Within the veterinary field there are many specialties. The numbers of careers are as varied as the requirements. Some positions require a college degree followed by four years at veterinary school. If you specialize in dentistry or ophthalmology, add another year of school. Other jobs, such as working in a pet store or shelter, require a high school diploma. Most other jobs, such as working in the development office of a humane society or working as an environmental educator, require a college degree.

 Fact

> While it's true that the majority of veterinarians work in private practice, they also work in large animal hospitals, on farms, and in zoos and wildlife centers. Did you know that NASA employs veterinarians to conduct experiments in space so they can learn about human and animal diseases?

The career field is large, and one that is constantly changing with the times. "As our concern for the environment deepens, we will have a need for environmental educators," says Christopher O'Sullivan, environmental educator at the Trailside Museum and Zoo at Bear Mountain State Park, which is part of New York State Parks and Palisades Interstate Park Commission. "I see this field changing because of our concerns about global warming and other environmental issues. As educators, we work with schools and corporations to broaden public awareness about our interaction with animals and our surrounding environments."

Susan Smith, a research and development director for Palisades Interstate Park Commission, agrees. "Corporations have taken a major interest in our parks," she says. "Filling out grant applications for various cleanup and restoration projects is more detailed. Corporations want to be green, and they want to associate with us. The forms are more detailed. They want to know where their money and manpower are going. It's a good situation for everyone involved."

 Fact

Most people are aware that corporations donate money to nonprofit environmental centers. However, many big businesses are also hosting volunteer days, allowing their employees to donate time. For instance, seventeen employees from USB Bank spent a day cleaning out Rockland Lake in New York State. Volunteer manpower is always welcome among nonprofits.

Another new field with lots of growth potential is working on the government level or for private research facilities. There are crime scene investigative (CSI) units for animals, disaster relief and response teams that rescue animals, and high-tech surveillance units that are working with insects to create bug-size spy drones. Spy technology or robot bugs (using real flies) sounds like something James Bond would employ. However, with the government's keen interest in homeland security, many new opportunities in the intelligence fields are opening up for people who want to work with insects and animals.

With new opportunities, many traditional jobs are also going through changes. Zoo directors and zookeepers have seen their surroundings vastly improve. The days of the small barred cages are over. Visitors to zoos want to see animals in their natural environments. That has opened up the field for zoo designers.

Traditional jobs of zoo director and zookeeper have also evolved. They have always been caretakers and educators. Now they also work closely with zoo designers to create the best home for the animals. Most important, many are working to study endangered populations and reintroduce them into the wild.

 Fact

A number of U.S. government agencies, private entities, and universities are creating cyber bugs—live insects with computer chips in them. The hope is to use these bugs as spyware. They are remote controlled, and could be used to follow suspects, guide missiles, or find survivors in collapsed mines or buildings.

The job outlook for zoo directors is among the most limited because zoos have a low turnover. However, zookeepers and directors have other opportunities. They don't have to work at a traditional zoo. Wildlife centers, natural history museums, and other nonprofits where animals are involved often look for people with zoo experience.

Number of People Employed

Numbers of people in each profession are as varied as the professions themselves. For instance, there are more than 86,000 veterinarians actively practicing in the United States, according to the American Veterinary Medical Association. On the other end of the spectrum there are just thirty-five safety representatives who work for American Humane on movie sets and television studios. Whether it's taking care of a family dog or cat or making sure that the lion in a blockbuster movie is kept free from harm, the prospects for finding work are excellent.

Should you be discouraged from applying for a job with just thirty-five slots—especially when twenty-five are part time? "Definitely not," says Jone Bouman, head of communications for American Humane's Film & Television Unit. "Working on a movie set with Johnny Depp in *The Pirates of the Caribbean* is exciting, and openings do occur. I look for people all the time, especially with equine experience."

Having a specialty gives you a leg up in getting your foot in the door. While 75 percent of all veterinarians in the United States are in private practice, many veterinarians specialize in a wide range of fields. That means extra schooling, and more opportunities. Veterinarians can work in nonprofit organizations, in government, at universities, on farms, and even in space.

 **Question**

Who was the first veterinarian to participate in an outer space mission?
It was Dr. Martin Fettman, who in 1993 was part of the space shuttle Columbia. He studied the effects of zero gravity on animals and people. The space crew's research proved beneficial to the health and safety of astronauts on later space missions.

Another growth field within veterinary medicine is veterinary technologists. They are like a nurse to a medical doctor. According to the Bureau of Labor Statistics, about 60,000 veterinary technologists and technicians work in the United States. Of that number, most work in private practice alongside a veterinarian. Others work at kennels, animal shelters, stables, grooming salons, and zoos, as well as at local, state, and federal agencies.

Veterinarians and veterinary technicians work in all sorts of places—even on farms, where they work closely with farmers, ranchers, and agricultural managers, who themselves also work with animals. Farmers, ranchers, and agricultural managers held nearly

1.3 million jobs in the past two years according to the Bureau of Labor Statistics. Of that number, 83 percent were self-employed. Most of these workers oversee crop production activities and manage live-stock and dairy production. A large majority of farmers and ranchers work part-time running small farms.

During the same time period, a large number of animal care workers held jobs at animal shelters and humane associations, pet supply stores, stables and boarding kennels, and research labs. Many worked as animal trainers. Those figures total about 172,000 animal caretakers nationally. About 27 percent are self-employed.

Other jobs with fewer people still draw a great amount of interest. The American Society of Ichthyologists and Herpetologists, dedicated to the scientific study of fishes, amphibians, and reptiles, has 2,400 members. The Association of Zoos and Aquariums has more than 200 institutions and thousands of individual members.

 Fact

According to data from the Department of Labor's Bureau of Labor Statistics, nearly one out of every three nonfarm animal caretakers is self-employed. This includes animal trainers, where three out of every five are self-employed.

Job numbers vary depending on the position, and those job figures change from year to year. All expect upward growth.

Do You Have to Relocate?

Jobs can be found around the globe. Here in the United States, positions are available in major metropolitan areas and small towns, near beaches and on farms. Where you work depends on the type of position you want. Veterinarians can work pretty much anywhere in the country. More opportunities are available in rural areas on farms.

Marine biologists will want to be around water—whether it's an aquarium in a large city or in a research facility close to the ocean. People who work in zoos go where the jobs take them; that could be a major city or a wildlife center at a national park.

Most of the people employed at American Humane's Film & TV Unit are located in Los Angeles, the film capital. Still, others who work on-call for the Film & TV Unit can live in a variety of cities. They just have to be ready to board a plane to take them wherever a movie is filming. The representative who worked on the Harry Potter films is an American who has spent most of the past five years living in England on movie sets making sure that the animals in these movies were treated humanely.

Leading a safari doesn't mean moving to Africa—although it could. Many wildlife safaris exist right here in the United States. William P. Rives, VMD and director of Six Flags Wild Safari, lives close to the Great Adventure safari in Jackson, New Jersey.

Animal welfare specialist Dr. Kenneth Gold, who works on-call with American Humane, travels around the country often. He doesn't always know where he will wind up; it all depends on where a movie, TV show, or commercial is being filmed. He likes the travel and the work. He resides with his wife in Chicago, and has worked as a general curator at the Singapore Zoo and at Apenheul Primate Park in The Netherlands.

Some jobs require travel, but most are local. These local positions—be it at a pet shop, doggie daycare center, pet hotel, shelter, veterinary clinic, or zoo—can be right around the corner from your home. Travel is not necessary. The lion's share of Jim Burwell's business is close to home, though he does travel on occasion. "I do get calls to travel, and it is fine every once in a while," he says. "One of the perks about this job is that I am local and make my own hours."

Salaries

People don't go into this profession for the money. Almost everyone who works with animals has wanted to do so since childhood. People in these professions almost always grew up with a family pet. Some lived on farms and developed close ties to farm animals. Working with animals is reconnecting with a part of that childhood. For people who love animals, it's a thrill to be around them on a daily basis.

It's also exciting working with a different species—one that communicates on a totally different level. For animal workers, it's a joy and, in part, a privilege to be around animals. That is not to say that the money is bad. In many cases, it is good—very good. Many animal workers are highly skilled at what they do, and they are well compensated for their services. Starting salaries for students fresh out of veterinary schools range from $30,000 up to $75,000 or higher, depending on the location and the position or area of specialty. Median salaries are $40,000 to $50,000. Veterinary technicians earn less. Shelter workers are paid hourly—often minimum wage or slightly better. This is slowly changing because there is a strong demand for shelter workers, which is forcing pay increases.

Dog-training salaries also run the gamut, from $30,000 to six-figure incomes. Burwell is making more money as a dog trainer than he did when employed as an executive in a bank. "Plus my hours are so much better," he notes. "I like being my own boss, and I enjoy the many people and dogs I meet. It's fun going to work.

"An in-home dog-training franchise requires less capital than most franchises," says Burwell. "It requires no investment in real estate. You just go to the client's home to do your training. Plus, an in-home dog-training franchise requires no investment in personnel other than you."

People who work in nonprofits writing grants are seeing changes in their salaries too. "I work for the state," says Susan Smith. "I'm a civil service employee, so salaries don't always match the private sector. Still, I'm seeing positive changes. Grant writing is a growing profession, and one that is highly valued in the nonprofit world."

Christopher O'Sullivan says, "The need to educate children and adults about our environment and our interaction with nature and animals is what drives my profession. Changes are happening and salaries are getting better."

Starting salaries in the nonprofit world as a grant writer, educator, publicist, or administrator are around $30,000. Directors at nonprofits earn more; their salaries can start at $50,000 and go up to $100,000 or higher—depending on the size of the organization and geographic location.

While salaries are improving, one thing remains constant—the perks. "It's a joy being around nature and animals," says O'Sullivan. "Working with animals, and educating the public about them, is quite rewarding."

Job Security

Animal service workers are among the most highly skilled workers in the country. They have specialized training—whether it is running a pet shop or grooming business, or working as a zoologist. Dog trainers and judges at dog and cat shows also are experts in their fields. Being an expert often equals job security.

Most animal care workers tend to hold on to their jobs. Zoo directors often remain in their jobs until they retire. Veterinarians can keep their private practices running for the full span of their careers. The demand for highly skilled animal service workers means that there are plenty of job opportunities and that once a job is attained, you can be in it for the long haul.

That suits many animal care workers well, because rather than being routine, every day brings new challenges. "It definitely is not a boring job," says Dr. Mary Burch, of the American Kennel Club. "I work with a wide range of professionals and see a lot of different types of dogs. It's quite exciting."

As long as people dote on their animals, opportunities for caring for animals will always exist. Susan Briggs, owner of doggie daycare center Urban Tails in Houston, explains. "People who bring their pets to Urban Tails love their animals. They lead busy lives and want to make sure that we are taking good care of their pets when they are at work or on vacation. I have seen this business grow because of that concern on the part of animal owners." She adds, "There are other doggie daycare centers and pet hotels opening up in nearby cities and across the country. The opportunities are here, and so is the security."

The self-employed, private, government, nonprofit, and college and university sectors all are seeing growth and strong job security for people who work with animals.

CHAPTER 3

Making Career Choices

Choosing a career is an involved process that takes a lot of time. You know you want to work with animals, but might not be sure which direction to follow. The best way to choose a career is to do a lot of research. Start by talking to a career counselor or—even better—a working professional. Shadow someone who is working in a field that interests you. You can take a part-time job or internship to get a taste of what this job is like. Talk to the professionals. Most will be happy to share their insights with you.

Self-Assessment and Evaluation

Deciding what type of career is right for you takes careful planning. It's important to think about your interests, values, personality, lifestyle, talents, abilities, and skills. Do you have any work or life experiences with animals? What about schooling? Does going to veterinary school on top of college intimidate you? It can be daunting. If you specialize on top of that, add another year or two of school. However, the need for education and the money to pay for graduate school shouldn't hold you back. In this chapter and the next, you'll learn more about education and financial aid options.

Working with animals takes commitment, creativity, smarts, skill, and plenty of determination. One of the best things about this field is the people in it. Ask them about the pros and cons of their profession. Most are willing to talk about the challenges they faced along the way. Talk to them. They will fuel your ambition.

Looking at your life to determine what you want to be means being truthful. "I think self-assessments and evaluations are an important consideration," says achievement expert Doug Vermeeren, "but sometimes it is hard to do an evaluation on yourself. Make a list of things you need and then the things you are passionate about. Next, seriously take a look at jobs, and while it's not always going to be a perfect fit, be honest and look at everything."

 **Question**

Can I go from docent to professional?
Having some experience and a good deal of knowledge is a great way to learn about a profession and get in on the ground floor. Sue Smith started as a docent at the Palisades Interstate Park Commission before moving to a career as research and development director. She did get her master's degree at Columbia University while she worked as a docent.

The Art of Caring Is Essential

The number one reason people choose a career working with animals is because they care deeply about them. Healing, training, and overseeing an animal's welfare are major concerns to people in this field. People who work with animals are also willing to go the extra mile. They will work long hours when needed, and they put their hearts and souls into their work.

From rescue work to repairing a broken leg to making sure that animal actors are treated fairly—all are part of a typical day for some animal service workers. At the American Humane, reps are hired to watch over animal actors, ranging from ants to elephants. Even cockroaches are not harmed.

The effects of caring individuals are being seen in the improvements in animal welfare at zoos. Life in captivity is changing. Just thirty years ago, zoos were like prisons. But today, because people have a hunger to learn about exotic animals and how they live, zoos and wildlife centers are designed to simulate the animals' habitats. People who visit zoos, as well as those who work with the animals in them, want the best environments for the animals. No one wants to see an animal in a small cage with steel bars.

Essential

When you are watching a movie and see a bug get crushed, you may wonder about the welfare of that animal. But in actuality not even bugs are harmed in movie making. When filming such a moment, the director will yell "Cut," and a fake bug will be placed in the scene. The actor stomps on an artificial critter.

Animal service workers also care deeply about people. Even those who work in research laboratories or in Crime Scene Investigation units interact with people. Animal caretakers must be compassionate about animals and people.

What Appeals to You about Animals?

Did you like watching documentaries about animals when you were growing up? Did you cry when Bambi's mother died, or sob while watching the movie *Old Yeller?* Did you ride horses, live on a farm, or have a pet as a child? Or maybe you liked to go snorkeling or deep sea diving to discover a whole new world of creatures in the ocean.

Many things draw us to animals. It can be companionship or the foreign aspect of learning about a new species. For William Rives, VMD and director of Wild Safari at Six Flags Great Adventure in Jackson, New Jersey, nothing is better than his job. Dr. Rives oversees all 1,200 animals at the 350-acre safari park. He grew up watching Mutual of Omaha's *Wild Kingdom*, and would catch all sorts of critters in the woods near his home, and the library books he read were always about animals. Thanks to his high school biology teacher, who interested him in animal sciences, he was hooked. He knew he wanted to be a veterinarian when he grew up. "The best part of this job is to come up with ideas and plans on how we can improve everything," he says. "It's such an awesome place."

 Fact

In the field of animal research, the American Veterinary Medical Association follows the "three R's" tenet. "These principles are: refinement of experimental methods to eliminate or reduce animal pain and distress; reduction of the number of animals consistent with sound experimental design; and replacement of animals with nonanimal methods wherever feasible," says Dr. May of the American Veterinary Medical Association.

Promoting a cause that is close to one's heart is what drives Kimberly May, DVM and the assistant director of the Communications Division of the American Veterinary Medical Association. She started her career as a board-certified equine/large animal surgeon and now she works with all sorts of people who want to know about careers with animals. "That takes many different forms," she says. "In this role, I write and educate the public about animal welfare and working with animals. I'm constantly learning in this profession, and I enjoy teaching everyone from young children to people who inquire about jobs as veterinarians. I'm still doing a lot of research about animals, and there is a lot of contact with people. Studying and educating the public about animals and animal careers is uplifting."

Being around animals, communicating with them, and helping them are what motivate people in this profession. "We also enjoy the positive feedback we get from the animals," says Jim Burwell, owner of Petiquette, a dog-training program in Houston, Texas. "With an animal you can tell right away if it likes you, if it is scared, shy, or angry. Just reading their signs and knowing how to handle and help them is a thrill."

Having a dog lick your face with gratitude or hearing a cat purr his "thanks" is rewarding. "It makes the job so beneficial," says Burwell.

Don't Be Deterred

Some students shy away from specific careers because the study of math and science can be intimidating. Not all careers with animals require biology, chemistry, biochemistry, and other sciences. If you are running a pet shop, you need to have a background in retail business. Dog trainers, shelter workers, and zookeepers don't need a heavy load of math and science in school.

A career as a veterinarian, veterinary technician, animal researcher, or behaviorist, among other professions, does require a certain amount of math and science. "Your major in college is irrelevant," says Dr. May. "We've had English majors apply and get into vet school. Veterinary schools look at the overall package. You need to have some experience working with animals before applying to vet school. That can be by working or volunteering at a zoo, animal shelter, or local veterinary office. Vet schools want someone with leadership skills.

"Yes, good grades are important, and you have to be well-rounded too," adds Dr. May. "Vet schools look closely at extracurricular activities. Just because math and the sciences are daunting to some, doesn't mean you shouldn't apply. If you want something badly enough, go for it."

Doug Vermeeren strongly agrees. "Many times people are afraid of the work," he says. "They want something; they dream about it; they hope for it; but they are afraid of the work it will take to get there. Anything worthwhile is worth investing your all into. Don't be afraid to work at it."

According to Dr. May and Vermeeren, only you can impede your success. "You can always find a tutor to help you with those tough courses," says Dr. May. "Not everyone in vet school finds science, math, or other subjects easy to tackle. If you want a career as a veterinarian or in a similar field, you shouldn't give up before you try.

"The same thing can be said about the cost of veterinary school," Dr. May continues. "After four years of college, there is vet school on top of that. It isn't cheap, but there are scholarships and student loans. The salaries are good, and are getting better because of those student loans. If you are thinking about applying to vet school, look at the big picture. The schools are here to offer advice too."

Narrowing Your Choices

You are sure that you want a job working with animals, but which career? The first step is to write a list of all career options that appeal to you. Do you want to work for a large company? Would you prefer owning your own private practice or going solo as a freelancer? How important is money? What about benefits?

Look at all of your priorities and try not to compromise. Your pro and con list will help narrow your choices. "Narrowing down job decisions is hard," says Vermeeren. "It doesn't come solely down to passion, but passion is a beginning stage. It may not be the only thing, but it matters because sometimes you are able to do what you enjoy but it's not meeting your needs. I speak about four specific areas when we talk about meeting needs, and those needs should be balanced in each area.

"The first one is wealth, and this doesn't just mean the amount of your paycheck; it also means prosperity. The second aspect is health. Will that job contribute or take away your health? What will it do to your stress levels, and what will be the physical difficulty associated with it? The third aspect is relationships. Will you have to give too much time to work? Will you be able to dedicate enough time to your family? The last aspect to consider is self-achievement. Will the jobs in consideration strike a chord with your core values? It's important to have balance, and receive fulfillment in all areas in the job you choose."

E ssential

When making career choices it is a smart idea to focus on transferable skills you most enjoy using. Often those skills can apply to the job you want. Many skills translate into a variety of jobs. All employers look for good communication skills, leadership abilities, enthusiasm, and willingness to take on new challenges.

Once you narrow your search down to two or three options, continue researching each field. With a list of pros and cons in hand, you will soon narrow the choice. "It is also okay to make changes while you are in grad school," says Dr. May. "Often you can take one set of skills and knowledge and apply it to other fields. You don't have to feel locked into something."

Reaching a Decision

You know what you want to be. It's a powerful feeling knowing what you want to do in life. "A friend once told me that, 'I can sell anything as long as I believe in it,'" says Vermeeren. "I think that sentiment can be applied above and beyond sales. You want to be wholly involved. You want to believe in the mission statement and customer service values, and you want to make sure they are congruent with the way you represent yourself in the marketplace."

Alert

Surround yourself with people who support your decision and offer you encouragement. Having a network of family and friends to lean on makes any process easier to handle.

With a clear focus, you can put all of your energies into having a career working with animals. While you are in school, your interests can change. "Don't be too concerned," says Dr. May. "Your knowledge, experience, and skills are always transferable. Learning is time well spent, and working with animals is being in an environment where you are constantly learning."

"I changed careers midway, and I am pleased with my decisions," she says. "When I worked with horses, I was happy. When I changed careers to work with the American Veterinary Medical Association, I was equally thrilled. We change, and so do our desires and needs. So, being open to all job opportunities is important."

CHAPTER 4

The Education Process

Depending on your career choice, it is quite likely that you will need a college degree. To specialize or become a zoologist, veterinarian, entomologist, or graduate school professor, you will need a doctorate. Having a good understanding and even an enjoyment of science and math goes a long way. Workers in all animal care professions, from shelter workers to those with an advanced degree, will benefit from having a background in the social sciences, such as psychology and sociology. Even though you will be working with animals, knowing how to interact with people is essential in all animal service careers.

Prepare in High School and College

Some people have always known that they want to work with animals. If you are in high school, it is a wise choice to start your research now. Look at undergraduate and graduate programs that specialize in your specific career. It's never too early to write, e-mail, or call the admissions office to request information about specific courses of study.

Talk to your high school guidance counselor. He may already have information in your school about advance degree programs.

Rebecca Humber, a certified animal safety representative with American Humane, knew as a little girl that she wanted to have a career working with animals when she grew up. "When I was in high school, I asked my parents to take me to Moor Park College," she says. "They have an Exotic Animal Training and Management program. It is the only one like it in the world. I lived in northern California. Moor Park is in southern California. We took a road trip. I talked to students, professors, and administrators at the school. Everyone was happy to share information. I knew this is where I wanted to apply." She did apply, and was accepted.

E ssential

Keep a calendar of all admissions deadlines on hand. You must get all applications and financial aid papers in on time. Colleges and grad schools do not accept late applications. Financial aid and scholarship forms also must be filed on time.

If you are in college and plan to go after an advanced degree, start looking at graduate schools. The one thing that all schools want—be it college, vocational, or graduate levels—is a well-rounded individual. Those extracurricular activities are essential. Are you head of the debate team? Do you belong to an after-school club? Are you a leader? Also, national and local professional associations have free pamphlets and information on their websites about different jobs within a specific category, and often post career opportunities online too.

If you are in high school or college, it is a good idea to intern for school credit or volunteer with either a professional or organization to get experience. Many people in graduate schools interned at zoos, shelters, and veterinarians' offices.

Technical or Vocational Schools

These schools offer careers for people who wish to become veterinary assistants or technicians, as well as a host of other specialties. Many of these programs provide classroom study with hands-on experience.

Community College

Many people take the community college route when they aren't fully sure of which direction to take. Community colleges offer a two-year associate's degree, and are often less expensive than four-year colleges and universities. Many four-year colleges and universities accept transfer credits. Before you apply, check to make sure that course credits are transferable. Every school is different.

Four-Year Colleges and Universities

It's true that many students study animal behavior, math, and the sciences in college if they are planning to pursue an advanced degree in working with animals. However, some start out with other majors. "We've had English and psychology majors apply to vet school," says Dr. Kimberly May, of the American Veterinary Medical Association, "and because of their well-rounded backgrounds, leadership skills, and good grades, they get accepted. You don't have to go the traditional route."

 **Alert**

> Before you visit a campus, take a virtual tour on the Internet. If the school appeals to you, then visit in person. Talk to students, professors, and admissions personnel to see if this is the right program for you.

Graduate School

Depending on the degree, graduate school can be one, two, three, or four years. Some people take advanced degrees, which means additional schooling on top of their doctoral degree. You can be a DVM (Doctor of Veterinary Medicine) and still continue your training toward becoming a large animal surgeon or dentist.

Going Back to School

You've been away from school for a couple or a number of years. You might be quite successful working in the corporate world. However, success doesn't always equal happiness. If you are considering a career change, you will have to go back to school.

Changing careers is common, and many people find happiness the second or third time around. The first thing to do is talk with professionals in the career that interests you. Second, talk to the admissions office at the appropriate schools that have a career track toward your goal.

"I firmly believe family is first," says achievement expert Doug Vermeeren. "The decision is not one you should make on your own. Get your spouse, family, or friends involved through the entire process. Look strategically at the needs of your family and how those needs can be met. Go back and forth and look at what the transition period looks like. How many months will it take to get comfortable in the new job? How can you survive financially? What are the things you need to be aware of?"

If you have a nest egg or rainy day fund, now is a good time to see if you can use that toward your schooling. You should talk to admissions officers at schools and find out about scholarships. You might be able to use some of your own experience toward college credits. You won't find out until you talk to college admissions officers. You can also work part-time while going to school, or take evening classes to start.

Choosing the Program That Is Right for You

It's a lot easier if you have a targeted goal in mind. That will dictate the type of school or program that is right for you. If you aren't fully sure, a liberal arts degree or one majoring in science or the social sciences will serve you well.

Make sure that you are attending an accredited college or graduate school. To find out if a school is accredited, simply ask. A school is accredited when an official review board evaluates the school's programs for quality of faculty, curriculum, and educational environment, such as classrooms, laboratories, and libraries.

E ssential

The best way to find a good fit is to ask everyone you know— friends, family, teachers, guidance counselors, and most important, people working in the field you are interested in. People like to talk about their work, and are usually happy to share information about which schools would be the right choice for you.

Finding the Right School

It always comes down to narrowing choices. If you have no idea of where to start, talk to high school guidance counselors and people in your desired profession. Look online at *www.collegeboard.com* or *www.petersons.com*. These are just two helpful sites that provide information about various schools and ideas on how to make smart choices. If you have an inkling or know what you are looking for, start with a list of likes and dislikes. Ask yourself what are you looking for. Following are a few considerations to put on your list:

- Do you plan on living at home or going away to school?
- Do you want to live on campus or off?
- What type of campus housing is available?
- Do you want to be in a large city or rural area?

- Would you prefer a large school or a small one?
- Do you want a private or state school?
- Which schools have the best financial aid and scholarship packages?
- Will you work while going to college?
- Can you attend part-time or take evening classes if you have to work?

Comparing Schools

After finding a handful or even a dozen schools that appeal to you, start drawing up another comparison sheet of pros and cons. Important information to record on these sheets should include:

- The cost of tuition, housing and meals, and books and supplies
- Your application deadline—include a space for when you sent it in
- Any other costs, such as travel expenses to return home during class breaks and car expenses (if you need to have a car)
- Duration of the program
- Other prerequisites
- Entrance exams and fees
- Contact names, phone numbers, and web address

With your lists in hand, start comparison shopping. You should try to visit as many campuses as possible. If you have a school nearby, even if it is not your first or third choice, visit it anyway. You will be surprised at what you can learn by visiting campuses.

Your Application

Your application is your first link to the school's admissions office. Think of it as an introduction. First impressions do count, so fill it out carefully. To ease the tension, get an early start. You need to send it in on time. If you miss the deadline, you will have to wait for the open application period for the following semester.

 Fact

Understand that with each application, you will have to include an application fee. This can get expensive. Most students apply to four or five schools—depending on their budgets.

Some students take a month, working on and off, to review and fill out their applications. Just give yourself plenty of time to complete and gather all of the information you will need. Most applications require written recommendations from teachers, employers, or volunteer directors who know you as a student and as a worker or volunteer. Give those people two to three months' time to write your letter of recommendation. Remind them about a month before the deadline. It is a good idea to tell them that you need it earlier than on the exact date. This way, you won't have to worry about them being late. Once you get the recommendation letters in hand, be sure to thank the people who wrote them.

During this process, keep in mind that even if you have a 4.0 grade average in school, it doesn't guarantee entry into an undergraduate, graduate, or vocational school. Before you fill out the application, read about the student population. As mentioned earlier, most admissions officers look for the well-rounded student with plenty of leadership skills and extracurricular activities.

Competition can be fierce. Veterinary schools, like medical schools, limit the number of enrolled students each year. That is why you need to apply to more than one school. You may be placed on a waiting list, or you may hear from the school within a few weeks. Most applications include information as to when you should expect to hear back. Try not to spend every waking minute focusing on it. Just relax.

Alert

Admissions officers read through thousands of applications. Try to make yours stand out by showcasing your talents and accomplishments. Be sure to fill in all of the requested information, and make sure everything is neat and tidy. When writing an essay for your application, give it plenty of thought. Go back and reread it to make sure it is well polished.

Financial Aid

The big question every student asks is, "How am I going to pay for all of this?" First you should determine how much your education will cost. Don't look just at tuition and housing. Consider the cost of books, extra spending money, and travel expenses.

Fact

You will receive a copy of your Student Aid Report (SAR) about three to four weeks after submitting your FAFSA. The SAR details your Expected Family Contribution (EFC), which tells you how much you will be expected to contribute to college costs. The schools listed on your FAFSA also receive copies of your SAR, so they can customize a financial aid package for you.

Once you figure out the price for the college of your choice, the next step will be to apply for financial aid. Do you qualify? Before you even hear back from the college of your choice, you should complete the FAFSA (Free Application for Federal and Student Aid). The FAFSA determines your financial need. To qualify for any state or federal aid including scholarships, work-study programs, grants, or loans, you must complete the FAFSA. To find out more information about FAFSA, visit the helpful website at *www.fafsa.ed.gov.*

E ssential

According to the American Veterinary Medical Association (AVMA), most veterinary schools require potential students to submit their applications through the Veterinary Medical College Application Service (VMCAS). For information about VMCAS and this process, log onto *www.aavmc.org/vmcas/vmcas.htm.*

When you are accepted for enrollment, the school will send you an award letter. Award letters outline the entire cost of attendance at each school, your Expected Family Contribution (EFC), and a financial aid package.

If you are a student in high school, check with your guidance counselor about scholarships and other financial aid packages. You can also find out about financial aid and scholarship from the schools you are applying to. In addition, there are helpful online resources. A good place to start is at *www.collegeboard.com.*

If you are employed, ask your employer about tuition assistance packages. Financial aid officers at the colleges that accept you also are a good source of information.

Surviving School

The course load can be a heavy one, especially if it includes lots of science and math. It can get intense, but it doesn't have to be overwhelming. You can choose to do this full- or part-time; it all depends on your financial situation. You might want to take a year off in between college and graduate school. Whatever you choose, plan on taking a few fun courses, and don't forget to schedule breaks.

Tips for Surviving College or Graduate School

Try these time-tested strategies for remaining sane while getting the most out of your college experience:

- When you register, give yourself some free time by not scheduling back-to-back classes. This way, you can use the free time in between classes to study, eat, and hang out with friends.
- Show up on time for all of your classes, and from the first day, take notes—even if you think you know what is being covered.
- For every hour of class time, you will need two for study time. You can find a study group on campus, and you should also spend time alone reviewing your notes, homework, papers, and course load.
- Whether you are in a dorm or at your home, find a study place with a desk, a comfortable chair, plenty of lighting, and lots of supplies. Make this your study area.
- Don't stay up all night studying; your body can only take so much abuse. A good eight hours of sleep each night is healthy, and you will wake up fresh and ready to take on lots of new material.
- Take study breaks. Get up and stretch. Eat a healthy snack or even call a friend. Just keep these breaks short—about ten to fifteen minutes each. After each break, you will return to work refreshed.
- Join a study group, and keep the number of participants small. Being in a study group is great for motivating you when you don't want to study. Each of you can bounce ideas off of the others, and help each other with difficult subjects.
- Find out about study resources on campus, and make use of them. Most campuses provide labs, tutors, computer programs, and additional textbooks for you to use. Get to know your professors and advisers, and work with them. If you don't know the answer to something, ask.
- Study the toughest subjects first. This is when you are most awake and able to tackle harder work. After you accomplish that, you can go on to less intense subjects.

- Reward yourself with a treat every once in a while. Go out with friends, and maintain a healthy diet.

Special Tips for the Mid-Career Change

If you are going back to school after a lapse of a few or several years, know that you are not alone. At first it might be stressful to think that you will be older than your fellow students. True, most will be in their early twenties, but being older has its advantages.

Remember that you were successful at your job and that you are a responsible person. Here are a few more tips for doing well when you return to school:

- Maintain relationships with friends who are not in college. True, your main focus is your studies, but you will need to be around friends your age who share similar thoughts.
- If you are in a relationship, talk about your finances, time together, and your dreams.
- Remember that many of your current skills will work for you in school and on your new job. You might be strong as a communicator, leader, or planner. Many of the skills you have are transferable.
- Before you go to school to train for a new career, see if a professional will mentor you for a short while so you can get a taste of what the new career will be like. Try volunteering part-time or one night a week at a veterinarian's office, at a zoo, or with a pet trainer.

Remember that exploring new opportunities, making discoveries, and following your dream can be energizing. The appeal of going back to school can be an adventure leading to a new career path. Just keep in mind that high school students going directly to college, or college students moving straight into graduate school, are not better prepared than someone who is changing careers. When it comes to juggling school, work, and social life, everyone is on equal footing.

CHAPTER 5

Careers in Veterinary Medicine

Having dogs, cats, birds, reptiles, guinea pigs, gerbils, and other household pets as clients makes for a challenging and interesting career. The majority of veterinarians work in private or clinical practice caring for dogs and cats. Some veterinarians work in zoological centers with exotic animals. These opportunities have many tiers. Veterinarians can specialize in dentistry, surgery, research, and other areas of animal medicine. Others may choose a career as a veterinary technician or assistant; openings for these jobs are plentiful.

Veterinarian

If you have a pet, you have probably visited your local veterinarian's office. Depending on the size of the office, private practitioners usually work with a team of technicians, assistants, and office managers. Veterinary offices can have a small or large staff.

"I got my first taste of what would be my life's work tagging along with a neighbor who happened to be a veterinarian," says Dr. Tony Kremer, a veterinarian and owner of Kremer Veterinary Services in Illinois, which oversees the day-to-day operations of Animal Care Center of Plainfield, Plainfield Veterinary Clinic and Surgery Center, and Mallard Point Veterinary Clinic and Surgery Center.

"I wasn't quite old enough to work, but I loved just being around all the animals," he says. He was thirteen at the time.

"He took me under his wing and I continued working for him, doing odd jobs nobody wanted, cleaning cages, feeding, and making sure there was enough water for the animals. I got to walk the dogs for several summers and really developed my love and respect for animals. During these experiences, I realized I didn't just want to tag along. Caring for pets had become my lifelong goal. I wanted to be a veterinarian. I attended the University of Illinois in Urbana, where I graduated with a degree in veterinary medicine."

With degree in hand, Dr. Tony (as he prefers to be called) went back to the same clinic to work. Working at the clinic was a joy. However, after a few years he started his own clinic. Today, he owns three veterinary clinics and has a staff of ninety—from kennel workers to associates.

He finds so many aspects of the job to his liking. "We do a lot of routine care, preventative medicine, wellness checkups, vaccinations, and surgeries," he says. "Every day is different because of the scope of the animals and people you are dealing with. Each and every one of them is unique.

"I have seen the profession change over the last twenty years," he says. "A lot of our office visits are spent educating pet owners about preventative medicine and vaccines. They care so much about their animals and take a deep interest in what we do. It's like a partnership of sorts."

E ssential

Most veterinarians need to learn basic managerial skills because they work with a team of technicians, assistants, and office workers. Even the small private practitioner with one assistant and office manager should learn basic business practices in order to run an efficient office.

Dr. Tony, who lives with his wife, Meg, as well as two cats, two dogs, fish, and a quarter horse named Tango, has grown the business to include grooming, daycare and boarding, behavior and nutritional counseling, obedience classes, and emergency and critical care. His advice to people interested in becoming veterinarians is to "intern, volunteer, or take a part-time or summer job working at a vet's office. This way you can see if this is work you really want to do."

 Fact

> Did you know that veterinarians help people too? While working to heal a fractured bone in a dog, Dr. Otto Stader, a veterinarian, created the reduction splint. Medical doctors took a look at the reduction splint, studied it, and adapted it to use on healing broken bones in humans.

Most veterinarians work late hours and on weekends to accommodate their clients. Others have a more normal schedule. In larger cities, emergency clinics are open throughout the night and early morning hours.

Veterinarian's salaries are rising. This is in part due to the high cost of veterinary school. Starting out, you can expect to earn anywhere from the mid-$30,000s to $50,000. Veterinarians in private practice or in hospital settings with more experience can earn over six figures, depending on where you live in the country. Remember that in addition to the salary itself, you need to consider cost-of-living factors.

Veterinary Technician

Veterinary technicians are similar to nurses. As nurses work under the supervision of doctors, technicians do the same with veterinarians. They are well educated in the care and handling of animals. They can draw blood, prep animals for surgery, and hold animals down while vets administer vaccines. In some instances, they can give vaccinations, but not the rabies vaccine, which by law a veterinarian must do.

Chrissy Zarony, a veterinary technician with Animal Care Center of Plainfield, went into the profession after completing nursing school. "People who know me know that I have a mothering nature," she says. "I always had an interest in caring for animals. My nursing background helps. I have a lot of contact with people. You need good people skills for this job. And the rewards from this job are amazing. It's unbelievable when you save lives. The downside is when you have to euthanize a sick animal. It is good for the animal if he is suffering, but it still feels sad."

Zarony works 7 A.M. to 2 P.M. "The hours are pretty steady at a hospital or large clinic, and you can go home and spend time with your family," she says.

When she started her career fifteen years ago, she learned hands-on. "My nursing background was somewhat transferable, and I was eager to pitch in and learn," she says. "Today, many schools offer certification to become a veterinary technician."

 Fact

Dr. Daniel E. Salmon graduated from Cornell University in 1872 with a BVS (Bachelor of Veterinary Science) and went on to earn his DVM from Cornell in 1876. It was the first DVM to be granted in the United States. The genus *Salmonella* was named after him, although it was actually discovered by Theobald Smith, a research assistant who worked under Salmon.

Many schools offer a two-year associate degree for veterinary technicians. Some schools promote a four-year baccalaureate degree. The degree programs focus on basic skills needed to assist veterinarians. Students learn about overall healthcare concerns, how to handle and restrain animals, how to diagnose certain illnesses for large and small animals, and certain surgical procedures. Most students study practical applications in animal anatomy and physiology, pharmacology, and pathology. They also learn about basic office procedures. Students with a four-year degree usually earn high salaries and have more responsibilities, but it depends on the place of practice.

Starting salaries range from $9 to $20 per hour, depending on where you live. Annual cost-of-living and performance raises are routine, and most veterinary technicians get health benefits.

Veterinary Assistant

In some hospitals and private practices, a veterinary assistant supports the veterinarian and veterinary technician. Assistants perform all kinds of work, from cleaning kennels to assisting in restraining and handling animals. They also feed and exercise the boarded cats and dogs. In addition, they do a good deal of clerical work.

Veterinary assistants do not need degrees. According to the American Veterinary Medical Association, there are no credentialing exams; however, training programs do exist. Many veterinary assistants start out in this position and work their way up to veterinary technicians or even go back to school to become veterinarians. Others stay in the position because the hours are fairly steady, and they get to work around animals.

Research Veterinarian

Many veterinarians use their experience and education to conduct research at laboratories for private corporations, universities and colleges, and governmental agencies. By working as researchers, veterinarians have helped control malaria and yellow fever, solved botulism, and produced an anticoagulant to treat some people who have heart disease. Research veterinarians help both animals and people.

Some work for pharmaceutical and biomedical research firms. They develop, test, and supervise the production of drugs for human and animal use. To become a research veterinarian you will need to specialize in pharmacology, virology, bacteriology, pathology, or laboratory animal medicine.

 Fact

It was a veterinarian who discovered the link between the fatal West Nile virus found in some animals and humans. Dr. Tracey McNamara, a veterinarian at the New York Zoological Society in the Bronx, New York, was the first person to determine that zoo animals and wild birds were dying from the same disease that was harming people in New York.

Orthopedic Veterinary Medicine

Simply put, an orthopedic veterinary surgeon treats broken bones, strains, sprains, and dislocations. Orthopedic surgeons work with dogs, cats, horses, and other animals. Because this is a specialized field, most veterinarians who go into this line of work must have an additional year of study on top of vet school and residency, and take an exam to become a board-certified orthopedic surgeon.

If an animal breaks a leg, he may be able to go to a local veterinarian. However, if the break is in an unusual place or requires nonroutine surgery, a specialist should be called in. Several private orthopedic practices exist. Some even offer sports medicine for pets. Just as athletes see trainers and sports doctors for preventive care, so do some animals. Working dogs, such as K-9 rescuers, assistance dogs, and show dogs, often need massage treatments, stretching, and possibly chiropractic adjustments to work limbs that are under pressure. Racehorses and other working horses also are looked after by orthopedic veterinarians. Even the active family dog who chases a Frisbee needs preventive care.

 Fact

The face of veterinary medicine changes constantly. Much like medicine for humans, veterinarians are looking at alternative practices. Some use acupuncture to treat a wide variety of ailments. The veterinarian knows specific points in the body that correlate to healing the animal. Most animals actually calm down when needles are applied. The needles are unobtrusive, and vets know where the calming points in the body are located.

Orthopedic veterinary doctors earn upward of $50,000 to $60,000 starting out, and can easily earn salaries over six figures.

Other Veterinary Specialties

Veterinarians are employed in so many different fields. There's zoological medicine, aquatic animal medicine, aerospace medicine, animal shelter medicine, teaching, and other professions.

Board-Certified Surgeon

Just like medical doctors, veterinarians wishing to become board-certified surgeons must complete additional schooling. This is a three-year residency program in which veterinarians must meet specific training requirements, perform research, have that research published in a medical journal, and complete a residency program. At the end of the residency, the veterinarians must pass a rigorous exam.

Veterinarians who specialize often earn higher salaries than those who don't. Also, the need for their specialty guarantees job security.

Regulatory Medicine

The U.S. Department of Agriculture's Food Safety and Inspection Service employs veterinarians. Veterinarians can also work in a state agriculture department. These veterinarians work to prevent animal disease and to promote food safety by ensuring that animal food products are carefully monitored.

Veterinarians also work for state and federal regulatory agencies to quarantine and inspect animals to make sure no foreign diseases are brought into the country. They supervise interstate shipments of animals and test for disease. They work hard to eradicate diseases, such as rabies and tuberculosis, that can have troublesome effects on human and animal health.

 Fact

Dr. Andre-Joseph Brogniez's deep love of and interest in horses led to the development of artificial arms and legs for humans. By studying the movement of horses, this veterinarian expanded his work to study human movement. He developed an early version of prosthetics.

Public Health

In addition to overseeing the safety of our food supply, veterinarians work as epidemiologists in city, county, state, and federal agencies, investigating animal and human disease outbreaks. They also work to ensure the safety of our environment by studying the effects of pesticides, industrial pollutants, and other contaminants on humans. They can work at the U.S. Food and Drug Administration (FDA) as well, studying the safety of food additives for human consumption.

The newest arena for veterinarians is with the Department of Homeland Security. Here they protect humans and animals by devising antiterrorism procedures.

Military Service

Speaking of antiterrorism programs, the U.S. Army Veterinary Corps is developing programs to protect United States citizens against bioterrorism. These veterinarians are responsible for our food safety and biomedical research and development.

The U.S. Air Force also employs veterinarians, in its Biomedical Sciences Corps. These veterinarians work as public health officers managing communicable disease control programs. They are working to stop the spread of HIV, influenza, hepatitis, and other infectious diseases.

Fact

According to the American Pet Products Association, the pet industry, which includes everything from supplies to veterinary services, reached $43 billion in 2007. Pet owners spent $9.8 billion on veterinary care in 2007.

Teacher of Veterinary Medicine

Some veterinarians use their experience to teach veterinary students about the profession. Some continue working as veterinarians and teach part-time at a college, university, or veterinary medical school. Others who have been practicing for years go into teaching full-time because the schedule is a lot easier, and they want to impart their love and knowledge of the profession to their students. Lots of opportunities exist for teachers at the nation's twenty-eight veterinary medical schools. Those specializing in advanced degrees are in even greater demand. Teachers can earn upward of $65,000 to start, and over $100,000 annually over time.

CHAPTER 6

Careers in Compassion and Conservation

The threat of global warming has been a wakeup call. People are purchasing cars powered by alternative fuel sources; environmentally friendly homes are being built; and concern for the environment is on the increase. Caring for the environment has become a movement for our elected officials. This has sparked a bounty of opportunities in the field of conservation, including careers related to animals and their habitats.

Animal Anthropologist

One of the most famous animal anthropologists is Jane Goodall. Goodall is noted for her work with chimpanzees in Africa. Through her work she has established sanctuaries for orphan chimpanzees, and has spoken out on a wide range of environmental concerns. Goodall is known as a primatologist, a person who studies the behavior of primates.

Animal anthropologists study the behavior of all animals—from single-celled organisms to invertebrates, fish, amphibians, reptiles, birds, and mammals. Animal anthropologists are also called animal behaviorists. They study the behavior, functions, and development of animals, how behavior changes over generations, and how that behavior impacts humans and the environment.

Most animal anthropologists need a master's degree and often a doctorate. They major in anthropology, psychology, or sociology. The majority of animal anthropologists work as university professors. Others work as researchers in universities and at government and private research institutions such as drug companies or government laboratories. Behaviorists conduct research to find out about the effects of new drugs and about the links between behavior and disease.

 Fact

As a child, Jane Goodall dreamed of going to Africa to study primates. "I had this dream of going to Africa. We didn't have any money, and I was a girl, so everyone except my mother laughed at it. When I left school, there was no money for me to go to university, so I went to secretarial college and got a job." She eventually took a job as famed anthropologist and archeologist Louis S.B. Leakey's secretary. He saw a spark in her and hired her to study wild chimpanzees in Tanzania.

Zoos and aquariums often have behaviorists on staff who work to improve the health and reproduction of animals. Some wildlife centers and conservation organizations employ behaviorists whose main jobs are to work with endangered animals in the hope of reintroducing them back into the wild. With increased support from the public, conservation organizations are growing in numbers, which means the job opportunities for animal anthropologists are on the rise.

E ssential

Wildlife Biologist

Some days Keith Hudson spends his time crawling into caves counting gray bats. On other days he soars with flocks of birds, keeping careful track of their numbers while also keeping his light plane a safe distance from trees. Sometimes he is indoors, in front of a computer screen recording his findings. "Sixty percent of the time I'm outdoors," says Hudson, a wildlife biologist who works on the state level at the Alabama Department of Conservation and Natural Resources. "The other 40 percent of the time, I'm indoors. I prefer being outside."

His love of the outdoors stems from childhood days hunting and camping with his father and uncles. Most weekends found them at a cabin close by a river in his native Alabama. He knew at a young age that he wanted to work with animals and to be outdoors as much as possible. "A lot of my work has evolved into endangered species work," he explains. "I have a number of projects from taking bird and bat surveys, which involves netting them (catching them to count them) with mist nests, recording their numbers, releasing, and monitoring them. I've seen the bald eagle and white-tailed deer populations restored. Gray bats are on the endangered list. Many people don't understand bats, but they are starting to understand why conservation is so important."

When working outdoors with wild animals, Hudson is on the animals' schedule. "Bats are nocturnal, so I take the surveys starting at dusk," he says. "This isn't a nine-to-five job."

 Fact

Gray bats are endangered because of damage to their habitats. They live in caves. Pollution, natural disasters such as flooding, overuse of pesticides, and any change to their caves affect the gray bat population. Hudson and other wildlife biologists are working to bring back the gray bat population.

He works with two other wildlife biologists in the nongame and endangered species division of the Alabama Department of Conservation and Natural Resources. He goes out with an assistant biologist. "I rarely go out in the field alone," he says. "It's safer as a team."

He notes that it would be nice having a larger unit. "The jobs are fairly scarce and the funding is low," he explains. "There are other wildlife biologists who work on the federal level and in other state or privately run agencies. I'm seeing opportunities slowly change thanks to the hunters. Their role in conservation is huge. Hunting permits and licenses partially fund state agencies to improve and preserve the land on which game live and roam. Hunters provide a lot of feedback about an animal's habitat, food supply, and general welfare.

"Each state differs on the number of wildlife biologists that they employ," says Hudson. "Even with state, federal, and private agencies, there aren't hundreds of jobs to be had, but wildlife conservation is a growing field. And if someone is interested, they should go for it. People go into this profession because of altruistic beliefs. They care about animals and the planet. And many of us 'hope to save the world.' I'm in this profession because I love nature, and because I want my children and grandchildren to experience the beauty of the outdoors."

Not too many people in this field leave their jobs. Hudson has been doing this for twenty-plus years. He and others make a good living. "You won't get rich, but the rewards of improving the planet are priceless," he says.

Alert

In all fields of conservation when dealing with the public, there is a saying: "it's easier managing animals than people." All of these fields require a good deal of contact with people. It's essential to be a people person when working with animals.

Wildlife biologists' salaries start at around $30,000 and can go up to $70,000 and higher—depending on where you live and the management level of the position. Most wildlife biologists hold master's degrees specializing in forestry, wildlife biology, or fisheries. Some have doctoral degrees.

Wildlife Conservation Officer

Wildlife conservation officers must love the outdoors. They work to protect, manage, and enhance the environment by spending most of their days patrolling lakes, mountains, streams, marshes, beaches, and parks. Being physically fit is essential, since this job requires a lot of hiking. The job can vary from day to day. One day an officer can be taking water samples and the next day arrest someone for an illegal dumping offense.

The hours are long, and usually include working on holidays and weekends when hikers and others are using the parks. Wildlife conservation officers must be good at taking data and filing reports. A college degree in the sciences is a definite plus to get a job in this field, and candidates must pass a state and federal exam.

Wildlife conservation officers attend police academies. They are the state police of the waters and the woods. While many patrol parks on foot and in cars, those who oversee public lakes and rivers get around on Jet Skis. They enforce drunk driving laws on the land and in the waterways. They investigate all boating and hunting accidents. They work under the U.S. Fish and Wildlife Service, and can enforce federal fish and wildlife laws and assist federal officers when needed.

Starting salaries begin between $25,000 and $32,000—depending on location—and can increase to $65,000 or higher with several years on the job.

Ecologist

If you ever observed a bug or watched an animal gather food for the winter, you studied a bit of ecology. Ecology is the study of organisms and their interactions in their natural environments. Ecologists study the effects of rainfall, pollution, temperature shifts, and industrialization. Through the use of scientific research, an ecologist can change the way people think about the environment. One of the most famous ecologists was Charles Darwin, who worked as a theoretical ecologist.

 Fact

Charles Darwin believed in the importance of humans and animals working together. He said, "In the long history of humankind (and animal kind, too) those who learned to collaborate and improvise most effectively have prevailed."

Ecologists work in zoos, wildlife centers and parks, and universities. Ecologists can specialize in working with plants or mammals.

Other ecologists work in universities as professors. Many have backgrounds in chemistry, environmental science, geology, biology, climatology, and statistics. They often hold master's or doctoral degrees.

The field is opening up, and many ecologists become environmentalists. It's an easy switch since both use their scientific and statistics-based backgrounds to lobby for positive changes within the environment.

Those with higher degrees earn more money. Most make comfortable salaries, and can earn upward of $100,000.

Environmental Educator

Teaching the public about how their actions affect the planet is what makes Christopher O'Sullivan thrilled to be an environmental educator at the Trailside Museum and Zoo at Bear Mountain State Park in New York. Issues such as global warming, pollution, and even littering are at the forefront of O'Sullivan's mind. As an environmental educator he can show students and their families how every action they take has an impact on their surroundings. "We teach school and camp groups," he says. "Some of our visitors live in the country, and others are city folk. It doesn't matter. What does matter is seeing them go from not being overly excited to wanting to take action to help the planet."

At the Trailside Museum and Zoo, which is a part of the New York State Parks and Palisades Interstate Park Commission, all of the animals in the zoo had been injured and would not survive if released back into the wild. "They are a great learning tool," says O'Sullivan. "We have an osprey that got caught in a fishing net. It can't fly. The kids and adults enjoy seeing the animals up close. That hooks them, and then we can educate them about the animals and about the environment; it's all connected."

O'Sullivan always wanted to make a difference, but he took a roundabout path to his career. He got his degree in psychology at the State University of New York at Binghamton. He suggests majoring in environmental sciences. His psychology degree serves him well. "We deal with people on a daily basis," he says. "It's true that I work in this amazing state park. It's not too heavily populated, and you can find quiet areas here. But we do get a lot of visitors. So, it is important to know how to deal with the public, and you really must like interacting with children and adults because that is a major part of the job."

He does get hands-on time with the animals when he is teaching, but the zookeepers have more interaction with them. "I do a lot of paperwork and coordinate our volunteers," he says. "Our volunteers are essential."

Working at a park, zoo, or environmental center—any place that is open to the public all year—means working weekends. "We put in a lot of time, but it's not overwhelming," says O'Sullivan, "and besides, the park is a wonderful place to be."

This is O'Sullivan's second job. Before this, he worked as an assistant educator at Stony Kill Farm Environmental Education Center in Wappingers Falls, New York. "You have to work your way up," he says. At the Trailside Museum and Zoo, he has a supervisor and no assistants, except for the volunteers. "This is a nonprofit state-run entity, so we don't employ a lot of people."

 **Question**

What is the difference between an environmental educator and an interpretive naturalist?
The answer depends on who you ask. Some people in the field believe that interpretation is the art of enhancing the learning experience and that an educational program is strictly a learning experience. Most educators, especially those who work with children, like to think of their work as a combination of presenter/ actor and educator.

"To work for a state or federal agency, you have to become a civil servant, which means taking an exam," he explains. "It's a few hours and covers a lot of questions on how to deal with people, so my psychology degree served me well. The salaries are fair, not great. If you are looking to get rich, this is not the field to go into. You do this so you can make a difference, and I see things improving as attitudes change. More and more people are interested in working to help the planet."

Starting salaries range from $25,000 to $35,000; it all depends on the location. Executive-level salaries can rise to more than $60,000 annually.

Environmental Manager

Environmental managers have some contact with animals. Their major concern is care of the environment. They monitor the delicate balance between nature and humans. Hundreds of new jobs have been created in the field of environmental sciences specifically because of catastrophes involving toxic waste, air and water pollution, and natural disasters. They work in government and private agencies, and many are employed by the Environmental Protection Agency or state departments of environmental protection. They work preparing environmental impact studies, and ensure that laws keeping the earth, water, and air clean are upheld.

Under the umbrella title of environmental studies are forestry technicians and park rangers. Preparation for all of these fields involves studies in biology, chemistry, environmental sciences, geology, hazard perception, emergency and disaster planning, and waste management.

People in these professions earn anywhere between $25,000 and $40,000 depending on where in the country they live. Managers with several years of experience can earn upward of $60,000 on average.

Forestry Technician

Forestry technicians work for government agencies, such as the U.S. Department of Agriculture and U.S. Forest Service. They are responsible for the care and maintenance of federally owned forest land. Large paper and lumber corporations also employ forestry technicians to conserve and maintain the thousands of acres of forests. It is a good idea to have a background in biology and geography to get a job as a forest technician. Attending a four-year college with a forestry program is a wise choice.

Park Ranger

The National Park Service, the U.S. Forest Service, and state parks hire park rangers. Depending on the park, there is some interaction with animals, but the main responsibility of a park ranger is to enforce environmental laws to protect our parks. A park ranger must have a good understanding of wildlife conservation.

Most rangers have a four-year college degree majoring in geography, biology, zoology, wildlife management, and forestry. Rangers are civil servants, so they must take state exams to become a licensed park ranger.

Wildlife Rehabilitator

If you've ever found an injured animal, taken it home, cared for it, and released it back into the wild, you are a wildlife rehabilitator. Most people who do this are volunteers, but there are a few who earn a living doing this type of work. Wildlife rehabilitators rarely have veterinary or medical experience. They do have a permit to care for wild animals. To become a wildlife rehabilitator you must pass a state exam. When you pass the test, your name is registered as a wildlife rehabilitator in a public directory; if people find injured animals, they will call you for help.

Jonathan and Susan Wood are founders of the Raptor Project, a premier raptor rescue and education center. They make their living teaching the public about these magnificent birds of prey. Jonathan, Susan, and their young daughter, Rachel, travel around the country in a large mobile home with their collection of raptors. The birds have come to Jonathan from a variety of places. People find injured birds, call him, and he mends them as best as possible. Some of them can't fly, but they are all in good condition. His road trips take him to parks, schools, museums, and wildlife centers. He is a personable guy who also makes regular appearances on television shows teaching people about these birds of prey. His collection features an assortment of owls, falcons, hawks, and other raptors.

He is a federally licensed master falconer, wildlife rehabilitator, raptor propagator, and game-bird breeder. He is also licensed to handle eagles and endangered species. He gives between 800 and 1,000 lectures each year. This is not a nine-to-five job. Wood and other wildlife rehabilitators can get calls all hours of the day from people who find injured animals. Other wildlife rehabilitators focus on snakes and lizards. Work is available for those who build up a reputation.

To become a wildlife rehabilitator, it is essential to volunteer with a trained wildlife rehabilitator or at a wildlife center. A background in biology and animal behavior is helpful. Most wildlife rehabilitators don't earn a lot of money. Wood, however, makes a good living because he travels the country giving lectures. It's a lot like booking shows for a theater performance. Susan does most of the booking and scheduling. People who do this can earn anywhere from $30,000 to upward of $100,000—depending on the amount of traveling and number of shows involved.

Working with Pets

If the biological aspect of working with animals does not appeal to you, there are many careers that focus on caring for pets, whether it be through proper training, grooming, exercising, or spending time with them while their owners are away. These jobs are plentiful and fun and offer rich rewards in assisting in the betterment of the animal's life.

Animal Behaviorist

There is a bit of an overlap among animal behaviorists, therapists, and even obedience trainers. They all study psychology and behavior, and have acute observational skills. They can work as private practitioners in an office or in their clients' homes. They also work in research facilities, zoos, and universities.

Most animal behaviorists are certified as either an associate applied animal behaviorist or an applied animal behaviorist. Associate applied animal behaviorists must have a master's degree in biology or behavioral science with an emphasis on animal behavior. The hands-on experience is essential in getting certification. In this case, students must have at least two years of professional experience in applied animal behavior. Applicants must be able to show that they can work independently performing studies and data analyses, formulating and testing hypotheses, and writing in a professional manner. They must have experience working with an applied animal behaviorist. Applicants must present at least three letters of recommendation from Animal Behavior Society members.

Applied animal behaviorists must hold a doctoral degree in either biological or behavioral science with an emphasis on animal behavior. In addition, they must have five years of experience or a doctorate in veterinary medicine, plus two years in a university-approved residency program in animal behavior. Applied animal behaviorists must also apply to the Animal Behavior Society. The application requirements are the same as those of the associate applied animal behaviorist. For more information, contact the Animal Behavior Society at *www.animalbehavior.org*.

Depending on the type of degree, animal behaviorists start out earning at least $60,000, and salaries can rise to over $100,000 with experience.

 Question

Which certification is more rigorous—associate applied animal behaviorist or applied animal behaviorist?
It is the applied animal behaviorist, because students applying for this category have a heavier education load and are required to have more hands-on experience.

Animal Therapist

How many of you are visualizing a dog or cat lying on a couch talking to a therapist? By using their instincts and keen observational skills, animal therapists have a good understanding of what is going on with your pet. They work with animals and owners by surveying their environments. You can learn a lot about an animal's behavior by simply observing its surroundings and interactions with its owners. Animal therapists act as counselors to pets and their owners, offering advice on preventive medicine. Providing advice on diet, exercise, and care all fall under the roles of an animal therapist.

Animal therapists specialize in massage and bodywork. Some do intuitive communications work; others work as behaviorists. It is good to have a psychology degree as well as certification in animal massage techniques. This is an alternative side of the animal care profession that is slowly catching on. For more information about this profession, visit the International Association of Animal Massage & Bodywork at *www.iaamb.org*.

Pet Shop Owner

A major change seen over the years at most local pet shops is that they no longer sell dogs and cats. (People are purchasing pets through reputable breeders and at local animal shelters.) Most carry an assortment of tropical fish, guinea pigs, mice, rats, ferrets, snakes, and lizards. Pet shop owners also stock a large selection of pet food, pet toys, and care products—everything from bubble bath solutions and clothing for dogs to scratching posts for cats. Some pet shop owners allow local shelters to come in with shelter puppies and kittens. The money for those pets goes directly to the shelter.

Owning a pet shop is similar to running any retail operation. It is important to know what you are selling, and in this business it is essential to have a business degree in retail or lots of hands-on experience working and managing a store. Taking business courses is extremely wise. You will learn how to write a business plan, how to obtain capital to set up shop, how to hire and manage employees, and how to market your business. It is also a good idea to take a basic psychology course because you will be interacting with the public. Getting experience is also a must. Take a part-time or full-time job at a local pet shop to see if this is the career for you.

Hours can be long, and depending on the size of your retail shop, you will probably work weekends. Salaries are like most retail operations. If you are in a good location and stock products people need, you can be quite successful.

Doggie Daycare

This is one of the fastest-growing businesses in the animal care world. "People care about their pets, and they care where they leave them," says Susan Briggs, owner of Urban Tails in Houston, Texas. "We board dogs and cats when people go on vacation and while they work. A lot of our clients drop off their dogs early in the morning and pick them up on their way home from work. While they are at work, they want to know that their animals are safe and are having a good time."

At Urban Tails, dogs are exercised, fed, and played with. There is even a television and daybed in each kennel. Most of Urban Tails' business, like that of other animal daycare centers, comes from dog owners. People do drop off their cats mostly during vacation time.

Before starting Urban Tails in 2000, Briggs worked as a vice president of mortgage at a bank. "While I was working at the bank, I owned a smooth collie and a golden retriever," she says. "I took both dogs to obedience training classes. I enjoyed the classes so much that I wanted to follow my passion. So I changed careers. I thought it would be wonderful working with dogs."

She took a few business courses and opened Urban Tails. She started with a small staff and now has twenty-two employees. That includes groomers, trainers, and front desk staff. Briggs looks for enthusiasm and strong animal and people skills. "We have a lot of contact with pet owners," says Briggs. "They care about their dogs. That is why they send them here. They don't want them at home alone. Here we exercise and interact with the pets."

The dogs go for runs in the outdoor area. Pets take naps in rooms that measure either nine by ten feet or eight by eight. Each room has a color TV. "We call these our luxury suites," says Briggs. "The staff reads to the dogs, gives them treats, and even takes them swimming. We have an indoor swimming pool. It's like camp for dogs.

"A lot of large cities are opening daycare centers for dogs," Briggs adds. "To do this job, you need to have an equally strong understanding of dogs and business. I have a business partner who has a background in dog training. I also attend expos and workshops run by the American Boarding Kennel Association (ABKA). At a pet services expo they held, I got information on how to get financing for my business and how to manage the business once it was up and running. We also attend Groom Expos, which are organized by Barkleigh Productions (*www.groomexpo.com*). You learn about grooming, pet care, and info on running a business. It's a good form of continuing education, and it's always important to stay on top of things to continue to learn."

Briggs also learns from the dogs. "Watching them interact tells you a lot about their personalities, which helps us make their stay here a better one," she explains. "I also learn about new breeds. The other day someone brought in a Spinone Italiano; it's a hunting dog with origins from northern Italy."

Running a doggie daycare center means long hours, but life got easier for Briggs because she trusts her staff. "I'm fortunate that my staff is made up of good and dedicated people," she says. "This allows me to go home and spend time with my family. I don't have to work long hours thanks to my staff. They work different shifts, and we are open on weekends and have evening hours. When I first opened, I worked around the clock."

Her biggest expense in addition to paying her workers is the mortgage for the daycare center. "It's a big place—a warehouse—and real estate today is costly," she notes.

Briggs says that doggie daycare owners can earn anywhere between $40,000 and $75,000 annually. She does well because of all of the extra services she provides. "We have overnight boarding, daycare when pet owners are at work, grooming services, training and behavior, and we sell retail items such as food, leashes and collars, and pet toys."

Staff is paid hourly rates. They can earn anywhere from $7 an hour up to $25—depending on the position, location, and size of the business.

Groomer

Groomers can work at pet retail shops, in their own private practice, at a veterinarian's office, or in a client's home. This profession has the potential to be lucrative; about 70 percent of dog owners take their pets to a groomer at least three or four times a year. In addition to grooming animals, groomers have become advocates for pets. Since they spend up to an hour or more during each visit, they learn to detect any unusual ailments. They can tell if a dog is healthy or not. They can report these findings to the veterinarian they are working for or directly to the pet owner if the groomer is self-employed.

If this field interests you, you should decide whether you want to perform only basic services, such as bathing, nail clipping, and general care, or want to delve further and work with show dogs, for which you need to learn specialized haircuts. You can get the necessary training at a vocational school that specializes in dog grooming. There are no laws requiring certification, but having a certificate will make getting a job a lot easier.

Once you have your certificate in hand, it is a good idea to join the National Dog Groomers Association of America (*www.nationaldoggroomers.com*). Like most associations, this group offers workshops to its members, covering everything from the latest grooming techniques to how to run a business.

Freelance dog groomers and those who own their own grooming retail shop can earn upward of $50,000 annually.

Horse Groomers

Groomers work in stables saddling and unsaddling horses, giving them rubdowns, and walking the animals to cool them down after a ride. Horse groomers also feed, bathe, brush, and exercise horses. They clean out stables and make sure there is enough hay for bedding in the stables. They polish saddles and clean and organize the tack—harness, saddle, and bridle. In addition, they store supplies. Many experienced groomers help to train horses.

Groomers usually are paid by the hour. Salaries vary from $9 an hour up to $25, depending on experience and location.

Breeder

If you think you are going to breed dogs or cats to make a lot of money, get out now. This is a business that people do because they love dogs or cats; they want to work with a particular breed; and because this business allows people to spend a lot of time with their canine and feline friends. If you are game, you have to decide which breed you want to work with. City dwellers often choose smaller dogs. If you live in the south, pick a shorthaired breed. If you have a lot of outdoor space, you can choose a breed that likes to run.

Once you've selected the breed, study all that you can about it. Talk to local breeders and check out the American Kennel Club (*www.akc.org*). AKC offers tons of information on its website, including literature about each breed of dog and the requirements that must be followed if you want your litters to be AKC registered. There also is information on how to breed a litter, how to choose a suitable mate for your dog, and how to help with the pregnancy.

 Fact

The American Kennel Club's Compliance department sends field inspectors out to ensure the integrity of the registry and to protect the welfare of purebred dogs. Their field inspectors do investigations, inspections, and DNA testing.

If you prefer to work with cats, check out the Cat Fanciers' Association (*www.cfa.org*). Its website offers a wide range of information, from how to get started to how to register your litters.

If you want to go into this business, don't underestimate the cost involved. Consider housing, food, and veterinary bills. You are raising quality purebreds, so you can't skimp by buying cheap food. If you expect to earn a decent income, you will have to be in this for the long haul. Depending on the breed, some dogs can sell for $800 and upward. Some dogs can have up to seven litters in a year. (The size of the litter depends on the size of the dog, and most breeders do not overbreed for fear of harming the health of their dogs.) Small dogs, such as Yorkshire terriers, usually have litters of up to three puppies. Larger dogs, such as Doberman pinschers, can have up to ten in a litter.

If you still want to work with dogs or cats, but don't want to breed them, consider being a field inspector with the American Kennel Club or the Cat Fanciers' Association. In addition, other opportunities exist within these organizations. Following are descriptions of a few AKC careers.

AKC Field Inspector

Penny Butler used to show Doberman pinschers. She has shown dogs for the past thirty years, and participated in conformation and obedience at AKC events. She is on her fifth-generation Doberman. "I love this sport, the AKC, and of course the dogs," she says. "The AKC is the largest purebred registry. It's a great organization, and I wanted to give back to the people in the organization. They have given me so much."

 Fact

AKC's Compliance department conducted 4,800 inspections of dog kennels, individual breeders, distributors, and pet stores last year. The staff of fourteen field inspectors travel across the country and conduct inspections within their territories.

Butler now works as an AKC field inspector. She is on the road four days a week driving from Georgia to Florida to South Carolina inspecting AKC-registered kennels. She travels with Lincoln and Brooke, her two Dobermans. "This job is so gratifying," she says. "I meet people who love their dogs and I get to travel with my dogs. The other day I walked into a Beagle kennel and saw four field champions. It was amazing."

As a field inspector, Butler can control how a litter is raised by making sure the conditions at a kennel meet AKC guidelines. Her main purpose is to make sure the lineage of the dogs is pure. She does this by taking DNA samples, keeping careful records, and sending the samples and her reports back to AKC headquarters.

"I work four days a week," she explains. "I have my cell phone attached to the hip, and am in constant contact with my office. It's a lot of travel, but I love it. I have made so many friends, and in some cases field inspectors get to teach breeders how to care for their litters. We want the best for these dogs."

 Fact

The AKC has the largest database of canine DNA in the world. DNA is collected to determine parentage and genetic identity. DNA samples are taken and compared to the DNA of the mother and father of each litter. These findings guarantee that puppies are from the same lineage.

With Lincoln and Brooke along for the ride, life on the road isn't lonely. The AKC pays for hotels, mileage, and meals. AKC field inspectors earn $50,000 to start, and there are annual cost-of-living increases and benefits. "It's a big stretch from my former life running a custom framing store," she says of the job she held for twenty years.

Butler suggests that if you are interested in this profession, "you should start by showing dogs. Get to know the people involved. Talk to AKC members and breeders. There aren't many openings, but people do come and go." Butler herself plans to stay for the long haul.

 Fact

Field inspectors can suspend all AKC privileges if they find poor conditions at a kennel. If they find dogs in devastating situations, they will revoke registration and impose a fine as directed by the AKC. Their goal is to teach breeders how to take excellent care of their champions.

AKC Judge

American Kennel Club has about 7,000 evaluators around the country. "We teach basic training and good manners to dogs," says Dr. Mary Burch, an AKC judge and the Canine Good Citizen Director at AKC. The Canine Good Citizen Program is a certification program that started in 1989. Members teach their dogs good manners. It is a two-part program that emphasizes responsible pet ownership. Dogs who pass the ten-step program receive a certificate from AKC.

"AKC is the largest registry of purebred dogs," says Dr. Burch. (United Kennel Club, the second largest, is another place that employs people who want to work in this field.) "As Canine Good Citizen Director, every day is different. One day I might be working with the media to promote an event; on another day, I might work on data, budgets, or helping to train evaluators at events." Dr. Burch is a certified animal behaviorist and dog trainer too.

"I have a PhD in psychology and worked with humans for years," she says. "My interest in AKC began when my husband got me an out-of-control Border collie. I took him to basic AKC obedience training, and got hooked. I learned how to become a trainer and got set up in a community Canine Good Citizen Program."

Dr. Burch also worked as an AKC judge. "The best way to start is to show your own dogs," says Dr. Burch. "You get involved at the local level by attending shows and events. Here you will meet judges. You will have to attend seminars and apply for a judging license. You can also ask a judge to mentor you."

According to Dr. Burch, judges specialize in a few breeds. "You have to start with one breed and become an expert on that breed. Each purebred dog has distinctive traits. For instance, Rottweilers have been bred for centuries to be very protective of their owners and can snap at strangers. If you choose to specialize in this breed you have to learn how to approach a Rottweiler. Same goes for other breeds." The Chow Chow provides another example. These dogs are quite reserved, and have limited vision because of their deep-set eyes, so judges and trainers know that it is best to approach them from the front.

AKC judges must have a license from AKC for each breed that they judge. Judging standards for each breed is different. For example, toy, miniature, and standard Poodles are extremely smart and enjoy being around people. They are retrievers by nature and may be judged on their retrieving skills.

Judges can earn about $200 a day; the day rate depends on where you work. Many judges spend a lot of time traveling to different cities to judge dogs at a variety of dog shows. Others do this as part-time work. They may be obedience trainers or hold other jobs.

Animal Obedience Trainer

Sitting behind a desk at a major bank, Jim Burwell contemplated being at work at 7 A.M. when the bank opened and staying till 9 P.M. on most nights. "I put a lot of effort into my job, but wasn't happy."

Burwell won a dog at an auction. "He was a misfit type of dog, full of energy and easily got into mischief," he says. "I decided that if I wanted to keep Charlie (a golden retriever), I would have to train him.

So Charlie and I went to obedience training school. I was amazed at the outcome. I had a good time during the training, and while I was working at the bank, I kept on thinking about a career as a dog trainer."

That was twenty-five years ago. Today, Burwell is known as the Dog Whisperer of Houston. "Before I left my job at the bank, I spoke to a good friend of mine who wrote for the *Houston Chronicle*," he says. "She told me that it was possible to be able to make house payments and earn a decent living as a dog trainer.

"Over the years the business has changed. In the beginning I worked weekends and evenings. Today, my schedule is more flexible because there are so many people who work in the comfort of their own homes. So, I can actually work more normal hours. I also cut back on my overtime, and started training people how to become obedience trainers."

When he started, he read everything he could on dog training. "In this business you are constantly learning," he says. "The dogs and the owners teach you a lot on the job. You go to people's homes and watch how they interact with their dogs. Right there you can spot problems and undo them. It's instant gratification. People in my obedience training classes love their dogs and want the best for them. They will work hard to make those behavior changes in their dogs, and they will have a good time doing it too."

Burwell has a franchise called Petiquette, where he teaches others around the country how to become dog trainers. He also trains cats and works on behavioral problems with cats and dogs—such as scratching furniture or jumping. In addition, he has trained animals for television commercials.

He says that in-home dog-training franchises require less capital than most franchises because you are often working at the client's home. His Petiquette franchise is a four-week training program. "You need to see the dog or cat in its home setting," he says. "That way you can observe any problems and correct them."

This business also requires no investment in personnel other than you. Obedience dog trainers need to be comfortable around dogs and people because they spend an equal amount of time with both. Trainers can expect to earn upward of $50,000 annually. Running a franchise obedience training program commands an even higher salary, sometimes reaching six figures.

Dog Walker and Pet Sitter

Dog walkers have always been employed in major cities and small towns. If you walk along Manhattan's Fifth Avenue near Central Park, you can see a few dog walkers walking up to six or even eight dogs at a time. Dog walkers perform a much-needed service, and there are many pet owners who will pay someone to walk and exercise their dogs when they are at work or on vacation. The service has expanded to include pet sitting, pet taxiing, and minor medical care.

Dog walkers and pet sitters find clients by posting flyers or leaving cards at local veterinarian offices, at pet hospitals, and even at supermarkets. A good portion of their business is generated by word of mouth. One pleased client will tell another. People in these careers can earn anywhere from $10 to $15 per walk. Extra income comes from taking dogs to doggie parks and exercising them. Pet sitters are usually paid by the hour, and that rate varies based on cost-of-living factors. Dog walkers and pet sitters develop close relationships with their clients, which is essential for repeat business.

The one requirement for these jobs is to have good dog and people skills. Having some background working with animals is also helpful. One way to earn more money in this business is to specialize. Stacey Karin walks dogs and sits for people's cats and dogs. She also can administer medication to animals. Her company is called Grateful Pets. "I have a medical background," she says. "I'm a certified EMT for surgical practices. I started administering medications to dogs and cats by working with my local veterinarian. He recommended me for other pet-sitting jobs, and it snowballed. If a pet owner has to go on a business trip or vacation, they want to leave their pets in good hands. Knowing that I can give various medications—like diabetic medicine to cats—gives pet owners peace of mind. I do this because I care about animals, and specializing brings me more income."

She also stays overnight at clients' homes. "Many clients want to keep their pets as comfortable as possible," she says. "That means keeping the pets in their own homes."

Question

Do pets suffer from separation anxiety?
Yes. Many pet owners will hire a pet sitter to come into their homes while they are away on vacation or business to ease that loneliness, and the major drug manufacturer Eli Lilly has launched its first dog drug to treat separation anxiety.

Most dog walkers and pet sitters have "menus" listing the fee for each service. An overnight stay may be $50, with an additional fee for a walk at night and in the morning.

Paul Mann, a pet sitter and dog walker, boosted his income when he formed his franchise company, FETCH! Pet Care, Inc., in Berkeley, California. "I started FETCH! Pet Care with the sole purpose of providing as-needed professional pet sitting and dog walking services," he says.

Begun in 2002, FETCH! expanded within two years to cover the entire San Francisco Bay area and grew to become one of northern California's leading pet-sitting and dog-walking services. Today FETCH! has thirty franchise locations. "My clients appreciate the level of service they receive," says Mann. "Our services include private dog walks, group dog exercise, daily pet visits, in-home overnight sitting, private in-sitter's home boarding and daycare, pet taxiing, yard pet waste removal, and home care," he says.

He has done full background checks on his staff. "Clients want to know that their pet and home are safe," he says. "They trust us with a member of their family." Every member of his staff has been fully trained by Mann. Some work part-time hours and others are full-timers. "Very few pet sitters do this as a sole source of their income," he says. "Depending on how much time they put in, most earn between $5,000 and $10,000 annually. Those working full-time hours can earn $35,000 a year or more.

"Many of my FETCH! franchise owners see a profit within a year in business. Earning $100,000 is doable within the first three to five years." The fee to purchase a franchise, which comes with training, is $8,000. "The investment is minimal because your staff works out of their homes," he says. "What's important about this business is not to look at one month or even one year down the road. It takes time to grow a business. People go into this business because they care about pets. They also like the flexibility of the job, and they want to have fun. After 9/11, I have seen many people change careers. They want to spend time with their family and with their friends. We have priorities, and one of those priorities is to have a job that you enjoy."

CHAPTER 8

Careers at Zoological and Wildlife Parks

Zoos and wildlife parks have undergone major renovations. The steel bars and small concrete cages have almost disappeared. Today, major zoos try to re-create the best of Mother Nature. For example, at the Bronx Zoo in New York, the African Plains area offers lions a safe place to roam; snow leopards can be spotted in the Himalayan Highlands habitat; and western lowland gorillas have made a home at the zoo's Congo Gorilla Forest. Wildlife centers also have designed their parks with the animals in mind. At Six Flags Great Adventure in Jackson, New Jersey, the 360-acre Wild Safari is home to more than a thousand animals.

Veterinarian

Dr. William Rives, head veterinarian and director of Six Flags Great Adventure & Wild Safari, loves his job. He knows all of the employees at the wildlife park—even the part-time seasonal workers—and he can rattle off facts about every animal in the park. That's impressive considering there are 1,200 animals, representing 57 species from every continent except Antarctica.

If anyone on staff is having a bad day, Dr. Rives tells them to take a drive through the park. "It cheers everyone up almost immediately," he says. "Just being around the animals and observing them is a thrill."

Dr. Rives got hooked on animal science in high school. His biology teacher suggested he go to school to become a veterinarian. He always had an interest in animals. "I used to watch Mutual of Omaha's *Wild Kingdom* and other wildlife shows when I was a kid," he says. "I also read every animal book I could get my hands on."

While in school, he worked part-time as a gate guard at Six Flags Wild Safari. He then went to the University of Pennsylvania to study veterinary medicine. In 1993, he returned to the Wildlife Safari park as the head veterinarian. A few years later, he was promoted director of Wild Safari.

E ssential

Without zoos, most people would never see a wild animal up close. The role of today's zoos is to educate the public about animals. The role of zoo veterinarians, vet techs, and zoo directors is to preserve the animal population—especially endangered animals. Many zoos and wildlife centers are working to reintroduce endangered species back into their natural habitats.

As head veterinarian, Dr. Rives oversees the care of all of the animals at Wild Safari. He is happy that he can rely on his staff. "When an animal is sick or injured, we all have to pitch in," he explains.

The natural response of veterinarians, vet technicians, and others who work with wild animals is the desire to care for and have a personal bond with the animals. With these wild animals, it is essential to keep a safe distance, and try not to domesticate them. It's in the best interest of the animal care professional to be as caring as possible without getting too attached. The animal care worker knows that these are wild animals and should not be treated as pets.

Animals in the wild—mostly pack animals—try their best to hide injuries and illness. If a prey animal is sick, the pack usually doesn't want it around because it calls attention to the herd. Predators usually go after the weak link, and that is often an injured or sick animal.

So, Dr. Rives and his staff keep a constant eye on every animal in the safari park.

Fortunately, Dr. Rives has a support system. "When you go to veterinary school, it would be impossible to learn about every single animal," he says. "You are constantly reading everything you can get your hands on, and you talk to your staff and colleagues at other wildlife centers."

 Fact

Zoo veterinarians practice all facets of veterinary medicine including surgery, internal medicine, anesthesia, pathology, preventive medicine, and radiology. While each zoo has a different collection of animals, most veterinarians who work in zoos and wildlife centers care for a broad range of exotic animals.

When he began on the job as head veterinarian, Dr. Rives felt pangs of nervousness. "It is okay to be a bit terrified when you are treating your first animal," he says. "It gets easier each time. In vet school, they train you to be on your own—even though there is always a support system around. I can always call or e-mail other vets and former professors to discuss how best to treat an animal."

It seems that the working relationship among veterinarians and people who work with animals is one of cooperation. People in this field share a few common goals. First, they want to improve the welfare of all animals. They also enjoy learning from the animals they work with, and they want to pass on their knowledge about the animals to the public—for the public's edification as well as enjoyment.

Being a veterinarian at a zoo or wildlife center is a major responsibility. Zoo veterinarians take care of a wide range of animals. To become a zoo veterinarian or vet at a wildlife center, one must complete veterinary medical school. Majoring in zoology is also recommended.

Dr. Rives and his colleagues suggest volunteering while in school. "Get as much on-the-job experience as possible," he says. "Even an internship or part-time volunteer position at a wildlife center will give you an idea if this is the job for you. Plus, we look for people who have worked as volunteers at zoos and other wildlife centers."

 **Alert**

There is no such thing as a typical workday for zoo or wildlife center veterinarians. Each day is different because of the wide variety of animal species. Veterinarians who work with exotic animals need to be especially creative and must be able to think quickly on their feet in order to solve a broad range of health problems.

With more than 200 accredited zoos, wildlife centers, and aquariums in the United States, opportunities are available for veterinarians from time to time. People who are employed at these institutions usually don't leave. They enjoy their jobs so much that they leave only when they retire. That's not to say there aren't opportunities. Jobs do open up.

It helps to be a member of the Association of Zoos and Aquariums or the American Association of Zoo Veterinarians. These non-profit member organizations post jobs on their websites (*www.aza.org* and *www.aazv.org*). Networking and the willingness to relocate for a job helps.

Zoo veterinarians also must be open to doing grunt work. It doesn't matter if you are the head vet or an intern; at a place like Wild Safari everyone pitches in. Hours can get crazy once in a while. If a birth is expected, the staff is on call. The folks at Wild Safari do get to spend time with their family. This isn't an around-the-clock job, but hours can be long if an animal is injured, sick, or giving birth.

Incomes are good, mostly falling in the mid-range. Dr. Rives gets a few calls each month from students asking about career opportunities. "If the first thing they ask is about the money, I tell them to look for another career," he says. "We don't do this for the money. We do this because we are passionate about animals."

Salaries range from $25,000 to $60,000 for veterinarians first starting out, depending on geographic location. Most wildlife parks and zoological centers have great benefit packages for their employees.

Veterinary Technician

While studying to become a veterinary technician, Kyle Covill, veterinary technical supervisor at Six Flags Great Adventure & Wild Safari, would volunteer to work with rabbits, rats, mice, snakes, an impala, kangaroo, and lion. "Ninety-nine percent of what we learned at school is centered on dogs and cats," he says. "Whenever I had the chance to work on an animal other than a dog or cat, I jumped at the opportunity."

 Fact

> The veterinary technical field is attracting more and more women. About 80 percent of veterinary technicians are women. Women, as well as men, are drawn to this semi-new field because they want to help animals. Veterinary technical school varies between a two-year and four-year degree program. Some vet techs don't have degrees—just on-the-job experience. Having a certified veterinary technician degree makes getting a job easier.

He actually first started showing dogs when he was nine years old. "I did that until I turned twenty-one," he says. "I would show dogs for professional handlers."

When he turned twenty-one he enlisted in the Marine Corps. After spending four years with the Marines, he went back to school to work with animals. While he was at school, Covill spent a lot of time volunteering at veterinary hospitals.

"Several years ago the job of veterinary technician wasn't well known," he says. "We are animal nurses, and we do everything a nurse does. I'm a certified veterinary technician [CVT]."

Covill got his CVT from the Northern New Jersey Consortium for Veterinary Technology. He says that when it comes to working with exotic animals, most of the education you will get is from on-the-job training. "Over time you will learn that a tiger is a tad bit different from a lion in the way he behaves. Each animal is different. Sometimes you can apply what works for one animal to another. Other times, you must be very creative."

Many states require two- and four-year vet tech graduates to take a licensing exam. According to Covill, the test is pretty broad, with 200 questions covering everything from domestic animal care to facts about pet food and medications. The National Veterinary Technician exam is offered in most states, and the license is transferable from state to state. For more information about this exam, contact the Association of Zoo Veterinary Technicians at *www.azvt.org.*

For Covill, working at Wild Safari is an adventure. "We can have a few hair-raising moments," he says. "Safety is paramount. When you are working with a lion that may be ill, you have to anesthetize him, and make sure that he is not moving. Before we open the pen, we tap on it to make sure he isn't moving. Before we do anything on the animal, we apply bite locks, so if they do bite down, we won't get bit."

Most of the time, Covill spends his day making rounds, driving through the safari park observing different behaviors. "Often, we let nature takes its course," he says. "Sometimes it is best for the animal to leave it alone, or let the mom take care of it. We step in when we need to—to do what's best for the animals."

When Covill comes across an animal that needs care that he is not familiar with, he consults with Dr. Rives and his staff. "If we are stumped, I can go online to my member organization and ask a question."

Covill belongs to the Association of Zoo Veterinary Technicians (AZVT), a nonprofit organization with more than 300 members. AZVT offers an annual conference to its members, has a job board, and lets members know about workshops to enhance their knowledge. "Once you become a vet tech, it's a good idea to be part of a national organization," says Covill. "It's a good place to learn more about the field."

 Fact

Veterinary technicians at zoos and wildlife centers often earn an hourly wage of $8 to $20, depending on geographical location and institution. Some start out with annual salaries of $25,000. After several years of on-the-job experience, vet techs can earn between $45,000 and $60,000. Most who get salaried positions receive a full benefits package.

Even with a good support system in place, vet techs can be on their own—especially when working with exotic animals. "Sometimes we come across a situation where there is nothing written," says Covill. "We can stump our colleagues with questions. That's when we have to try different methods to see what works and what doesn't work. There is a lot of creativity that goes into this job."

Even when he is stumped, he enjoys the challenge of treating a wide assortment of exotic animals—especially the hoofed stock. "I like working with the antelope species," he says. "We have several endangered ones here. The trick for me is not to get too attached."

Zoological and Wildlife Parks Director

When Dr. William Rives was asked to become the director of Six Flags Great Adventure & Wild Safari, he jumped at the opportunity. "I did have to talk it over with my wife," he says, "but I took the job because I knew that I could affect policy. The major concerns here are the welfare of the animals and the enjoyment of our guests. We want this place to be a sanctuary for the animals and a place of learning for the people who drive through the park."

He still works as the head veterinarian at Wild Safari. As director of the safari park, he oversees a staff of veterinarians, veterinary technicians, animal trainers, wardens (zookeepers), and seasonal workers. Wild Safari is open from April through November, but staff is kept busy taking care of the animals year-round.

Dr. Rives also attends a good number of meetings. He likes hearing suggestions from his staff and enjoys coming up with ideas to enhance the park and park experience for visitors. His favorite part of the job—hands down—is driving through the safari and tending to the animals.

The path to a career as a director in a zoo or wildlife center can be serendipitous. Some positions require a bachelor's degree; others require a PhD or veterinary degree. Often people in the zoological world start out in an entry- or mid-level position and work their way up. The one certainty to obtaining a job in this field is to start out part-time as a volunteer—even if that means doing grunt work, like cleaning cages. When you volunteer and do a good job, people who are hiring notice. When a job opens up, you will definitely have an edge.

Jim Anderson, director of the Fort Wayne Children's Zoo in Indiana, started at the zoo as a seasonal worker. "I was home from college as a music major looking for a summer job," he says. "I happened by the zoo and thought, 'That would be an interesting job.' I was hired as a summer seasonal, driving the train, mowing grass, cleaning restrooms, and feeding and cleaning the animals. That was thirty-two years ago. I moved up from summer employee to zookeeper, supervisor, curator, assistant director, and now director.

"I loved that first summer at the zoo," he says. "I liked being in the role of caregiver. I liked learning about animals—in the wild and at the zoo. I liked the public aspect of the zoo—showing people animals and seeing them enjoy their experience while they learned a little."

Anderson advises people interested in the profession to make sure it is the right calling. "Working in a zoo isn't just watching monkeys swing on the vine all day. Make sure you have the right character attributes, personality, and skill set for the position you seek. Then learn all you can and seek experience where you can find it."

He recommends joining the Association of Zoos and Aquariums (AZA), which posts jobs on its website, *www.aza.org*. "Be willing to start from the bottom, gain experience, and work your way up," he adds.

In addition to getting a bachelor's, master's, doctorate, or veterinary degree, it helps to have a business background. Additional schooling in business, marketing, and/or communication is a big plus. "The zoo business can be tough to get into," says Anderson, "but the former director here used to say, 'There's always room for the good ones.' It is a very tight profession, but there are opportunities. Some success may depend upon good timing."

Zookeeper

Jodi Carrigan has a fancy job title at Zoo Atlanta in Georgia: level III keeper in the zoo's Primate Department. She oversees the interns and volunteers and has more responsibilities than a level I or II keeper. Carrigan also is the secretary of the American Association of Zoo Keepers *(www.aazk.org)*. At Zoo Atlanta, her daily duties entail training, enriching, cleaning, feeding, and caring for the primates. In addition, she is responsible for public speaking, which includes educating the public, and also for educating a staff of interns and volunteers.

She started as a volunteer at the Pittsburgh Zoo and Aquarium while she was in college. "I volunteered to get some experience and to see if this is what I'd enjoy doing for a living," she says. "I fell in love with the profession and the animals, and was extremely lucky enough to get a job right after graduating college at the Miami Metro Zoo working with primates. From there, my boyfriend at the time— and now husband—moved to [Zoo] Atlanta, where he worked with the giant pandas. I obtained a job with the Primate Department. I followed a dream I had for working with primates."

At the zoo, Carrigan works with gorillas. Zoo Atlanta has twenty-three of them, which makes it the second-largest gorilla collection in North America. She also studied and works with eleven Bornean and Sumatran orangutans, which make up the largest orangutan collection in the country. "We practice protected contact with our apes, which means we do not go in with them," she says. "There is always something in between us and the animals. For one thing, apes are several times stronger than humans, and we want them to be animals and socialize among themselves. We only intervene if it's absolutely necessary, for example if a mother rejects its newborn or if there's a serious injury or illness. We want them to be among gorillas and orangutans, and when you add a human to that mix it changes everything."

E ssential

Some schools, such as Santa Fe Community College, offer an associate's degree in zookeeping. Carrigan says that while some zoos hire keepers with an associate's degree, having a four-year bachelor's degree is the way to go, considering the stiff competition. Some zookeepers can move up into a higher position with a master's or doctoral degree.

At times, she does have hands-on contact with many of the animals. She has to check and brush their teeth, listen to their breathing with a stethoscope, file down nails, take temperatures, and vaccinate them.

Carrigan got a bachelor of arts degree in anthropology from Indiana University of Pennsylvania. She says that most institutions require keepers to have a bachelor's degree in a science-related field—zoology, anthropology, animal science, or biology. Carrigan says that being a zookeeper caring for primates is very competitive.

"Most people love what they do and stay there for the duration, which doesn't leave too many positions available," she states. "Many people interested in working with primates can't get a job working with them right off the bat and often obtain a position in some other area of the zoo, for example working with small mammals, and even in the commissary where the animals' diets are made. They get their foot in the door and their face known."

Salaries for zookeepers vary among zoos and wildlife parks. "Anyone that works with animals will tell you that they don't do it for the money," says Carrigan. "It's not a high-paying profession. I love what I do. I am lucky enough to say that I have a job where I wake up in the morning and I really love going to work to be with the animals. Not many people these days can say that about their profession."

Educator

In order to teach the public about animals, zoos and wildlife centers are hiring educators. Some zoos have classrooms where visitors can listen to a lecture and observe—and in some cases even pet—an animal. At Turtleback Zoo in West Orange, New Jersey, children and their parents fill a classroom to learn about tarantulas, snakes, and small birds. Some fearless children walk right up to the tarantulas and snakes. Others cower behind their moms and dads. All come away with a bit of new knowledge.

The goal of most zoos and wildlife centers is to make their institutions user friendly. At Cleveland Metroparks Zoo in Ohio, visitors not only learn about an animal and its habitat, they can watch a few medical procedures—from routine checkups to emergency surgeries. "My job is to stand on the people side of the glass and explain what's happening," says Victoria A. Putnam, education assistant at the Cleveland Metroparks Zoo. Putnam works out of the zoo's new state-of-the-art veterinary hospital, the Sarah Allison Steffee Center for Zoological Medicine. "It's pretty cool stuff. I love it because the information I can share with the people is endless. I can talk about animals, the environment they come from, conservation of that species, how the zoo cares for our animals, zoo careers, medical treatments, and what zoos are doing to improve wildlife for the animals."

Putnam got her bachelor's degree in biology from Mount Union College in Alliance, Ohio. From the time she could pronounce the word "biologist," she wanted to work with animals. Upon graduating, she found that getting a job was a lot harder than she imagined. She worked part-time at the Cleveland Clinic at night and as a waitress during the day. "Waitressing paid the bills," she explains. "It helped me get by. I didn't enjoy the work at the Cleveland Clinic because there was too much testing going on; I just didn't enjoy that aspect of the job."

 Fact

Several zoos have educators on their staff. Some also use volunteer docents to teach the public about the animals. At some zoos, the education person might also handle other duties, such as marketing and public relations. The number of people working in a marketing, education, or publicity department depends on the size of the zoo.

She also took a seasonal job as a counselor at the Cleveland Zoo. "It was the first year that the zoo started a day camp," she explains. "By the end of the summer, a position in the education department opened up. I applied for it and got the job. It was quite exciting because the zoo had just built this state-of-the-art 24,000-square-foot veterinary facility."

The public part—called the learning lab—also includes an exhibition space. It's here where Putnam spends most of her day. "The public lines up to watch our talks," she says. "They like getting a behind-the-scenes look at the zoo—how the veterinarians take care of the animals. We draw crowds from schools, camps, and general visitors."

Putnam recommends that if you are interested in a career as an educator at a zoo or wildlife center, you should minor in education and get your bachelor's degree in biology or animal science. Zoo educators can earn between $34,000 and $42,000 with benefits.

Animal Trainer

Animal trainers at zoos and wildlife centers are taking on new roles. In addition to training a seal to balance a ball on its nose, coax a dolphin to jump through a hoop, or have a capuchin monkey perform on cue, animal trainers are working closely with wildlife veterinarians to identify unusual behaviors. If an animal is sick, a veterinarian will sometimes call on the animal trainers to assist with calming the animal.

Jessica and David Peranteau, senior supervisors of animal training at Six Flags Great Adventure & Wild Safari, train a variety of animals from small birds and reptiles to kinkajous, dolphins, and sea lions. When an animal is out of sorts, the Peranteaus are called in to get the animals to cooperate—kind of like a mom sitting with her children in the pediatrician's office.

"The animals we train know us," says Dave. "They let us take blood samples. Most animals have to be anesthetized or restrained in order to take blood samples. The dolphins we work with let us use gastric tubes to take stomach fluids. We can also get them to let us do voluntary ultrasounds on them."

"The reason they do this is because they trust us," says Jessica. "These animals know us, and we make a game out of these necessary tests. It's better for the animals not to restrain them. There is less stress involved for them and for us. Everything they do is voluntary."

The Peranteaus use positive reinforcement on all of the animals they train. Developing a relationship based on trust is essential. "Animals cannot tell us when they are under the weather," says Jessica. "The staff here really relies on us to let them know if we notice anything out of the norm. We can see signs or precursors before they get sick by observing their behavior. We spend a lot of time around the animals, so we know when something is off."

 Fact

> Most people don't realize that animal trainers need to have excellent public speaking skills. According to Jessica Peranteau, "Animal trainers are the ambassadors of the animals they represent. We want the audience to have a good time. We also want them to come away with a good understanding about the animals. So, public speaking is a major part of this job."

Dave says, "We do want our audience to know the animals. Through knowledge comes caring, and this work is all about caring. This is not a job; it's more of a lifestyle. Jess and I are lucky that we ended up working together. Many people in this business end up in close relationships since we spend so much time together doing something we truly enjoy. This is not a nine-to-five job. We are on call if an animal is pregnant or sick. The vet staff relies on us."

"We helped hand raise a few baby monkeys that were brought to us," says Jess. "We took turns bottle-feeding them every couple of hours throughout the night. Not all nights are like this, and many people outside of the animal world don't always understand the dedication that is needed for this job. It's just so cool to be around the animals. We are also lucky that we can work together as a couple."

Jess got her bachelor's degree in behavioral psychology from Kent State University. Dave got his bachelor's in marine ecology at Gettysburg College in Pennsylvania. In his senior year in college, Dave went to the Caribbean to study sharks. He also interned with the National Aquarium in Baltimore, where he worked with dolphins and seals, doing outreach educational programs with visitors to the aquarium. He was then hired at Sea World in Ohio.

Jessica also applied and was hired at Sea World. "A lot of people don't realize that there is a Sea World in Ohio," says Jess. (In 2001, the company sold the Ohio property to Six Flags.) As a child, she went to Sea World often with her family. "Every summer, my family and I went to the Cleveland Zoo, Columbus Zoo, or Sea World," she says. "I was in high school when I went up to the trainers and asked them how I could pursue a career training animals. They suggested a background in animal sciences, animal behavior, and hands-on experience."

"Nothing is as important as hands-on experience," says Dave. "Many schools for animal training have internships. Volunteering at zoos, aquariums, and wildlife centers is essential. Some parks even have shadow programs where you can follow a trainer around for a day. It's a good way to tell if this is a job for you."

Getting a job training exotic animals is possible. "We found a way," says Dave. "It helps to volunteer—even if it means interning or volunteering at a shelter or veterinarian's office working with dogs and cats."

Jess says that when applying for a job to train animals, you should be open to all situations. "You might not be able to train monkeys or killer whales. You might be able to train sea lions. The basics of all training principles are the same. Never close doors, because each experience is a learning one, and if you are working with one species, a good deal of what you learn will apply to another species."

As with most jobs, salaries depend on experience and geographic location. Trainers of exotic animals with at least five years of experience can earn between $40,000 and $50,000.

Zoo Designer

When you design a home for an animal, you have to please five clients—the animal, the zookeepers, the visitors to the zoo, the donors, and government officials. First, the animals should be housed in a comfortable environment that works for both the animal and zookeeper. Animals must be able to roam in as natural a setting as possible. They usually spend a good deal of time outdoors. Their enclosures have to be easy to operate—meaning doors should open and close without any fuss for the animal, and the zookeeper must be able to get to the animal in order to feed and care for it.

Visitors to the zoo want to see the animals in natural settings. They also want to be able to see the animal without any obstructed views. Donors, who have become extremely important to zoos and wildlife centers over the last decade, get more of a say in the design process. Some landscape architects are designing behind-the-scenes viewing areas just for major donors.

Then there are government officials. "Building a zoo or habitat for an animal is very different from building a warehouse or zoo gift shop," says Nevin Lash, ASLA (American Society of Landscape Architecture) and principal at Ursa International, a design and planning firm that specializes in zoological projects. "There aren't codes written for designing animal habitats. When working with government officials we have to explain and show them why a door has to swing a certain way. It has to be easy for the animal to operate. We don't want a frustrated animal that can't get into his shelter because of a faulty door."

E ssential

The old zoos of yesteryear are a thing of the past. New construction of zoos and wildlife parks mimics natural settings. Gone are the steel-bar cages. They are replaced with landscapes that resemble, as much as possible, the animal's natural home. In some cases, even the temperatures of indoor exhibits are controlled to create appropriate conditions.

Lash's company has designed habitats for many zoos including Zoo Atlanta, Chimp Haven, Roger Williams Park Zoo in Rhode Island, Zoo New England, Dallas Zoo, North Carolina Zoo, Cape May County Zoo in New Jersey, Dian Fossey Gorilla Fund International in Africa, Cochrane Polar Bear Conservation Center in Ontario, and Jamaica's Hope Zoo. Lash has thirty years of experience as a landscape architect. When students ask him about zoo design, he tells them "First work as a landscape architect."

Lash followed his own advice, working as a landscape architect for ten years designing gardens for homeowners, office parks, and shopping malls. "I got bored silly after a while," he says. "A friend told me about a firm in Philadelphia that specialized in designing zoos. That was in 1986 when zoo design consisted of creating lushly illustrated drawings."

He applied and got the job. What he loved was that the atmosphere was casual. "My boss wore sandals and shorts to work in the summer," he says. "I didn't have to starch my shirts any more."

 Fact

One of the biggest changes in zoo design is green building. Companies like Lash's are using more environmentally friendly materials in their designs. Often a solar roof will be hidden to make the habitat look more natural. Landscape architects are trying to design nature-inspired settings that are good for the animals and planet.

What he learned on the job was that the zookeepers, biologists, and zoo directors were the experts. He fully understood architect-speak—the language of his trade. However, designing a home for a client who doesn't speak can be a challenge. "It's a lot like designing a kitchen or an outdoor park," he explains. "Your clients know what they want. You have to work with them to make it possible."

For example, zoo habitats can be lush and beautiful on the exterior. The shelter part of the exhibit that the public doesn't see is a different story. "Most of the floors are concrete," he says. "They have to be easy to clean. However, we put down a lot of hay and soft areas for the animals. We also design spaces with skylights. We have to make the interior as comfortable as possible, and easy to get in and out of. Some interiors have pools and others have ropes for swinging and climbing on. Both interiors and exteriors have to be extremely sturdy so the animal doesn't destroy it. There is a lot to take into consideration."

Zoo designers need a four-year degree in landscape architecture from an accredited college, plus five years of training as an apprentice with a licensed landscape architect. Then they take a state exam to become a licensed landscape architect. Every state does its own licensing. If you want to work in a particular state, you need a license in that state. Lash is registered in three states— Pennsylvania, Georgia, and Texas. It is also possible to work in other states by collaborating with landscape architects who are licensed in those states.

Lash has seen the industry change and grow over the last two decades. About twenty years ago, there were just a handful of landscape architectural firms that designed zoos. Today, there are twenty. He works with his wife, Gail Y.B. Lash, PhD, co-owner of Ursa International. She has a degree in biology and has worked as a biologist, which gives them an edge. "What I love about this job is that I get to learn about animals and their habitats," Lash says. "Designing zoo habitats is a great field that's very fulfilling. Every job is different and challenging. Plus, it's high on the moral scales from my point of view. Once you get involved with an organization like a zoo, you meet dedicated, caring people with huge hearts."

Fundraiser

Fundraisers are the behind-the-scene stars at wildlife centers and zoological parks. Without them, zoos and wildlife centers just wouldn't exist. Most institutions hire fundraisers to write grants, pitch letters to their membership, and organize a host of events and galas to raise money. The fundraiser's role has grown because part of the job is to promote the names of the donors. Most donors, except for those few who want to remain anonymous, are treated as celebrities. Just walk through most zoos and wildlife centers and you will see signs highlighting the names of the donors on each exhibit. Donor names are often as large as the name of the exhibit. Some even have information about the individual donor or company posted next to the exhibit. In many cases, fundraisers who write grants stipulate that the donor's name and company information will be publicized.

Even with promises of recognition for the donors, writing grants is a tough business. The competition is fierce. Every institution feels it is worthy of receiving funds. Fundraisers, also called development officers, must feel good about the organization and projects that they are promoting. Depending on the size of the institution, some companies hire a development director, who often reports to the executive director, while the development director oversees the work of the assistant development director, grant writer, and an assistant. Development staffs are often small. Some can be one person who does it all—even the publicity and marketing.

 **Alert**

Many people are in awe of those who ask others to donate money. It's not uncommon to hear, "I could never ask for money." That is just a portion of the job, but an important one. Developing ongoing relationships with donors is essential in this business. If asking for money is difficult for you, consider going into another field.

The median salary for development directors is $78,000. Development directors or fundraisers must have a bachelor's degree in communications, public relations, marketing, business, or finance. You must possess excellent writing and speaking skills. It also helps to join a professional organization such as the Association of Fundraising Professionals (*www.nsfre.org*).

Researcher

What do animals think about? How can we learn about them? How can we learn from them? Why do they behave in a certain manner? Researchers, who can be scientists and behaviorists, are employed at a large number of zoos and wildlife parks in the country. Their objective is to understand animal behavior and to educate the public about those behaviors.

The National Zoo in Washington, D.C., is home to Think Tank, a place where visitors to the zoo can learn about the tools an animal uses, its language, and how that animal interacts with others. Think Tank researchers study an animal's behavior. As part of the National Zoo's Orangutan Language Project, visitors can watch researchers teaching orangutans to use symbols and syntax to express their thoughts.

Researchers at the San Diego Zoo in California study animals, their habitats, and their social behaviors as well. Most of their work involves teaching the public about the animals' behavior. By becoming educated about animals, people often wind up caring about them. Many zoos have programs that educate the public about endangered species.

 Fact

Gorillas, Siberian tigers, pandas, and elephants are just a few of the endangered animals listed on the Red List of the International Union for Conservation of Nature and Natural Resources. The Red List includes 15,589 species that face extinction. Research scientists are working to educate the public about this crisis and its effect on the public. To learn about the animals on the Red List, go to *www.iucnredlist.org*.

The San Diego Zoo's center for Conservation and Research for Endangered Species (CRES) is the largest zoo-based multidisciplinary research team in America. CRES, which formed thirty years ago, has grown from a small research institution to one that includes international field conservation programs in more than twenty countries. From the center's inception, CRES scientists have worked to gather and disseminate research about the conservation and recovery of endangered species.

Competition for researchers at zoos and wildlife centers is intense. Having an advanced degree, either a master's or doctorate in biology and animal behavior, is necessary. It also helps to have excellent writing and public speaking skills. To get your foot in the door, volunteer in the research department at a zoo or wildlife center.

Starting out in this profession, expect to make between $35,000 and $45,000. With several years of experience on the job, salaries jump to $60,000 to $90,000, depending on the size and location of the institution.

CHAPTER 9

Jobs in Entertainment

From ants to elephants, animal actors include all kinds of species—even cockroaches. Lassie, Mr. Ed, Morris the Cat, and others work on the big screen as well as the small. The animals may act or be part of a documentary. Horses and dogs can be found entertaining crowds at circuses. Many of these animals work with trainers, groomers, and certified animal safety representatives. Then there are jockeys who ride horses, and reporters who cover the races. Not all of the animals have a starring role, but they are essential in the world of entertainment.

Animal Trainer for Film and Television

Many film reviewers said that in the movie *Eight Below,* it was the animals who stole the show. The six Siberian Huskies and two Malamutes in the film play sled dogs. For each dog, there were six to eight stunt doubles. Dog trainers worked with the dogs to teach them tricks for their roles in this film. "Animal trainers have a close relationship with the animal actors," says Rose Ordile, a film and television animal trainer who is the 9Lives Morris the Cat handler.

Ordile has worked on the sets of *Eight Below, South of the Border,* and other movies and television shows. "Ever since I was eight years old, I knew that I wanted to work with animals," she says. "The only trouble was that I didn't want to be a veterinarian or vet technician. I wanted to be an animal trainer for TV and films. I grew up watching *Lassie*, *Petticoat Junction*, and *Green Acres*. I told my high school guidance counselor that was what I wanted to be. He said those types of jobs didn't exist. Growing up in New Jersey, we really didn't know about other opportunities working with animals other than vet or vet tech."

Since she didn't know she could work in film and television with animals, she went for an associate's degree as a veterinary technician, and also majored in art. While at school, someone suggested she study grooming. After graduating, she enrolled in a grooming school in Las Vegas. "There I learned about grooming and coloring techniques," she says.

While studying to be a groomer, she learned about Moor Park College in California, where students can get a degree in exotic animal training and management. Ordile didn't go to Moor Park, but she did move to California. "The tuition at the time was a bit out of reach," she says. "But I went to California hoping to get into the film industry. While I was there, I worked as a groomer."

"I tried to get my foot in the door, but it wasn't easy," she continues. "Through my work, I met a girl who said she had a friend who was looking for people to ride ostriches in a movie. I called and the producer asked me if I ever rode an ostrich. I told him I was a city girl from New Jersey and New York and the only animal I ever road was a taxi. He laughed and asked me if I could ride horses. That I could do. So, I went down and got the gig. It helped being 103 pounds. They needed lightweight people for that role."

After that, film work dried up, but she had her grooming business to fall back on. In the meantime, she volunteered on movie sets cleaning kennels. "That was fine with me," she says. "I was able to meet people and I weaseled my way in as a volunteer. Still, I didn't have steady work."

When she heard that the same producer was looking for someone to train exotics, she called him. "He asked me if I worked with exotics," she says. "I told him no, but that I have worked with domestics—just cats and dogs. He said 'no,' but I didn't give up. I called him once a week for a few months. He finally gave in. I worked hard and showed that I could do the work."

In this business you get jobs through people you know. "You just have to get your foot in the door; then it gets easier," she says. "The best way to start is to volunteer. Show people that you can do the work—even if that means cleaning kennels. I don't mind that work at all. Actually, I get to spend more time around the animals, and they get to trust me. You can also work as a second or third trainer to the main trainer. Again, you will do some grunt work, but you are getting experience."

Show business isn't steady. Animal trainers work from production to production. One constant in Ordile's life is working as Morris the Cat's handler. She, Morris, and Morris's double travel the country making live appearances as part of Morris' Million Cat Rescue. The rescue started in September 2006. On their travels, Ordile teaches the public about animal care and the importance of taking care of and adopting shelter cats.

 ## Question

Where was Morris the Cat found?
The original Morris was found in a shelter in Hinsdale, Illinois, in 1968. He retired in the late 1970s after working almost twelve years. The second Morris also was a shelter cat. He was discovered at a New England shelter and stepped in as spokescat for 9Lives.

The salaries for animal trainers range from moderate to more than six figures. It depends on where and how often you work. Ordile does well thanks to her work in film, television, and with Morris.

Colorists

Ordile also works as a colorist in Hollywood. As a groomer, she learned a lot about hair color. She creates animal-safe dyes so animal stunt doubles can look like the star. In a film where a zebra befriends a small child, Ordile actually colored a white horse to look like a zebra. "Zebras are ornery," she says. "They have bad tempers and don't always cooperate." For this show, she dyed the horse's white coat with black stripes. Voila! a zebra was created. "Animals lick their fur, so I only use my own dyes, which are animal-safe."

 Fact

Many animal actors began their lives as strays. Fang, the drooling Neapolitan Mastiff from the Harry Potter movies, was rescued from a junkyard and adopted by his trainer. Max and the six different dogs who played the same role in the film *How the Grinch Stole Christmas* also were shelter dogs.

In the film *Eight Below*, each dog had six stunt doubles. "The dogs are not exactly alike," she says. "That is where a colorist comes in. You can dye an animal's fur to match the star." (You can see samples of her work at *www.animalcolorist.com*.)

Colorist's salaries are similar to those of animal trainers. Being a certified groomer is a way into the industry. Ordile notes, "The path into this industry is to volunteer and network. You really have to know people."

Certified Animal Safety Rep

Certified animal safety reps are on film and television sets making sure that no animal is harmed during the filming of a show, that the animals get breaks, and that they are treated with the utmost respect.

Many people outside the industry question the protection of some animals—say, a cockroach. "It's all about where we draw the line," says Jone Bouman, head of communications for American Humane's Film & Television Unit. "Should we make the cutoff at guinea pigs or dogs or larger animals? We have to protect all animals without discriminating. Our goal is to watch out for the welfare and safety of each and every animal on the set."

American Humane started working in the film industry in the 1920s and '30s. "At that time, there were several instances of wire-tripping of horses in westerns," says Bouman. "It was the film *Jesse James*, starring Henry Fonda, that had a chase scene where a horse had to jump over a cliff. The horse was forced over the cliff and died. That was in 1939, and because of that situation, American Humane was able to rally a public outcry. We weren't officially recognized on film sets before that time. The Film & Television Unit officially opened its doors in 1940."

 Fact

The year 2007 marked the 130th anniversary of the American Humane Association. It has two divisions: one protects children from all forms of child abuse, and the other focuses on the well-being of working and farm animals.

So when you are watching the end credits of a film and see the statement, "No animals were harmed in the making of this film," you know that a certified animal safety representative was on the set watching out for the animal actors.

Certified animal safety representatives are part of the Screen Actors Guild. They are not hired by the studio, producer, or director. "That would be a conflict of interest," says Bouman. "We aren't beholden to the people who make the film. Our reps are on the set working for American Humane. Their salaries come from grants from American Humane."

Working with major film stars can be exciting. Rebecca Humber, who works as a full-time certified animal safety representative for American Humane, has met many A-list stars. However, she gets an even bigger thrill from the animals. "I enjoy working for the animals," she says. "Each day is different, and often we don't know where or which set we will be working on."

 Fact

> For the film *How the Grinch Stole Christmas*, reps from American Humane were on the set from the start. They actually monitored the preproduction training as well, and made sure that the dogs' costumes were comfortable. Max and the other six dogs that played the same role had to wear antlers and long, floppy ears for the film. These headpieces were just a few ounces in weight, and didn't seem to bother the dogs at all.

Being in Los Angeles or Hollywood is important, because that is the film capital of the world. However, American Humane employs reps throughout the country, and many travel overseas to work on film sets. For instance, the film *Chronicles of Narnia* was filmed in New Zealand. The Harry Potter films were on location in Great Britain. "We go were the work is—it's an adventure," says Humber, who recently worked on a television movie set keeping a close eye on a mountain lion.

American Humane hires ten full-time reps and between twenty-five to thirty-five on-call and part-time safety reps. "We keep them as busy as possible," says Bouman. "We host trainings once a year. It is a tough job. It can entail a lot of travel, hard work, and long days with a lot of sitting around."

Full-time reps earn $40,000 a year to start. Part-time reps are paid by the hour. It can be as low as $15 or up to $25 an hour. Food is usually provided on the set, and hotels and transportation are paid for by American Humane if you are on the road.

Humber got her degree at Moor Park College. "I'm from northern California," she says. "I learned about Moor Park's animal training and management programs from trainers at Sea World. After the shows, I would stay and ask all kinds of questions—mostly how they got into this business. When I was in high school, I contacted the school for information. Toward my senior year, my parents and I took a trip to the campus. I applied and got accepted. I think what helped was that I volunteered at local rescue operations."

Even though the staff of reps is small, "we are always looking," says Bouman. "Not everyone is comfortable with the amount of travel and unpredictability of not always knowing what set you will be working on. This type of schedule does lead to openings. I'm always looking for people with equine experience or trainers who work with livestock. Being able to work with dogs, cats, horses, and other animals gives you a leg up in this job."

Theater

Training an animal for the theater is a bit different from training one for the movies or television. True, both have a lot of distractions on the set. However, in a theater there is the audience to contend with. The animal actor has to be completely comfortable in front of a live audience as well as know when to interact with the actors on stage. One noted animal trainer is William Berloni, who began his career in 1976 with Sandy, the original dog in the Broadway production of *Annie*.

Rescued from a shelter, Sandy appeared in the production for seven years. Sandy was the first animal to have a starring role in a major Broadway production. After working with Sandy, Berloni trained other animals for careers in theater, film, and television.

Animals and their trainers have a strong bond. "It is in the trainer's best interest to make sure that the animals they are working with are well cared for," says Rose Ordile. "After all, a happy, well-cared-for animal gives the best performance. No one wants to work with an overworked, tired animal. It doesn't benefit anyone. So good trainers take good care of the animals they work with."

Ordile has made live appearances with Morris the Cat. "A cat sleeps about 70 percent of the day," she explains. "However, getting them to lie still or react positively to a crowd takes a lot of training.

The dynamics of a live appearance are similar, but not the same as a filmed production."

Most animal trainers work with animals in film, television, and theater. Basically, the same skills are needed for each, and the education is similar. Most are certified animal trainers. Salaries are also in the same ballpark.

Circus Trainer

Each morning Yasmine Smart tends her six Arabian horses and one pony. She has a staff of three trainers but likes to be involved in the care and feeding of each animal. As a star performer in the Big Apple Circus, each day is different. Some days she, her staff, the horses, and the rest of the circus are on the road, traveling by trailer from city to city. (The Big Apple Circus performs 250 shows a year, and makes ten city stops.)

Training starts at 9 A.M. sharp, but her day begins around 7 A.M., when she and her trainers feed and care for the horses. She likes to mix things up by introducing new routines every so often, and there is a new show every year. "We get a repeat crowd," she says. "We don't want to present the same show every year. The audience would be bored, and so would the horses. They like learning new moves, and it makes it more interesting for everyone involved. We get to be creative by introducing new steps."

Yasmine was born into the circus. Her grandfather was the legendary Billy Smart, a circus performer from England who crossed the Thames on a wire in 1951. Her father, Billy Smart Jr., ran the Billy Smart Circus in England, and her mother was a high-wire acrobat. At a young age, Yasmine learned how to walk on the high wire and how to swing on a trapeze by watching and studying with her parents.

"I have always enjoyed living in the circus, being with the performers and the animals," she says. "It was exciting and is familiar to me. Growing up in this industry was my norm. I was always drawn to the horses. Like a lot of little girls, I always loved horses. At eleven,

I convinced my parents to let me train the twelve black Shetland stallions. They thought I would grow out of it, get interested in boys, and do other things teenage girls do."

Not so. Yasmine rose early every morning before school and would clean out stables, and feed, wash, and exercise the horses. She also trained them. "My parents saw how serious I was about working with horses," she says.

She worked in her parents' circus, and then toured with other circuses. She has been with Big Apple for the past four years. Artistic Director Paul Binder discovered Yasmine at a festival in Monte Carlo and invited her to join Big Apple. It is a hard life on the road, but one she enjoys. Workdays usually start at 7 A.M. in the stables, and performances end either at 7 or 9 P.M. depending on the day. Then there's the work of putting the horses back in the stables for the night.

"Circus horses tend to live long, healthy lives," she says. "They get a lot of exercise and care. If you are in this business, you must love being around horses." Her dedication to performing and putting on entertaining shows is evident, but that is secondary to her love of horses and her concern for them. "It's a good life if you don't mind the travel," she says. "Circus performers can be a close-knit group because we spend so much time traveling together. We also hook up with friends after a show when we travel from city to city."

Getting a job as a lead trainer/performer in the circus can take a few different paths. "Just because you are born into this business doesn't guarantee you a job," she says. "You have to show that you can do the work. It's like any profession. You have to be good at what you do, and you have to be willing to work hard and start at the bottom."

Yasmine suggests waiting around after performances to talk to trainers, going to school to become an animal trainer or groomer, and volunteering at stables. Her three assistants all had experience working in stables.

Star performers can easily command six-figure salaries. Salaries for groomers don't pay much. It is an hourly gig that pays around $15 an hour. All room and board are taken care of by the circus.

Documentarian

Did you grow up watching Mutual of Omaha's *Wild Kingdom?* Are you hooked on one of Animal Planet's special documentaries? Watching animals in their natural setting has wide appeal, and has introduced many people to animals in the wild. Working on a production is even more thrilling than watching one on TV. Producers, directors, film crew, and all those involved with the making of animal documentaries have a risky and exciting job.

People who make wildlife documentaries should have a strong background in animal science and film. Lacking the latter, they can hire a film crew. In the case of wildlife conservationist Chris Morgan, chance played a major role. While Morgan was leading an expedition of tourists through Katmai National Park in Alaska, a filmmaker from PBS (Public Broadcasting System) started filming, unbeknownst to Morgan. The filmmaker, Joe Pontecorvo, captured Morgan and his tour group closely watching about a dozen bears dining on local salmon. The tourists' eyes opened like saucers being so close to the bears. After Morgan talked about the bears, Pontecorvo stopped filming and told him he got great footage. Afterward, the two went to a local pub for a beer and discussed working together to make a documentary called *BearTrek*.

"I was quite lucky to happen upon Joe," says Morgan. "Actually, my career studying bears has had many twists along the way."

He got his first glimpse of bears while working as a camp counselor in New Hampshire's White Mountains. He was eighteen years old at the time and was planning to attend school when summer camp ended. His plan was to return to England, his native home, and attend a university to become a computer graphics artist. "Everything was set," he says. "I had this summer job in the States, and was planning on going to art school."

Plans changed when a wildlife conservationist who studied bears gave a talk to the kids at the camp. Morgan stayed for the lecture, and afterward asked the conservationist about "a million questions," he says. "I got his number and kept on asking him to take me out with him."

One day he got a call in the evening, and was told to be ready at 9 o'clock that night. The bear expert showed up in his pickup truck and took Morgan to a garbage dump. "I saw fourteen black bears," Morgan says. "We watched them and tracked them. It changed my life. I knew I couldn't go to art school. I had to study bears."

When he returned home, he found a school that offered a program in conservation management. After college, he got a master's degree in advanced ecology. His work focused on carnivore research and bear ecology. Within the past twenty years, he has worked on bear research and education projects on every continent where bears are found, in regions including northern Spain, the Pakistani Himalayas, the Canadian Arctic, Ecuador, the Canadian Rockies, and Borneo. He is currently living in Washington State, where he started a nonprofit company called Insight Wildlife Management. Insight offers research, education, and ecotourism products and services that focus on the eight bear species in the world. Morgan relies on raising funds through Insight and other nonprofits for completing and showcasing *BearTrek*.

BearTrek will cost about $1.6 million to make and promote. Of that sum, $400,000 will be donated to several major bear conservation projects—including those groups that are profiled in the film. To raise the money, Morgan established a production company called Wildlife Media and hired a grant writer. "It's a big part of getting this project off the ground and keeping it afloat," he says.

Pontecorvo and the rest of the documentary crew will film Morgan as he travels to different parts of the world exploring bears in their natural habitats and the people who work on behalf of bear conservation. The documentary will also show how bears impact our environment on a local level.

Morgan enjoys working on the film because he gets to bring his message to the public and he gets to be around bears. Being out in the wild can get lonely. He and his crew have formed tight relationships. Living outdoors and in sparse conditions doesn't seem to bother Morgan or his crew. "It's an adventure," he says. "I have what I need on a material level. Being surrounded by this beauty is amazing. Plus we get to meet incredible people from different cultures who share our concerns."

He has been doing this work for just over twenty-one years, and his enthusiasm is still as fresh as when he spotted his first bears in New Hampshire's White Mountains. Finances are secondary to the pleasure of being around bears and the people who are working to protect them. There have been times when he would just scrape by, but that doesn't seem to bother him. He loves his life and the fact that he can create a documentary explaining the importance of the bear population in the world, and how that population affects mankind.

Horse Trainer

Training horses for professional racing is somewhat similar to training horses for other forms of entertainment. A career as a horse trainer is time-consuming and can be somewhat dangerous. Even the best trainers have been bitten and kicked. You really have to know how to handle horses. Horse trainers start out low on the totem pole, taking care of the horses, grooming them, and exercising and saddling them. Riding comes later, or can be done off-hours. Having in-depth knowledge of equine health and psychology is essential for this job.

If working at a race track is what you really want to do, you should start by hanging out near the stables and introducing yourself to the trainers. Ask if you can volunteer. That might mean cleaning out stalls. Show that you really want to be there and are willing to do all jobs to advance in this profession.

Once you are interning, volunteering, or working with a professional trainer, you will want to apply for a license through your state's racing commission. When taking the exam, you will be tested on racing rules and regulations and horse knowledge. For more information, contact the American Quarter Horse Association at *www.aqha.com*.

Jockey

Jockeys are usually self-employed. They work with thoroughbred racehorses. This sport has two basic forms, flat racing and steeplechase. In flat racing, jockeys ride horses on a flat or leveled track for a predetermined distance. Steeplechase is racing over hurdles. In either case, you must know horses and must be a top-notch rider in good physical shape. Jockeys cannot weigh more than 115 pounds, so that a horse can easily carry you as you race on the track.

Jockeys need a recommendation from horse trainers and owners to get a job. You will probably start out as a groomer, making sure the horses are brushed, cleaned, and ready to ride. Most groomers oversee the care of three or four horses. If you prove yourself to be a good groomer, you will advance to riding the horses, for exercise purposes only.

 **Alert**

Jockeys must keep their weight at or under 115 pounds. Steeplechase riders can weigh a bit more—but no more than 140 pounds. This has led many to suspect that some jockeys don't take care of their health. Some have had problems with anorexia and bulimia. A jockey must maintain good health in order to do a good job.

The next step is to start competing in small races. Here you learn how to get out of the starting gate and race. You will also need to apply for a license through the racetrack; the license is valid at racetracks nationwide. You can also attend a trade school to become a jockey. For more information about schools and the profession, visit *www.jockeysguild.com*.

Columnist/Writer

Writing books, newsletters, or magazine and newspaper articles about animals is a great way to work with animals and share information with readers. Joan Lowell Smith, columnist for the Star-Ledger in New Jersey, writes a weekly column called "Concerning Animals." As a reporter with thirty-five years of on-the-job experience, she has covered everything from nuclear physics to features on theater arts. For the past twelve years she has focused her writings on animals.

As a columnist, she spends a lot of time with animals. "I have a tremendous amount of contact with animals, or I'd be worthless as a pet columnist," she says. "I've been passionate about dogs and cats all my life. Some interviews are conducted on the telephone, some online, but most in person. I'm constantly covering events large and small."

With newspapers cutting editorial space, writing about animals can be a challenge. Lowell Smith wrote about animals every chance she got when she was freelancing covering human interest stories. "When the opening developed at the *Star-Ledger*, I gathered a bunch of articles I'd written about animals and submitted the portfolio," she says. "Many articles were from minor newspapers, but the *Ledger* was only interested in content, so I guess my message would be that no one should be reticent to submit work from minor media, since one would assume that a writer always does her best, whether the readership is 6,000 or over a million like the *Ledger*."

Lowell Smith suggests joining Dog Writers Association of America (*www.dwwa.org*) and Cat Writers' Association (*www.catwriters.org*) to learn more about jobs and events.

In addition to writing for newspapers, animal lovers can write for magazines, newsletters, and websites. Many nonprofit wildlife associations have newsletters. All need editorial staff. To become a writer, columnist, or editor at a publication, it is a good idea to major in journalism or English at an accredited college or university, and to start out as a staff intern. You also could start by writing articles in your spare time, and submitting them as freelance pieces.

Another career path for writers is to specialize in some form of animal behavior or science. Many scientific journals will publish well-written articles on animal-related topics.

Staff writers earn between $35,000 and $55,000 annually. Editors earn more; salaries may start at $50,000, depending on the size of the publication.

CHAPTER 10

To the Rescue

From finding lost children to busting criminals for smuggling narcotics to controlling crowds, animals play a major role in law enforcement. K-9 dogs are used in search and rescue operations. Police officers use dogs to sniff out everything from bombs to LSD. Military personnel also work with a variety of animals, from flies to dolphins, to keep us safe. Then there are those who rescue pets from disaster areas, and others who relocate exotic animals from one zoo to another to populate the species. All of these rescue workers help humans and animals.

Animals in the Military

Animals work in every branch of the armed forces—and they have since the beginning of time. Horses once carried soldiers into battle. Today, horses in the military are basically used for show in parades and at funerals. In battle, horses have been replaced by tanks and other vehicles. Dogs, on the other hand, are used for sniffing out drugs and explosives. They were used in Vietnam for scouting, tracking, sentry duty, flushing out the enemy, and detecting mines and booby traps. Dogs in K-9 units are used today in Iraq.

The U.S. Navy has used dolphins for surveillance and mine detection in Vietnam and in the Persian Gulf. Using dolphins is controversial. Many animal rights groups have opposed the military on this issue. It is in the best interest of animal trainers—in the military and in civilian life—to take the best possible care of each and every animal they are working with. However, in military service animals don't always survive. Just like a soldier, an animal that is placed in a dangerous situation may not come out alive. For instance, chickens were used in Kuwait to detect chemical and biological weapons. Unfortunately, more than half of the birds died from heat exhaustion from the harsh desert sun.

On the other side of the issue, the military treats its animals as valuable members of its team. They are an asset used to help protect multimillion-dollar ships and their most precious cargo—the sailors.

Members of the armed forces who wish to work with and train animals for search and rescue and defense areas need to have at least a year of military service before requesting assignment to animal training. While there is a need for animal trainers, animal rights groups are pressuring military personnel to use alternatives in place of animals.

Training Police Dogs

One of the most exciting positions in police work is being part of the K-9 unit. Dogs have been used to recover bodies from lakes and rivers, to sniff packages for drugs, and to detect bombs. Dogs are utilized for their keen sense of smell. Because of their great olfactory senses, they can sniff out old and new smells, including those that are masked to the human nose.

K-9 dogs make routine checks of postal packages. While searching packages at a UPS office, a K-9 Springer Spaniel named Aza found ten kilos of cocaine was wrapped in several layers of Saran Wrap, sprayed-on insulation, and mustard powder (to throw off the scent). All of this was packed in a Styrofoam cooler. She also found three kilos of cocaine hidden inside a VCR. "Drug dealers are constantly shipping stuff like that," says Raymond D. Humphrey, a retired police officer who served for twenty-eight years—twenty of those with the K-9 unit in East Windsor, Connecticut. "Our dogs find drugs in the mail, on people at airports, and even in coffins. There is no honor among drug dealers."

"Working with K-9 dogs is exciting," says Humphrey, who now runs the Penny Harris Foundation, a nonprofit organization based in Connecticut that trains dogs for police work. The foundation also raises money to train officers and to donate dogs to units around the country. "Every day is different because we encounter all sorts of crime."

On one of his last days on the job, he was called on a domestic violence case. When he showed up at the house with his K-9 assistant, the abuser took off. The dog found the suspect hiding in a cemetery a few blocks away.

 **Question**

How much keener is a dog's sense of smell as compared to a human's?
While humans have about five million olfactory receptor cells, a bloodhound has one hundred million. These dogs can even easily detect bodies at the bottom of a lake.

Dogs are trained differently for each task. Most people associate K-9 dogs with sniffing out narcotics and bombs. Other dogs are used to track criminals. Arson detection dogs can find traces of gasoline, kerosene, or other accelerants that are used to start and spread fires. K-9 dogs are used for search and rescue to find hikers who are lost in the woods.

In addition to an acute sense of smell, dogs hear much better than humans. Some dogs are used to find people—both alive and dead—in burning buildings, collapsed buildings, and in earthquakes. There is even a special unit that works with dogs to find cadavers, in the case of people who are missing and presumed to be dead.

"Working with dogs can be tough," says Humphrey. "You develop a close relationship with them. They are—in a sense—your partner.

You know they are going to go into a serious situation; they can be harmed or killed. We develop attachments to them."

The training can take from three to six months. "We have to train the dogs and the police officers," says Humphrey. Most trainers like to work with young dogs that they find at shelters. The majority of K-9 dogs are German Shepherds.

To work with a K-9 unit, you must be a police officer. "You have to prove yourself," says Humphrey. "So, you should be on the job for about a year or two before moving to a K-9 unit. In most cases you will start by volunteering to help your K-9 unit. When a job opens up, then you can apply for it."

People who work with K-9s work all over the country. Salaries are similar to those of regular police officers. In this line of work, advancement comes with experience, attitude, and showing that you are a good police officer.

Training Police Horses

In small towns and large cities, people admire police horses. Even in the roughest neighborhoods, mounted officers on horseback are easily approachable. "Nobody wants to pet a patrol car," says Jim Barrett, a retired police officer who worked as a captain in the Ventura County (California) Sheriff's Department. He worked as a police officer for thirty years, and for twenty of those years had the pleasure of being in the mounted unit. He now works as a manager at Police Horse Pros, LLC, a company that trains horses and riders for police work.

"The key to training horses is to desensitize them to a variety of stimulation," he says. "Horses don't like loud noises. The training involves getting them used to different sounds and a variety of obstacles. We may have horses walking through an area filled with plastic bottles because when they are working, they are exposed to all sorts of situations."

Equally important to training horses is to train the riders. According to Barrett, you must be a horse person to join a mounted unit.

"And you must do your time in a regular unit before applying to a mounted one. Salary depends on where you live and on your level of experience. You aren't going to get rich, but you will be comfortable. Besides, you get to work with horses."

Question

What type of horse is used for training?
Most mounted units prefer training American quarter horses. The horses have to be desensitized to a variety of stimuli, and training can take up to a year. About 25 percent of the horses that go through the training don't make the cut. Instead, they are sold to private owners for use at dude ranches or for riders who use them as pets.

Animal Crime Scene Units (CSI)

It's true that animals cannot talk. However, animal DNA collected at crime scenes is quite telling. Crime scene investigative (CSI) units rely on information found from either a victim's or suspect's pet. During an assault case, the victim's dog relieved itself on the attacker's car. Police took a urine sample from the car and matched it to the dog's DNA. Thanks to this evidence, prosecutors were able to convict the attacker.

In another case, a serial murderer lived with half a dozen cats. Police found two bodies next to the house of the serial killer. The killer confessed that he buried other women nearby, but would not say where. The detective from the CSI unit collected hair from the cats, because the hair they shed often attaches itself to bodies and clothing. K-9 dogs picked up the scent of the cats' hair and found the bodies, putting the criminal behind bars.

CSI personnel can also be called ETs (evidence technicians), CSTs (crime scene technicians), SOCOs (scenes of crime officers), and CSAs (crime scene analysts). Regardless of job title, CSI personnel gather evidence by examining, identifying, documenting, and collecting physical clues at a crime scene. They usually start out with at least a year as a police officer, so they have to attend police academy. Many can go straight from high school; some tend to go to college for either a two- or four-year degree first. A background in biology and forensic science is important.

 Fact

The Foundation for Biomedical Research (FBR) and the American Veterinary Medical Association work hard to educate the public about animal testing. The goal of both organizations is to improve human and veterinary health by promoting humane and responsible animal research. For example, FBR works to inform the public about the essential need for lab animals in medical and scientific research.

People applying for this job must have strong stomachs. Being around corpses and crime scenes is not for the weak of heart. However, the work is quite rewarding because you help solve crimes. Salaries are on par with that of police detectives. Starting salary can be anywhere from $25,000 to $50,000, depending on where you live.

Disaster Relief and Response Teams

When Hurricane Katrina ravaged parts of New Orleans, disaster relief and response teams were called in to find, move, and relocate people and animals. When the wildfires in Southern California spread, many rescue workers were called in to rescue horses and household pets.

The Humane Society of the United States (HSUS) Disaster Response Unit helped relocate a few hundred pets from Louisiana to

American Society for the Prevention of Cruelty to Animals (ASPCA) shelters in Texas. HSUS Disaster Response Unit workers also helped find homes for animals lost in the 2004 tsunami overseas. HSUS is the largest animal protection agency in the country, with more than nine million members. HSUS is a nonprofit organization that works to protect animals in every manner, from disaster preparedness to wildlife and habitat protection to protecting farm animals. In addition to sending workers out into the field for rescue work, HSUS works to educate the public about animal welfare issues.

Another major component of HSUS is the workers who bring about new laws to protect animals. Among other goals, HSUS workers are working to protect dogs and cats from being sold to researchers by illegal means. They want to end the sale of random-source dogs and cats for experimentation. In addition, they want to stop imports of sport-hunted polar bear trophies in the United States.

 **Alert**

Animal relief workers must be comfortable working with pets that are scared and may bite. In the event of a disaster, everyone—even animals—can be terrified. The animals can be territorial and may not want to be moved. It is important to get the proper training from an organization such as HSUS to learn how to handle animals that may attack out of fear.

HSUS's Disaster Response Unit works closely with the American Red Cross, which works to protect people from natural disasters. Other animal organizations, as well as agencies run by state and federal government, also have a hand in rescue work. For example, the Department of Animal Care and Control in Los Angeles, California, organized and trains the L.A. County Equine Response Team to rescue horses.

Many response teams are made up of volunteers. Others work in fire and police departments. HSUS mostly uses trained volunteers, but they do need people to run these training programs. To find work, check out *www.hsus.org*, and look under Disaster Services.

Paid members of disaster relief units earn salaries equivalent to police officers and detectives. Salaries rise with experience.

Pet Relocator

When a zoo wants to find a suitable mate for an animal, it checks with other zoos. Animals in one exhibit at a zoo may all be from the same family, so mating them is out of the question. Once a potential mate is found, the question of how it travels from one zoo to another comes up. In addition, private individuals moving from one part of the country to another for work want to know how to relocate their animals.

Pet relocation companies have been around for a long time, though there weren't many companies doing this type of business. One thing is certain—whether you transport a gorilla for a zoo or a poodle for a family, the field brings many surprises and adventures.

Imagine seeing Kevin O'Brien's face when he was asked to move 3,000 mosquitoes from a research facility in California to one in Texas. He had to find the quickest and safest route possible. He also had to make sure that these 3,000 mosquitoes were well packed and would arrive alive and buzzing. "We found the quickest flight available," he says.

As head of PetRelocation.com, he knows which airlines are animal friendly and open to transporting animals. Depending on where the animal is going, it might be easiest to drive. In other cases, air travel is the only option.

In this do-it-yourself era, it is possible to go online and read the "traveling with pets" column on each airline's website. However, companies like PetRelocation.com know how to cut through the red tape. "We are all so busy, and at the same time, quite concerned about transporting our pets safely from one place to another," says O'Brien. "Our customers call us and only speak to one person—all hours of the day. That person is responsible for making sure their pets will travel and arrive safely to the desired destination."

If a family is moving overseas for work, pet relocation services will make sure all the necessary pet papers are in order. "Some countries quarantine pets for a few months before they are allowed into the country," says O'Brien. "That's so hard on the pets and the families."

By working several months ahead of time, O'Brien and his employees make sure the animals have all the necessary shots and papers. Rabies shots are mandatory; other requirements vary by country. Pet movers have employees in several parts of the country, and some overseas. "The Internet has made this work possible," says O'Brien. "I have connections everywhere. Many of my staff specialize in certain countries. They know the laws, which saves my clients time and grief. If a document is wrong, a pet may be denied entry into a country or may be quarantined for a long time. Having all of the right papers ensures a smooth process."

 **Alert**

All pet relocation workers must have background safety checks before getting hired. Individuals and companies hiring pet relocation services want to make sure that their pets or exotic animals are in good hands before they entrust them to a pet relocation worker.

Working for a pet relocation service requires someone who likes flexible hours. Workers are on call, and regulars are kept constantly busy. Some pet relocation companies are now part of employee benefits package. "If a company wants to hire an executive, they need to have all of the perks to entice that person to move from their home," says O'Brien. "That means relocating the pet as well as the family. Moving the family pet is the largest part of our business. Yes, people care about their furniture arriving safely and in mint condition. However, that is so minor compared to moving the family pet."

Pet transporters must have a driver's license and passport. They must be well versed on all of the rules and regulations concerning air travel, security, and entry into a foreign country. Plus, they must be comfortable being around animals.

"Most of the pets we transport are in crates," says O'Brien. His company sells crates of all sizes, which can easily fit in a car or on a plane. He even sells a product called Hydration Gel, which is a gel form of water. "Dogs, cats, and other animals need water," he says. "If they are on a long flight or in a car, water can slosh around. Dogs don't tend to be neat when drinking water. If water spills, the dog can't drink it. So having the Hydration Gel ensures that the pet will be well hydrated throughout the flight and upon arrival."

Other pets, such as the dart frogs that were transported to a lab in Switzerland, the cougars to a zoo in Belgium, and the horses to Honduras, were all safely caged at their starting destination. "Often it is the zoos or labs that properly cage the animals before we get them," says O'Brien.

The Internet has made this a growth business. Pet relocation companies constantly monitor flights to check for any possible delays. Companies such as PetRelocation.com have a place on their websites where clients can track flight services—and keep track of their pets—at all times.

Pet transporters were kept quite busy during Hurricane Katrina. According to O'Brien, his company was the only private one allowed to land a Boeing 737 in Louisiana to save dogs. "We landed our aircraft in Louisiana, during a time when no other commercial airline could even fly human passengers," he says. His company saved eighty dogs.

To become a pet relocation worker, start by contacting the Independent Pet and Animal Transportation Association (IPATA) at *www .ipata.com*. IPATA, founded in 1979, has grown from six U.S. pet shippers to more than 200 offices in thirty countries.

Pet relocation workers can easily earn between $50,000 and $60,000 a year. Some drivers can earn between $50 and $100 an hour depending on where they are going and what they are shipping. Running such a business takes very little capital, since a relocation service can be run out of a home office. What is necessary is a handful of computers with all of the right software. Owners of pet relocation services can expect to earn upward of $100,000 a year.

Animal Researcher

Animals are used for research. They are subjected to a variety of experiments relating to human psychology, injuries, and medical treatments. A lot of testing is controversial. Some are in favor of animal testing because of the human benefits—finding cures for diseases. Others strongly voice their opinions against such testing because of the stress and harm to the animals. Many people who work for nonprofit organizations, such as the Humane Society of the United States and the Anti-Vivisection Society, are educating the public about the welfare of the thousands of animals that are used in experiments. These organizations hire researchers to study animal behavior.

Jonathan Balcombe, PhD, a senior research scientist with the nonprofit Physicians Committee for Responsible Medicine, has devoted his work to studying animals and their behaviors without experimenting on them. He says he is a research scientist who doesn't wear a white lab coat or test on animals. "I study animal behavior, research scientific literature, write books, prepare research papers for lectures, and publish scholarly papers," he says. "I'm fortunate enough to be with Physicians Committee because they promote alternatives to animal research."

Balcombe, a vegan who loves studying animals, feels quite fortunate that he found a niche for himself in the animal world. His recent book, *Pleasurable Kingdom*, which explains to readers that animals do indeed experience joy, has opened many doors for his work. "The message in my book, which is geared for the public, is in line with my work at Physicians Committee," he says. "The book shows readers that animals experience a wide range of emotions—including happiness."

Because of the popularity of his book, he gets to tour the country speaking on behalf of the animals and the work of the Physicians Committee for Responsible Medicine. "I wrote *Pleasurable Kingdom* independently of my work at Physicians Committee," he says. "However, the message in my book coincides with that of Physicians Committee. Prior to my work on this book, the subject matter was grossly overlooked by most biologists. The research benefits animals and provides credibility to the issue that animals experience pleasure. I enjoy that I can work as an ambassador for them."

 Fact

Animal rights organizations have changed the research industry. For instance, they have stopped the military's cat-shooting studies, DEA (Drug Enforcement Administration) narcotics experiments, and monkey self-mutilation programs. Because of the efforts of Physicians Committee and other humane organizations, more than three-quarters of all U.S. medical schools have dropped their animal labs for medical students.

Prior to working at Physicians Committee, he worked as an associate director of the Humane Society. Balcombe suggests that students who want to work as researchers take an equal number of animal biology, behavior, and communications courses. "Writing is essential to this job," he says. "You have to know how to write grants, how to write for the public, and how to write scientific papers."

Having a bachelor of science degree is a start, but most animal researchers also have an advanced degree. Graduate students with a master's or doctorate can apply either to nonprofit organizations or to academia. Salaries at colleges and universities are often higher than those at nonprofits. Someone with a PhD can expect to earn in the low to mid-$50,000s to start. Mid-level researchers earn $60,000.

CHAPTER 11

Assistance Trainers

It's a proven fact that animals make people feel better. When pets make rounds at a hospital, children and adults both respond positively. A child on the low end of the autism spectrum may not communicate with his parents. However, his first word may be the name of his therapy horse. An Alzheimer's patient may sit in her room all day in icy silence, and then crack a smile when a therapist makes the rounds with a few dogs and cats. Animal-assisted therapists get to see miracles every day.

Guide Dogs for the Blind

Ever since Keith McGregor was a kid he knew he wanted to work with dogs. As director of training and supervisor of the deaf and blind programs for Leader Dogs for the Blind, he graduates between 260 and 270 guide dogs each year. The job combines an equal amount of time being around dogs and people. "You have to know a lot about dogs and about people," he says. "So having a background in animal and human psychology helps."

In college, McGregor studied zoology and animal psychology. He took a part-time job at a hardware store to pay bills, and volunteered at a local K-9 unit caring for the dogs. "I was observing and learning about the process of training," he says. "If you want to go into this field, or any field working with animals, you have to spend time around them."

After volunteering with the dog care staff, he applied for apprentice training, which is a three-year course. He learned how to train dogs and how to teach other people to train dogs.

After finishing his training, McGregor wanted to work with visually impaired people. "The sense that I am helping people who need help with their mobility drew me to this line of work," he says. "Being able to provide services for blind and deaf people is very rewarding."

 Fact

There are several schools around the country that educate people on how to train Seeing Eye dogs and their potential owners. The four leading dog guide schools are Leader Dogs for the Blind (*www.leaderdog.org*), The Seeing Eye (*www.seeingeye.org*), Guiding Eyes for the Blind (*www.guidingeyes.org*), and Guide Dogs for the Blind (*www.guidedogs.com*).

According to McGregor, the field has many opportunities for people who want to train guide dogs and teach the people who will eventually own the dogs. The process at Leader Dogs is similar to other guide-dog training programs for the visually and hearing impaired. Leader Dogs trains its dog handlers. The first month, student handlers teach the dogs to get used to wearing the harness and to walk in a controlled manner.

The following month the student handlers, and the dogs, are taught how to stop at curbs and raised surfaces and how to avoid obstacles in their paths. It gets trickier after that, when students are taught how to maneuver around traffic. The next month, students and dogs go into cities, and students take dogs on trains. They learn how to use escalators. During the last month, the students and guide dog trainers work with clients, teaching them how to work with the dogs they will receive. Staff, dogs, and clients take rooms in a hotel to put all of the training into action. "We are available around the clock that month," says McGregor. "After the training is complete, the clients go home with their guide dogs, and me and my staff start the process all over again with new clients and dogs."

A small number of the dogs in the program don't respond to the training. They may be a bit overanxious, jumping up instead of remaining calmly at the side of the trainer. These dogs usually are adopted by the general public. According to McGregor, there is a waiting list of people who want to adopt these trained guide dogs as pets. The dogs are great; they just didn't make the cut as guide dogs. So for each training period, there are always backup dogs. Most guide dogs are golden retrievers, labrador retrievers, and German shepherds.

Apprentice instructors, who are students learning to become trainers, earn between $25,000 and $35,000 a year. Instructors make between $32,000 and $45,000 annually. Leader Dogs has a staff of twenty-four instructors, plus field reps. Representatives go into the field after training is complete to check on clients. Their job entails a lot of travel, and they earn between $25,000 and $45,000 depending on how long they have been with the organization. Supervisors earn more—between $50,000 and $65,000—depending on location and size of the organization.

Hearing Dogs

Training dogs for the deaf and hearing impaired population is a lot like training Seeing Eye dogs. The main difference is that most hearing impaired people don't give verbal commands, so trainers must learn sign language to communicate with the dogs and with their clients. Most trainers who work with the deaf also work with the blind, and in the latter case, knowing sign language is an extra skill.

Guide dogs for the hearing impaired and deaf are trained to respond to all sorts of sounds. If a doorbell rings, the dog will place its paw on its owner's lap and gently nudge him to the door. If the telephone rings, the dog reacts in the same manner. Dogs are trained to alert their owners to all sorts of sounds—from a baby's cry to a smoke detector going off.

Many nonprofits for the blind also serve the hearing impaired community. Companies like Leader Dogs for the Blind train dogs for the hearing impaired too. There are numerous organizations that employ trainers just for the hearing impaired. One such nonprofit is Dogs for the Deaf (*www.dogsforthedeaf.org*). The organization rescues young dogs (ages eight months to three years) from shelters, and works with them to become guides for the deaf.

Salaries for trainers of guide dogs for hearing impaired people are the same as those for trainers of Seeing Eye dogs.

Medical Response Dogs

Medical response dogs are also called service dogs. Medical response dogs work with a broad range of people and perform a wide range of duties including turning light switches on and off, fetching help from another family member or neighbor, or pressing a life-line button to alert people about the owner's state. These dogs work in partnership with disabled people.

 Fact

Researchers at the University of Florida conducted a survey whose findings indicate that 10 percent of epileptic patients with service dogs were alerted by their dogs right before a seizure was about to happen. These patients could then take necessary precautions to prevent or minimize those seizures. These researchers believe that the dogs detected subtle changes in body chemistry or behavior in their owner.

Under the umbrella terms of medical response dogs and service dogs are seizure response dogs. These dogs have been trained to react when a person with epilepsy is having a seizure. They may bark to notify a neighbor or lie down next to the owner to prevent him from harm. They are also taught to move dangerous objects away from the owner, and even revive the owner if the person loses consciousness. These service dogs are trained to alert a person right before a seizure is about to occur as well.

Service dogs also assist people with psychiatric conditions such as bipolar disorder, post-traumatic stress disorder, autism, schizophrenia, and anxiety disorders. The dogs are taught how to recognize warning signs, such as changes in an owner's behavior. Dogs also remind their owners to take their medications.

Dogs are even being trained to detect different forms of cancer—from skin melanomas to prostate cancer. At the Sensory Research Institute at Florida State University, researchers are training dogs to sniff out different forms of cancer. Two dogs, Daisy and Tangle, were taught how to detect the unique odor of bladder cancer cells in urine samples. At the Pine Street Foundation in Northern California, dogs had a 97 percent accuracy rate in detecting lung cancer in patients. They had an 88 percent accuracy rate in finding breast cancer among patients. They were able to do this by smelling the breath of each patient.

Training service dogs is similar to training Seeing Eye dogs. It's best to start by researching various dog-training organizations that have assistance training divisions. One good place to look is the American Dog Trainers Network, which has a link on its website for Service and Assistance Dogs (*www.inch.com/~dogs/service.html*). The site lists service organizations in most states. Opportunities are growing in this field because people with disabilities want to be as independent as possible. They are relying on working with their dogs to be able to work outside of their homes, support themselves, and take care of themselves.

Mobility Assistance and Other Therapy Dogs

Mobility assistance dogs bring independence to people in wheelchairs and those who have trouble walking and standing. These dogs assist their owners by picking up dropped items, carrying groceries, and opening and closing doors. By helping people do what might be termed simple tasks, these dogs are giving them the ability to work, socialize, and have a life. "My dog Ben makes my disability invisible," says Karen Shirk, founder and executive director of 4 Paws for Ability.

"Before I had Ben, no one would approach me to start up a conversation, and in stores people went out of their way to avoid me," she says. "Now, with Ben at my side, it could take me an hour just to get milk, because of everyone stopping me to inquire about him."

When Shirk became disabled, she found that she wasn't able to get an assistance dog because she uses a ventilator. "That was the excuse I was given," she says. "So I founded 4 Paws for Ability."

Most Seeing Eye and other assisted therapy nonprofits will not give dogs to children. According to Shirk, children are the largest underserved population. Ninety-eight percent of her placements are with children. She placed one of the first dogs to work with an autistic child.

 **Alert**

Being an assisted therapy worker isn't a typical nine-to-five job. When training clients, some workers are on call and can work late into the night. Usually trainers know ahead of time if and when they are going to work late. As an assisted therapy animal trainer, you must be open to flexible hours.

Her dogs are trained with a reward system, similar to most training programs. However, the training is different because the dogs are supposed to be playful with the children and they have a variety of tasks to perform. "Training depends on the situation," she says.

For instance, she trained a few dogs to work on tracking autistic children. In some severe cases, autistic children will wander away from home. One child with a dog from 4 Paws for Ability went outside on a cold Pennsylvania night. It was -20°F and the child was naked. The dog found the child in a neighbor's yard in less than three minutes. The dogs are trained to alert parents if a child wanders off, and to interact with children. Many children on the autism spectrum respond better to animals than to people.

Often the dogs are tethered to children, so the children can have some freedom without wandering far. These dogs are also used to snuggle with a child and to prevent autism meltdowns.

For children in wheelchairs, these dogs retrieve items, turn lights on and off, alert parents to the child's needs, and offer companionship. Companies like 4 Paws are in constant need of trainers—not because of job turnover, but because of the growing number of children and adults with disabilities.

 Fact

According to the Centers for Disease Control, 1 out of every 150 children born in the United States will have some form of autism. In New Jersey, that number is 1 in 96. No one is sure why these figures are growing. Some theories state it is hereditary. Others say it is due to environmental factors. In any case, this population is in need of services.

Shirk started 4 Paws in 1998, and has a waiting list of families requesting dogs. She gets her dogs from shelters, and places them nationally. She is based in Ohio. She recommends that to become a trainer, you should have a background in social work and be well versed in issues affecting the disabled community. She also recommends taking assistance training classes, which can be found at a variety of websites. For information about 4 Paws, see *www.4pawsforability.org.*

As executive director of 4 Paws, Shirk has found business classes helpful. She also has a degree in social work, and handles grant writing for the organization. Shirk says that executive directors can earn about $65,000 annually. Trainers can earn $25,000 to $40,000, depending on experience.

Therapy Horses

Horses are the second most popular animal used in assisted therapy programs (dogs are the first). The actual term for horse therapy is "hippotherapy," from the Greek word hippo, meaning horse. Physical, occupational, and speech therapists use hippotherapy to help their clients with motor skill disabilities and speech delays. Hippotherapy is a form of therapeutic riding. Clients are placed on horses in a controlled environment—usually in a riding ring with a trainer. The purpose of interacting with horses is to improve one's sensory skills and neurological functions.

 **Question**

Why are horses good for therapy?
A horse's gait is rhythmic and repetitive. The horse's movement is much like our own. The pelvis moves in the same manner. Plus, riding a horse improves balance, posture, and mobility. Hippotherapy has been around for a long time; however, with the increase of autism and other disabilities, and the positive effect of these treatments, more and more hippotherapy centers are opening.

In addition to working with autistic persons, hippotherapists work with people diagnosed with cerebral palsy, multiple sclerosis, developmental delays, traumatic brain injury, stroke, depression, psychological problems, and learning and language delays. The work can be quite moving on an emotional level. "You see so many miracles when you pair a rider with a horse," says Lisa Gatti, owner of Pal-O-Mine Equestrian, a nonprofit therapeutic horseback riding program that teaches individuals with disabilities how to ride and compete.

Gatti founded Pal-O-Mine in 1995. She grew up riding horses in Long Island, and loved everything horse-related. She knew at a young age that she wanted to work with horses, and she also wanted to work with special needs children. Her mom was a special education teacher.

After attending Mary Washington College in Virginia and then going for her teaching degree at St. Joseph's College in Long Island, she taught an at-risk population of emotionally disturbed children. She really liked working with these kids. Still she missed being around the horses. While working as a teacher, she started Pal-O-Mine, and had many of her students help her. Many of the kids in her classroom spent their afternoons training as volunteers instead of joining gangs. "The work made them feel extremely worthwhile," she says. "These are the kids that fall through the cracks. They're good kids who just needed to succeed. They were able to do that by helping me at Pal-O-Mine."

 ## Question

What is the difference between hippotherapy and therapeutic riding?

In hippotherapy, a physical therapist, occupational therapist, or speech therapist works with a patient on a horse to improve motor skills and speech. In therapeutic riding, a certified therapeutic riding instructor is teaching a special needs person how to ride. Both have beneficial effects on the rider.

Gatti combined her special education background with her riding background and created an academic curriculum that incorporates the subjects of Character Education and Cowboy Ethics. Her husband is a former cowboy, and he often helps Gatti with her work.

She describes Cowboy Ethics as a form of self-respect and respect for others. Her curriculum is used in several classrooms in New York.

While practicing how to ride and how to care for the horses, the students learn about patience, building trust, and self-esteem. Gatti has five full-time staff members and 150 volunteers running Pal-O-Mine. She and her staff put in long hours and are able to get by on what they earn. "Living on Long Island can be difficult," she says. "Average salaries for my full-time staff are $25,000 a year."

She writes a lot of grants to keep Pal-O-Mine in the black. She just applied for and received a grant for $143,000. In addition to paying a mortgage for the land, needing funds for upkeep of the property, and paying her staff and herself, taking care of the horses can be expensive. Feeding, medicines, vaccinations, health supplements, veterinary bills, farrier bills (horses need their hoofs checked and trimmed at least every six weeks), dental bills, riding equipment, and insurance for her riders can get expensive. When it all adds up, it can easily cost up to $1,500 per horse per year.

"This is something you really should want to do," says Gatti. "I enjoy my work because I'm around wonderful people and, of course, I get to be around horses. I also see so many positives each day from our clients."

One aspect of Pal-O-Mine that sets it apart from other therapeutic riding stables is that Gatti and her staff host competitions between people with disabilities and able-bodied riders. "If you can sit on a horse, it doesn't matter if you are blind or have cerebral palsy, autism, a speech delay, or are able-bodied; on a horse you are equal in riding abilities," she says. "So we hold competitions. Many of our riders have competed elsewhere, and won too. It's so encouraging watching a competition. Our riders have goals—to overcome and/or manage their disability and to compete."

Therapy Animals

While most people respond positively to dogs and horses, other animals are used in assisted therapy programs. Cats, guinea pigs, birds, and fish help people with physical and emotional problems. More and more hospitals are opening their doors to organizations, allowing them to bring pets in to visit sick and terminally ill patients. Depending on the illness, the person with the pet can either approach the patient or stand near the door of the patient's room. The goal, which is often achieved, is to brighten the patient's day.

Animals are also used in prisons and detention centers for juveniles. Hardened personalities can soften when caring for an animal. For example, in a maximum security hospital for the criminally insane, a patient who refused to speak was given a pet bird. The bird lived in a cage next to the man. After being with the bird, he started talking to it. Then he started conversing with the staff and other patients.

 Fact

Pets can lower one's blood pressure level. The University of Maryland Hospital conducted a study that proved heart patients with pets had a better chance of surviving after they left the hospital than those who did not have pets. The study, which was conducted in 1995, involved 392 people and discovered that heart attack patients with dogs were eight times more likely to be alive a year after their attack than people without dogs.

People go into this field because they want to help others and because they want to work with animals. Many hospitals use volunteers to bring in therapeutic animals. However, due to the positive effects the animals have on patients, the field is growing for professionals. People interested in working with therapeutic animals should have a degree in social work with a minor in animal studies. Taking psychology courses also helps. If you want to be an executive director of an animal assisted therapy program, management courses are important. Check with the numerous programs to find the training that's best for you, and, as advised for other careers, volunteer first to see if this is really what you want to do.

CHAPTER 12

Nonprofits for Animals

Many people are leaving corporate America to take jobs at non-profit organizations. They are changing careers to do something that is meaningful and to get away from the sixty-plus-hour workweek. Often moving from corporate America to a nonprofit organization means a cut in pay. However, those who have made this career decision seem quite happy.

Executive Director

The main attraction to heading up a nonprofit organization is being able to promote an inspiring mission. Just think about getting up each day and going to work to advocate for a cause that is close to your heart. That is what motivates most executive directors and chief executive officers at nonprofits. Working to improve the welfare of animals and the environment is what fuels many of the people who work for nonprofits.

Executive directors have to see themselves as operating for change that will have an impact for the greater good. Unlike their counterparts at corporations, executive directors at nonprofits have to please the public sector, while executives at for-profit companies are working to benefit the private businesses they lead. At a nonprofit, an executive director may run the show, but he has to answer to a board of directors, its members, and its donors. Also, because of their role in accepting donations for their nonprofits and in some cases trying to make key changes in our laws regarding animal welfare issues, executives at nonprofits are also under greater scrutiny from the government and the press.

E ssential

Nonprofits have smaller budgets than do their corporate counterparts. That often translates to leaner staffs in the non-profit world, requiring executive directors to wear many hats. In addition to heading the organization, the executive direc-tor will also take a lead in fundraising, communications, team building, and advocacy.

People become executive directors by taking an entry-level job at a nonprofit and working their way up. They can also start their own small nonprofits. Others are hired by board members after working as an executive at another nonprofit or for-profit company. Many people who are unsatisfied in the corporate world do transfer their skills to the nonprofit world.

To become an executive director at a nonprofit, it is essential to have a business background. A master's degree in business will put you on the right career track. Taking courses in management, gover-nance, fundraising, finances, marketing, and grant writing are man-datory. Executive directors must be excellent public speakers and communicators. Understanding animal welfare issues is also key to getting a job in this field.

In addition to having a business background and an agenda to promote a cause, executive directors at nonprofits have to include their board members and staff in the decision-making process. It's true that executive directors must take the lead. However, the pro-cess of implementing change can take longer at a nonprofit because of all the levels it has to go through.

Just like their corporate counterparts, women who lead nonprofits earn less money than do male executive directors. For example, female directors with a budget between $5 million and $10 million earn an average of $85,000 a year; their male counterparts earn an average of $95,000 annually. More women than men work as executive directors of nonprofits with budgets of $100,000 or less. They usually earn between $50,000 and $65,000 annually.

Animal Welfare Economist

The question most people ask Jennifer Fearing, chief economist at the Humane Society of the United States (HSUS), is why she left her $200,000 job as an economy analyst at Econ One Research to take a job that pays $65,000 with an animal advocacy nonprofit. The answer is an easy one for Fearing, "I initially left the private sector to take a leadership role at United Animal Nations out of a desire to merge my business and personal interests," she says. "As I learned more about issues beyond those facing dogs and cats, I realized there was a need to merge my education and training into the mix as well. And it was clear that no one else with economics training was focused on this application. When, in mid-2004, I reviewed and responded to an economic analysis of a proposed ban on the exhibition of wild and exotic animals in circuses in Denver, it really crystallized for me how badly this approach was needed by the movement."

Despite a few comments from colleagues about leaving Econ One to run United Animal Nations (UAN), she knows she made the right decision. "My thesis is, I wasn't unhappy," she says. "I just wasn't totally happy. I'm shocked at how heroic people seem to think what I did is. It's one or the other. You're crazy or you're amazing."

She says that at Econ, "Everyone worked hard and was really smart." Her business degree from Harvard University and her work at Econ proved to be the right mix for her job leading UAN.

After a few years at UAN's helm, she wanted to make even more inroads in the world of animal advocacy. "As hard as it was to leave UAN, a role I cherished, I knew I needed to focus if I wanted my life's work to result in real tangible changes for animals. And the HSUS, with its large size and commitment to putting resources into solid research to support advocacy, was the obvious choice. I pitched the idea to the senior leadership and joined HSUS a few months later."

She became involved with animal nonprofits when she and a friend found a dog running loose in her neighborhood. She took the dog to a nearby shelter. Entering the shelter "freaked me out," she says. What upset her was how poorly managed the shelter was. She thought that she could put her economics background to use, and started volunteering. In 1999, she founded the Sacramento Area Animal Coalition. She spent most of her free time working on behalf of animal rights. As chief economist at HSUS, she sees herself working for a social movement, not a nonprofit.

Animal Welfare Lawyer

In the traditional sense, animal law covers the rights of animals. Nonprofits fighting against whaling in Japan or the use of exotic animals in circuses or the length of stay before animals are euthanized in shelters are all parts of animal law. Lawyers at animal welfare agencies are working to improve the lives of animals. A new branch of animal law is also on the rise. It can include custody decisions in divorce cases, housing disputes when pets are not allowed in certain buildings, and wrongful death or injury to a pet.

In recent years, working on behalf of animal rights has become a growth opportunity. More and more nonprofits are either hiring outside lawyers on a case-by-case scenario or are employing full-time lawyers.

Like animal welfare economists, animal welfare lawyers can earn a decent living. However, you will make more money in private practice or working for a large corporation. Those who go into this profession do it because they are passionate about animals and want to improve the lives of animals.

 Fact

Because of the growing interest in animal welfare issues, many law schools are adding animal law to its curriculum. Harvard, Stanford, UCLA, Northwestern, University of Michigan, and Duke are just a few of the ninety-two law schools that teach animal law. Animal law committees have recently been added to many state and local bar associations. Animal law covers tort, contract, criminal, and constitutional law.

To become an animal welfare lawyer, you will need a four-year bachelor's degree from an accredited college, and you should have a high GPA. After college, you will have to study for and take the LSAT (Law School Admission Test). You can take courses that will prepare you for the test.

After passing the LSAT, you should apply to at least three different law schools. Admission is not impossible, but it can be tough. Good grades are essential to being accepted. Make sure the schools you apply to are recognized by the American Bar Association (*www.abanet.org*).

Law school is a three-year program. While you are in law school, get involved in as many extracurricular activities as possible. Look for internships or write for the school's law journal. As with any career, being a well-rounded individual helps to land a job. After you graduate, you will receive a Juris Doctor (JD) degree. Then you have to pass the state bar association exam. Each state's bar requirements differ, so check with the bar association in the state where you want to be licensed to find out about fees, dates of exams, and other information.

Question

Who founded the Animal Legal Defense Fund?
In 1979, Joyce Tischler, a lawyer, created the Animal Legal Defense Fund to promote the field of animal law and to protect and defend animals.

Development Officer

After executive director, the development officer is one of the most important positions at a nonprofit. Simply put, development directors are fundraisers responsible for getting funding for various projects and for keeping the organization afloat. They work on short- and long-term plans to raise money for the nonprofit. Development directors in the animal world must be committed to the organization's ideals. They must possess excellent fundraising and management skills, and must be strong communicators. They need to conceptualize plans that appeal to donors and board members.

Depending on the size of the nonprofit, a development director can take on many roles. In smaller nonprofits, development directors will also handle communications and public relations. They write reports, press releases, and brochures educating the public about why donors need to support the organization. In larger nonprofits, the development director works closely with the communications or public relations officer, again to raise awareness and funds.

Development directors are part salesman. They have to sell their company to donors, and do it in a way that makes the donor feel good about giving. Asking for money is an art; not everyone can do it. For every positive response from a donor, there will be several negative ones. In addition to having a good fundraising plan, you have to have a thick skin and, more important, a passion for the project.

Susan Smith, development director for Palisades Interstate Park Commission in Bear Mountain State Park in New York, wears several hats. In addition to fundraising, she organizes events and handles public relations. She has a master's degree in historic preservation and a master's in architecture. She started as a docent, volunteering her time conducting tours of the area before coming on board. The goal of the commission is to promote and expand the awareness and preservation of the park's natural, historical, and cultural resources for the benefits of the public.

 **Alert**

Working for a state-funded agency requires passing a civil service exam. Each state's exam is different. In New York, Susan Smith had to pass an oral exam that covered various state regulations and information about historic preservation. For information about federal jobs, contact *www.federaljobs.net/exams .htm.* For information about state exams, contact your local town hall.

Smith relies on volunteers to help her with manpower. "In addition to writing grants for money, I ask for volunteers to work on various projects," she says. "Right now, corporations want to be affiliated with green organizations. This is a growing field."

Smith works with her volunteers and has one full-time assistant, as well as a part-time administrative aide who puts in about ten hours each week assisting with paperwork. She is thankful to the volunteers of the Friends of the Palisades Parks Conservancy (*www .friendsofpalisades.org*). "They have a lot of enthusiasm because they love the park and the projects we are working on," she says.

This isn't a nine-to-five job. Since she organizes events, she occasionally puts in long hours. Some fundraisers are after-hours, too;

Smith recently attended a fundraising dinner. "I enjoy these events, and I enjoy being surrounded by the beauty of the park," she says.

Having a foundation in business is ideal for a development director. Development directors must have a bachelor's degree in business, finance, or communications. A master's degree helps, but is not necessary. Depending on the size of the nonprofit, development directors can earn anywhere from $35,000 to $100,000.

Communications Director

Christopher Cutter, communications manager with International Fund for Animal Welfare (IFAW), used to work on the corporate side. He started out as a journalist covering high-tech topics, then switched to public relations promoting technology companies and gadgets. Work was good, but the hours were long. He was spending too much time away from his family, and something was missing. Switching to the nonprofit world proved to be the right move for Cutter. Since joining IFAW five years ago, he has traveled to places near and far in the quest to end Canadian seal hunting, stop the elephant ivory trade, and save whales from extinction.

IFAW works to improve animal welfare, prevent animal cruelty and abuse, protect wildlife, and provide animal rescue around the world. IFAW's headquarters are in Cape Cod, Massachusetts, and it has an office in Washington, D.C. Cutter is based in Cape Cod. "Working on the nonprofit side has really changed my lifestyle," he says. "I used to commute to Boston. Now, my family and I live on Cape Cod and my commute is fifteen minutes. It's beautiful out here, and I get to spend more time with my family. Sometimes, I work a fifty-hour week, but the work is so fulfilling. My salary is not as high as when I was on the corporate side, but all around I have a better quality of life; there is less stress in my life, and I go to bed with a clean conscience."

As communications manager, Cutter interviews people all over the world who work for IFAW. He writes reports, press releases, brochures, and other marketing materials with the goal of promoting

IFAW's mission. Having a journalism background is a plus. "A large part of my job is writing stories," he says. "It's a lot like writing for a newspaper or magazine."

The topics can be tough and not for the faint of heart. He witnessed animal rescues in Tabasco, Mexico, and New Orleans, Louisiana, after the hurricanes, oil-spill cleanups in Russia, and seal hunting in Canada. "Everyone responds differently," he says. "I go in and know that I am getting a story that has to be told. So, I can put some of the emotions aside. Some people cry. Others get angry. It can take an emotional toll on some."

By approaching his job like a journalist, Cutter makes sure that the local media gets all the video footage that is needed for the evening news. He works to get the facts and all of the details to the media. Keeping abreast of each reporter at all of the major media outlets as well as media in several local bureaus and news outlets can be a full-time job in itself. Journalists come and go, and knowing who to pitch a story to is essential to the job.

 **Alert**

A common complaint from workers at some nonprofits is that there is often a disconnect among departments because of limited resources. For the nonprofit to run smoothly, all of the departments must work together to share ideas and information. Teamwork is critical.

The work entails some travel, and a lot of writing, marketing, and communications. Cutter also attends a lot of meetings with people from around the globe. "Being part of an international organization lets me meet with people from all over the world," he says. "At our meetings, we hear from people who are working on behalf of animal rights in Africa, Canada, Europe, Asia, and other countries. You have to be able to listen, and be open to other people's points of view. I tend to get inspired by my colleagues."

Being open to other ideas from different cultures is essential if you are working for an international organization. Having a background in journalism, marketing, and public relations often is required. Cutter took a slightly different route. He got his bachelor's degree in English literature and his master's in creative writing. Being able to write and speak well are essential in both public relations and marketing. Many communications departments are eager to hire journalists who want to switch to public relations/marketing. It's not a big leap. Both disciplines require excellent writing, reporting, and interviewing skills.

A communications department can have many tiers. It all depends on the size of the nonprofit. Smaller companies have fewer staff, and some workers can take on many roles. In larger nonprofits, there can be a communications director, manager, and assistant. Some personnel may handle public relations—writing press releases and brochures and pitching stories to the media. If the agency is large, there will be separate marketing and membership departments. The role of the marketing staff is to shape and advertise the company and its goals. Marketing, public relations, membership, and even development all overlap and work together to promote the agency and its message to the public and the press.

Starting salaries vary, and can range from $30,000 to $40,000, depending on the size of the nonprofit. After a few years on the job, communications managers can earn between $50,000 and $65,000.

Environmental Educator

At a state park in New Jersey, crowds of children and adults watch as a team of educators talk about snakes, box turtles, lizards, and birds of prey. Several hawks and owls are on display, and one educator walks through the crowd holding a boa constrictor, showing off its lovely patterns and talking about its features and habits. He has the attention of even the youngest members of the audience. Hands are raised and questions are answered.

Environmental educators show up in a lot of places. They work in national and state parks, at zoos and wildlife centers, and at schools. Their job is to teach the public about animals and their environments. One impacts the other, and the field is opening up because of the concern about global warming and the environment.

Alert

Environmental educators work for the government, schools, and nonprofit organizations in camps, parks, nature centers, environmental programs, and museums. Most of the educators work in beautiful outdoor settings. Many give tours while on boats or hiking on nature trails. A downside is that the majority of these opportunities are part-time and don't pay a lot of money.

Environmental education is a hot topic today, thanks in part to the media and to our government leaders. Al Gore, former vice president, has used his influence to call attention to this issue with his documentary, *An Inconvenient Truth*. While documentaries and books about global warming reach a large audience, environmental educators for the most part work on a smaller level. They usually spread their message to a smaller audience, reaching fewer people but leaving a large impact.

At the New Jersey state park, environmental educators talked about the animals and their habitats, and how the changes in those habitats affect us. By bringing the message home, educators help people to understand the problem. Once it impacts them, change can occur. It starts with seeing an animal up close. The educator has the audience's complete attention. Then he can start talking about why change is needed.

Having a teaching degree with a major in science, animal science, or environmental science is a sure way to get a job in this field. You also can start out as a volunteer, giving lectures about animals at environmental centers and parks. Classroom teachers at parks and environmental centers tend to work full-time. If you want to work in a park setting, you can find out if there is a full-time position open for you. Some of the larger parks and environmental centers do have full-time educators on staff. Or you can contact the parks, museums, and other centers to see if they would be interested in booking your services on a for-hire basis. It's a bit like acting. You have to call, make an appointment, show up, and let the organization know what you can do. In this case you will also have to travel with the animals, which means having enough space at home to care for them.

Field Researcher

A field researcher is part detective and part scientist. Field researchers are responsible for collecting data for studies relating to anthropology, archaeology, astronomy, biology, botany, geography, geology, oceanography, paleontology, and zoology. Nonprofits are among the largest organizations that award grants for scientific field research. National Geographic's Committee for Research and Exploration funded the works of Jane Goodall, Dian Fossey, and the Leakey family. Earthwatch Institute has awarded grants to researchers investigating the habitats and conservation of Asiatic black bears in China, indigenous tortoises in Japan, cheetah conservation in Namibia, and aquatic ecosystems on the Upper Mississippi River.

 Fact

Organizations such as Earthwatch receive hundreds of research proposals each year. Out of those proposals, Earthwatch funds between 130 and 140 projects. Its total grant budget is around $4.2 million per year. National Geographic's Committee for Research and Exploration awards 250 grants each year. The average amount given is between $15,000 and $20,000.

As the name implies, field researchers spend a lot of time outdoors. Conditions are far from fancy. Observing the habitats of the sun bear in Borneo or cheetahs in Namibia means spending time at wildlife reserves and living in tents. You must be fond of camping and hiking.

Field researchers must have a bachelor's degree in science, animal sciences, or environmental science. The field is competitive, so having a master's degree will definitely give you an edge. Volunteering with organizations such as Earthwatch allows you to get a foot in the door and find out whether this is work that you really want to do. Field researchers rely on volunteers to gather data, and Earthwatch has programs designed specifically for volunteers.

Field researchers rely on grants to earn their living. Many go into teaching at colleges and universities. Most earn between $35,000 and $65,000, depending on experience and project. It is a competitive field that is slowly opening up because of our concern for the environment.

Tour Guide

Tour guides give visitors an inside view on animal behavior, their habitats, and why people should be concerned. They work at zoos, wildlife centers, national and state parks, safari parks, museums, and nature centers, giving visitors an overview about the animals and the environment, as well as a bit of history.

Alert

Tour guides must be comfortable around crowds. If you don't enjoy public speaking, consider another profession. You have to interact with your tour groups and be able to think quickly on your feet, as tourists will ask a wide range of questions. Enjoying activities such as being outdoors in all sorts of weather, performing before crowds, and answering questions are essential.

Most tour guides present programs about the area an animal is from, how it survives in the wild, how long its species has survived, what it eats, how it hunts, its mating habits, where it lives, and more.

Often tour guides work directly with animals. At local zoos, tour guides can work in a classroom or outdoors on the premises, showing and giving talks about specific animals. Some tour guides work on boats giving lectures to tourists about whales, dolphins, and other sea creatures. At state and national parks, guides conduct tours about the local flora and fauna.

Tour guides double as educators, and depending on the size of the institution, the tour guide may wear both hats. They teach the public about the animals, the location, and conservation efforts. Conservation is a big topic—now and for the future—which means that opportunities are opening up at many national and state parks.

E ssential

If you like sharing information, but don't enjoy hiking, consider being a tour guide who gives tours by boat, horse, bicycle, bus, or minivan. You can also conduct driving tours through national forests.

Ecotourism is the fastest-growing area within the travel industry. Before you become an ecotour guide, it is a good idea to take a handful of nature trips to see if you like them. You can also learn a lot by being part of a tour group. Study how the tour guide mingles with the group and how he imparts his knowledge.

It is a good idea to have a bachelor's degree in animal sciences and conservation, but it is not mandatory. You must have an intimate knowledge of the location where you want to work. Taking some psychology classes is also a good idea because you will be working with people. Sometimes these eco-adventures can be awe-inspiring and life-changing, so knowing a bit about the human psyche helps.

A good tour guide keeps his audience in mind. Travelers today make up a wide range of people. You will get people who are interested in education and history, social travelers, nature travelers, campers, and weekend travelers. Knowing how to gear your talks to each specific group will make your job more rewarding.

To become a tour guide, contact several eco-adventure companies. Start with the International Ecotourism Society (*www.ecotourism.org*). Or you can start by contacting a local university or college to see if you can lead tours around your neighborhood. Even if you live in the city, leading a tour will help you get a taste of what it is like sharing information and being responsible for a group of tourists.

In addition to introducing tourists to animals and their environments, ecotourism enlightens tourists about cultural differences. People on ecotours often learn about the locales' environmental, social, and even political concerns. Host countries often benefit from ecotourism because tourists spend dollars, which go directly to the economy.

 *Question*

What's the fastest-growing travel business in the U.S.?
While ecotourism is just 5 percent of the travel industry, it is estimated to be a $77 billion market. More people are traveling to national parks now than in the past. Attendance at national parks rose from 256 million people in 1990 to 277 million in 2004.

Tour guides can earn anywhere from $20,000 a year to $45,000; this all depends on where you work. Tour operators—the owners of tour companies—earn a lot more money. To run a tour company, it is essential to have a business background as well as a background in wildlife services, biology, or animal sciences. Several universities offer tourism degrees. Most are under the label of hotel and tourism management. A successful tour operator can earn a six-figure annual salary.

CHAPTER 13

Careers in Farming

In 1862 Abraham Lincoln created the United States Department of Agriculture (USDA). Back then, 90 out of every 100 Americans were farmers. Today, 2 out of every 100 Americans work as farmers. The USDA still does the same work that it did when it was first formed. This government-run organization oversees the safety of meat, poultry, and egg products. It conducts ongoing research on human nutrition and on the latest crop technologies, and also helps ensure open markets for U.S. agricultural products. When most people think about careers in the farming industry, they tend to think of farmers. Other opportunities exist including farm managers, 4-H Agents, farm instructors at a high school or college, and agricultural inspectors.

Farmer

While the USDA's goals and missions are the same, the role of farmers has changed over the years. Up through the early 1900s, farmers oversaw the production of many crops. Each farmer would plant oats, wheat, corn, and barley, and raise chicken, cattle, and hogs. Many would sell eggs and plant a variety of vegetables. In the mid-1800s, the average size of a U.S. farm was about 80 acres. All work was done by hand, horses, and simple machinery.

That all changed with automation in the 1900s. Farms got bigger, and farmers began specializing in just a handful of crops. Some would be cattle farmers and might also sell soybeans. Others just raised hogs, cows, and corn.

Finding ways to supplement a farm income has become almost mandatory today. Many farmers are opening their farms to the public, attracting city folk and people from nearby small towns who want to spend a day on a farm picking crops. The farmers even welcome school trips, allowing kids to go on tractor rides and watch a cow being milked by hand. Many farms that invite the public to pick fresh fruits, flowers, and vegetables also sell baked goods and cheeses. In addition, farmers may sell their goods at local farmers markets.

Some farmers even open bed-and-breakfasts on their property. In the morning, visitors can feed goats and sheep, see a cow being milked, and take a tractor ride. Children can go to the henhouse to gather eggs, which often are used for that morning's breakfast.

Farming is a tough business. The days are long; farmers usually work from sunup to sundown. Most of the work is outdoors, and if the weather doesn't cooperate, the crops and animals can have a bad year.

Farmers are self-employed. As is true for most independent businessmen, a farmer's income is based on what he produces. Farmers can make anywhere from $50,000 a year to a few million dollars. It all depends on what he produces, the size of his farm, and the demand for the crop. The majority of farmers earn in the $50,000 range.

 **Alert**

Farmers must invest a lot of their income in their land and machinery. They also are responsible for paying property taxes, maintenance on machinery and housing, fuel (which can easily cost more than $400 a day for diesel depending on the fluctuating market), seed, fertilizer, health insurance, liability insurance, and crop insurance. Then there are veterinary bills for the animals.

People who farm love being around Mother Nature and the animals. Most farmers are born into the industry. Children of farmers learn the trade at an early age by participating in chores on the family farm. Those who want to go into this profession can take agriculture courses at school. Many high schools in rural communities have 4-H clubs and courses on farming. It is also a smart idea to take business courses at a local university. If you want to see what a farm day is like, you can stay at a farm bed-and-breakfast, but because of liability issues, you will not be able to handle machinery. You can only observe others doing the work.

Farm Manager

Farm managers work with farmers, helping them to optimize their finances and maximize their assets. The managers advise farmers on everything from crop and livestock production to commodity marketing, soil conservation, financial analysis and accounting, and real estate brokerage. Farm managers are hired consultants. They must have a business degree with expertise in agriculture and finance. They will devise financial plans and budgets for farmers, and offer guidance on whether farmers should participate in government programs. Basically, they show farmers how to increase profits and lower operating expenses. Nationally farm manager salaries range from a low of $33,000 per year to a medium average of $42,000 per year to a high of $61,000 annually.

Agriculture, Extension, and 4-H Agents

There is a bit of overlap among these positions. Agriculture agents often work for the United States Department of Agriculture, inspecting farms, farm animals, slaughterhouses, milk plants, and other places where food is grown. In addition, they work closely with farmers to help them set up and operate a farm. Extension agents, who are usually affiliated with 4-H clubs and other farm organizations, also work closely with farmers. They may help the farmers to produce more crops by running specific tests on the soil, or help increase milk production by changing the dairy cows' diet. 4-H agents oversee and run volunteer 4-H clubs. They all can operate out of county extension offices.

All of these agents have expertise in production, processing, and distribution of agricultural products. They are well versed on environmental and conservation issues. They may also handle marketing by educating the public about farm concerns. Some teach, and all work closely with farmers, ranchers, agribusinesses, and commodity groups. In addition, they are on top of economic trends.

Question

How much milk can a cow produce in a year?
A dairy cow produces enough milk to fill 26,000 glasses. Depending on the size of the cow, she will have to be fed ten to forty pounds of hay and grass each day. A cow also needs to consume a half-pound of grain for each pound of milk she produces.

For the most part, 4-H agents work with youngsters ages nine through nineteen. They educate them on all aspects of farming through 4-H clubs. Most 4-H agents, agricultural agents, and extension agents started out as members of their local 4-H clubs in elementary and high school. To become a 4-H agent, it is essential to rise in the ranks of your local 4-H club and have a teaching background.

Agricultural and extension agents should have a master's degree in agriculture, family and consumer science, education, or science/technology. Several colleges and universities offer degree programs in agriculture and extension work, including Texas A&M, Virginia Tech, Penn State, and Purdue University. For a more extensive list see *www.oneglobe.com/agriculture/agcolleg.html.*

Salaries for agriculture, extension, and 4-H agents range between $30,000 and $65,000, depending on your experience, location, and the size of the department.

Agricultural Instructor

Depending on where you live in the country, there may be high schools that teach agriculture. Most of these schools are in rural areas. Instructors at these schools teach freshman courses in animal science, plant science, and environmental science. In the sophomore year, students interested in working with animals take basic courses in animal care, handling, and grooming. They learn about horse management and take introductory classes about birds, fish, rodents, and reptiles.

Junior-year students are asked to choose a career path. They can choose to major in agribusiness (this deals with a wide variety of animal-related businesses, canine training, kennel management, and canine and feline first-aid techniques), veterinary technology, or equine management.

 Fact

Agriculture programs are taught in high schools and colleges in rural areas. All have hands-on opportunities for students to work with animals. Equine management is just one of the courses taught as part of an agriculture management degree. The course includes riding techniques, barn management skills, and basic first-aid training.

"When I Googled 'ag high schools,' I got results showing over 50 million hits," says Laurie Walton, an agricultural instructor at the Essex County Agricultural School in Hathorne, Massachusetts. "That tells me that there is a need and that there are positions to be filled for anyone interested in working as an agricultural instructor."

According to Walton, many high schools are expanding their curricula to provide students with a wide range of career options. "The school is set up like a working farm, and components of the curriculum revolve around the farming aspect of instruction," she says. "Our school is actually comparable to a farm in the sense that we house horses, cattle, sheep, goats, and llamas here on campus. We're also in the process of bringing back some pigs as well."

To entice even more students into the field, Essex County Agricultural School is offering courses in companion animal grooming, veterinary technology, kennel management, and canine and equine training. "We used to be more of a farm-type operation," she says, "but in order to provide the necessary training for our students to find entry-level positions in animal careers prevalent to this area we have changed over the years, and are continuing to change on a regular basis."

New fields include hazmat training (dealing with hazardous materials, containment, and spills) and biotechnology. Some high schools also offer programs in greenhouse production as part of an environmental science major.

People who work in these fields often live in rural environments. To become an agricultural instructor it is essential to have a teaching degree with a minor in animal and environmental science. Salaries are akin to other teaching incomes.

Large Animal Veterinarian

According to the American Veterinary Medical Association, veterinarians who specialize in large farm animals are highly sought after. The majority of graduates from veterinary school care for small domestic animals—mainly dogs and cats. They tend to work in metropolitan areas, unlike large animal veterinarians who work on farms and in country settings. Those who choose this route can earn a handsome yearly salary because the need is so great.

If you think you would like to specialize in caring for farm animals, you should spend some time around a farm or on a ranch. Volunteer or see if you can find part-time work. Most of the work for volunteers will be grunt work—cleaning out stables and feeding and grooming animals.

If your high school offers elective programs in animal science, animal husbandry, or livestock management, take as many electives as possible. You should major in these courses at college, and try to get an internship or part-time job on a farm or ranch. You will have to apply to veterinary medical school and specialize in large animal veterinary medicine. Students must graduate with a Doctor of Veterinary Medicine (DVM) or Veterinary Medical Doctor (VMD) degree from a four-year program at an accredited college of veterinary medicine. Upon graduating from veterinary medical school, you must pass a state examination to obtain a license to practice.

 **Alert**

Large animal veterinarians work outdoors in all kinds of weather. They spend a lot of time on the road commuting from home or office to farms and ranches to treat animals. Therefore, it is ideal to live close to farms or ranches to cut down on your commute.

Veterinary Farm Technician

Veterinary technicians—whether working with farm or domestic animals—work under the supervision of a licensed veterinarian. Vet techs are equal to nurses in the medical profession. They can handle a lot of tasks, but they don't perform surgery, diagnose diseases, or prescribe medications.

The first thing they do is work closely with farmers and pet owners to get information about an animal. They can do initial physical exams, take blood cell counts, conduct urine analysis, fill prescriptions for the veterinarian, operate x-ray machines and develop x-rays, and assist veterinarians with surgery (just as a nurse assists a doctor). They also may manage staff schedules, hire employees, and take care of bookkeeping and inventory.

Like large animal veterinarians, there is a demand for veterinary technicians on farms and ranches. The job of veterinary technician is gaining more and more recognition. Salaries range anywhere between $35,000 and $60,000 a year, and depend on location.

E ssential

Veterinary technicians can get a two-year or four-year degree at an accredited college. Vet techs who specialize in farm animals also need hands-on clinical experience working with animals on a farm or ranch. Upon completion of school, they graduate as certified veterinary technicians. Others, who forgo the degree, can work as veterinary assistants, garner a few years of experience, and move up to become veterinary technicians.

Equine Manager

People who work with horses do it because they love the animals. They are not in this field for the money. Equine managers often live on the farm, and usually get free board and meals in addition to a salary, which can be about $20,000 to $30,000 a year. Some managers earn more if they oversee a large stable of horses, while those just starting out may be paid less. Managers who work on farms and ranches that are family owned and operated are usually treated like one of the family.

Equine managers are responsible for caring for, grooming, feeding, and training horses and riders. Veterinarians are called on to make sure the animal is in good health. The equine manager works with the veterinarian to inform him about the general health of the animal.

Managers must be able to ride well and know a good deal about caring for horses. They can obtain a degree in equine studies. However, most equine managers learn on the job. They start out as ranch or farm hands.

 Fact

Horses need routine care to prevent parasites such as worms. An equine manager will make sure the animal's coat is brushed often and his stall is cleaned on a regular basis. This helps reduce the number of worms. Equine managers can administer medicines every eight to twelve weeks to de-worm the horses. They also work closely with the veterinarian to maintain proper preventive health programs for the horses.

Breeding Manager

A breeding manager can also be a farm manager on some farms and ranches. Breeding managers can oversee the breeding of horses, goats, cows, pigs, sheep, chickens, and other farm animals. They are in charge of the animals' overall health in conjunction with a veterinarian, and are responsible for record keeping. Other skills may include shipping semen, artificial insemination, embryo transfer, and lab work.

Formal training to become a breeder varies. Breeders of livestock need either an associate's or bachelor's degree in agriculture or animal sciences, and experience working with farm animals. Under the umbrella of animal sciences, animal breeders should take courses in animal breeding, reproductive science, and genetics. Some technical schools and two-year colleges offer associate degrees in animal breeding, and there are many four-year college agriculture schools that offer programs for animal breeders. Typically, those with four-year degrees earn more than those with less education and experience.

E ssential

Did you know that 85 percent of animal breeders are self-employed? The rest are employed on farms and ranches. Since the demand for breeders is great, most breeders work long hours.

Since most animal breeders are self-employed, they often take additional courses in business and marketing. Knowing how to market your business is essential for making a living. A minority of breeders work for large farms. The ones on large farms often get benefits such as sick days and health insurance.

Horse Breeder

A purebred horse, like a purebred dog or cat, is worth more money than a mixed breed. Purebreds, which are called thoroughbreds in the world of racing, must be listed in a breeding registry in order to race. The breeding registry is filled with information about the horse's background and health. Raising thoroughbred horses is an expensive business. You need land, housing for the horses, veterinarian and farrier services, and money for food. Because it can get expensive, not too many people enter this profession.

It also takes a long time to raise a racehorse. To raise a winning racehorse, you have to be in this for the long haul.

Not everyone raises horses for racing purposes. Darby Herrington-Reiter, owner of Fenrevel Farm in Louisiana, has been around horses all of her life. As a child, she spent a lot of time on her grandparents' farm in Texas. There she learned a lot by observing, asking questions, learning to ride, and later on taking courses. She owns eight horses and breeds the Paso Finos with her male Andalusian. "My idea was to crossbreed to get a different kind of horse," she says. "Paso Finos are smaller and feistier horses. They take a lot longer to mature. By breeding them with an Andalusian, they produce calmer, bigger horses."

She is a one-woman operation. Though she does hire a farrier and uses a local veterinarian, on a typical day she may repair a broken fence, clean and groom her horses, haul supplies to the barn, and assist with a birth. "There is nothing like seeing a horse born," she says.

Raising horses has changed over the years due to science. A handful of universities around the country have equine centers that offer degree programs in assisted reproduction services and breeding management services. For instance, at the University of Massachusetts Equine Center, breeders perform embryo transfers, collect semen from stallions for sperm analysis, and handle examinations of mares or stallions with infertility problems.

 Fact

The thoroughbred racehorse is believed to have been created in the early 1700s. At the time, breeders used Arabian horses because of their streamlined size, which made them swifter than larger, bulkier horses. Most thoroughbreds are bay, chestnut, brown, black, or gray, weigh about 1,000 pounds, and can be sensitive and high-spirited. Lexington, Kentucky, is the breeding hub today.

Many breeders have on-the-job experience. To become a breeder it is essential to understand equine science, so getting a degree is helpful—though not always necessary. You have to start by working on a farm or ranch taking care of the horses and training with a breeder. Once a breeder knows you are sincere, he may let you assist him.

If you don't know any breeders—and even if you do—going to college for a bachelor's degree in equine science will put you at an advantage. However, even with a degree, you will need hands-on experience. All of the college programs offer internships or have farms located right on campus.

Alert

The cost of a horse varies greatly. It largely depends on the horse's age and level of training. Most important, before you purchase a horse, make sure that horse is fully examined by a veterinarian.

Some breeders of racehorses can earn six-figure salaries, but those jobs are quite rare. The horse world is small, and a lot of people in the breeding industry know each other. It takes time—even with a degree—to become a breeder. After you have your equine science degree and have spent a few years on a farm or ranch doing grunt work, you will have to apprentice with a breeder. People don't go into this field with high hopes of financial gain. They do it because they love and want to be around horses.

Broodmare and Foaling Managers

Broodmare managers take care of the mares up until birth. A foaling manager's job is to care for the foal as soon as it is born. Often one person can do both jobs, and breeders can also be broodmare and foaling managers. It all depends on the size of the farm. Larger farms may hire one person for each task. At Fenrevel Farms, Herrington-Reiter is the breeder as well as broodmare and foaling manager. She makes sure the female horses are well cared for during their pregnancies, assists in the delivery of the foals, and makes sure each foal is healthy. She calls a veterinarian as soon as a foal is born.

Once a foal is born, imprinting begins. The foaling manager will introduce the foal to sounds around the barn, gently stroke him, tap on his feet so he will get used to wearing shoes, and get him used to wearing a halter. "You have to start all of this early, so the horse can be trained," Herrington-Reiter says. "They won't fight you if you start early. They are prey animals and can be scared. You have to make sure early on that they know you are not a predator."

Salaries depend on where you work. Large farms pay more money and tend to have their broodmare and foaling manager on staff. Some broodmare and foaling managers are self-employed, and many work as breeders.

Stable Hand / Farm Worker

There are about two million farms in the United States. Large farms and ranches hire farm and stable hands. Farm and stable hands do all sorts of jobs, from making repairs and running equipment to planting and harvesting crops and taking care of farm animals.

Often farm hands and stable hands live on the farm. Their room and board are often covered, and they earn about $20,000 a year. Like farmers, they work long hours, mostly outdoors.

 Fact

Living expenses for most farm families exceed $50,000 a year. Making a decent living as a farmer or farm hand is tough. According to the U.S. Census Bureau, fewer than one in four farms in this country produce gross revenues in excess of $60,000.

Farm hands must love working outdoors and should enjoy being around animals. Having a high school degree, being physically fit (farm work is hard on the body), and knowing how to operate and repair farm equipment and tend to animals are requirements for the job.

Farrier

Simply put, farriers take care of horses' feet. They trim and balance a horse's hoof to make sure that the shoes are a perfect fit. They must have a keen knowledge of equine anatomy and the physiology of the lower limb to care for horses' feet, and they must know how to care for injured and diseased hoofs. They can work on farms and ranches. They usually are self-employed and live in rural areas. Some farriers who work at racetracks can live in or near big cities.

 Question

What is the difference between a farrier and a blacksmith?
In Colonial times, farriers and blacksmiths were synonymous. In addition to making shoes for horses and caring for horses' feet, farriers made and repaired tools. Today, farriers specialize in horseshoeing and foot care for horses. Although blacksmiths can make horseshoes, they now mainly make and fix tools.

Because they are self-employed, farriers usually charge by the visit. Rates vary according to location. They can earn about $35,000 to $60,000 a year, depending on how much work they do.

If you are interested in becoming a farrier, you can attend a trade school. Most offer six-month programs in equine science with a concentration in anatomy, equine care, and forge work. Some schools also offer basic marketing skills for farriers. Knowing how to publicize a business is always a smart idea for those who are self-employed.

After completing the course, students can get certified through programs with the American Farrier's Association. For more information on becoming a farrier or to learn about school programs and certification, contact the American Farrier's Association at *www.americanfarriers.org.*

CHAPTER 14

Jobs under the Sea

About two-thirds of the earth's surface is covered by water. Because of their vast expanse, less than 10 percent of earth's waters have been explored. Beneath the ocean's waves is a whole world filled with exotic fish, powerful polar bears, enormous whales, playful penguins, colorful coral reefs, and more. Career opportunities are broad and include everything from educating the public about the ecosystems to protecting sea life.

Veterinarian

For as long as Felicia Nutter, DVM and PhD, can remember, she wanted to be a veterinarian. Her mom, who worked as a nurse, tended to the injured birds Nutter found and brought home. As a child, Nutter watched every animal documentary on television. "My mother said that when I was four, I told her that I wanted to be a veterinarian and take care of an assortment of animals," she says.

Nutter, who works as the staff veterinarian at the Marine Mammal Center in California, spent several years studying gorillas in Africa. When an opportunity opened up at the Center in February 2007, she applied and got the job. She was ready to return to the States, and wanted to work with sea animals.

Now, Nutter oversees the clinical care of animals along a 600-mile range of California coastline, running from Mendocino County to San Luis Obispo County. If a marine mammal is washed up on the beach or is in distress, a volunteer will call the Marine Mammal

Center. Nutter and other staff then rush to the site to try to save the animal. "We have a network of over 800 volunteers," she says. "They have been trained to help injured or sick sea animals."

Depending on the season, she has encountered California sea lions, elephant seals, and Pacific harbor seals. "These are the most common," she explains. "They are stranded on the beach for a variety of reasons. It can be malnutrition. Seal pups may be separated from their moms before they are fully weaned. Or it can be some sort of illness."

Once the animal is captured, Nutter and her team collect blood samples and in some cases take x-rays and ultrasounds. Everything goes back to the lab for research.

The Marine Mammal Center is the biggest marine hospital in the world. The staff sees 500 to 1,000 patients each year. That's a lot of work for a staff of three full-time veterinarians, three veterinary technicians, and three research assistants. The Center has other departments with marine biologists, researchers, and educators. The Center relies on its volunteers to assist in spotting and capturing stranded animals. The staff and volunteers work to release the healed animals back into the sea, and also do cleanup of waters in the area.

Nutter's day starts off between 7 and 8 A.M. What she loves about the job, in addition to working with the animals and the volunteers, is that no day is typical. She does her rounds in the morning, checking on all of her patients. Some days are filled with paperwork, while others are spent out on the beach rescuing animals and overseeing cleanup operations.

Nutter says that with a greater concern placed on global warming and other environmental issues, opportunities for jobs like hers are opening up. On the downside for job seekers, people who work in this field tend to stay in it for the long haul. "We like what we do and don't really think about changing," she says. "However, there are plenty of aquariums and a few marine wildlife sanctuaries around the country for people who want to work with sea creatures."

To become a veterinarian specializing in marine mammals, you will need to attend four years of an accredited veterinary medical school. Upon completion of veterinary school, the common route, according to Nutter, is to enroll in a one-year internship or three-year residency program, which is followed by board exams. In addition to her DVM, Nutter earned a PhD in zoological medicine.

Nutter suggests that if you want to find out about the different professions within veterinary medicine, the American Veterinary Medical Association's website at *www.avma.org* is a good place to start.

Working with sea mammals or animals other than cats and dogs is an adventure for someone like Nutter. "I like dogs and cats, but it is exciting being in contact with more exotic animals," she says. "Salaries are good, but most organizations that hire someone like me are nonprofits." Average salaries can be in the $50,000 to $75,000 range for a veterinarian who works with sea mammals.

Educator

Educating the public about marine life is a growing business. Marine mammal hospitals and aquariums are hiring educators who specialize in marine life to teach students and the general public about life in the sea. Teaching visitors about marine ecosystems isn't new. Many aquariums have been doing this for decades. What's new are the programs that take the public behind the scenes for a close-up view. Some aquariums have programs that allow visitors to swim with the sharks. Others employ educators to take tourists out on whale-watching expeditions. A few are teaching volunteers how to assist in rescue operations. The bottom line is that educators are needed to work with the public.

At the Marine Mammal Center in California, Doreen Moser Gurrola works as the assistant director of education. She teaches everyone from pre-K to high school students about ocean life. "I take students out on the water to take water-quality surveys," she says. "They also do sand crab surveys, plankton surveys to identify different species, and even track harbor seals."

She works full-time at the Marine Mammal Center and also contracts herself out to lead whale-watching and nature tours. At the

Center she works both outdoors and in the classroom showing students how to identify, care for, and tag animals. "I enjoy being able to share this knowledge with students who are eager to learn," she says. "They have a real interest in marine mammals, and even the tough ones who at first seem uninterested quickly come around when they see an animal."

Because of the success of the program with students, the Marine Mammal Center began offering education workshops to the public in 2008. Now visitors can learn about sea creatures in an up-close and personal setting. The Center's educators teach visitors about ecosystems, diseases that affect the animals, the animals' immune systems, and the impact the environment has on the animals.

 Fact

Approximately 80 percent of all life on earth is under the sea, and less than 10 percent of the ocean has been explored. That means there are a lot of opportunities for workers to discover life in our planet's bodies of water.

Educating visitors has boosted funding to various organizations. Most wildlife centers and aquariums are nonprofits that rely heavily on donor support. By reaching out to the public, letting them have a greater understanding of what's going on the behind the scenes, and sharing knowledge about the animals, these nonprofits have strengthened their funding and membership.

Workers at the Marine Mammal Center cannot see the organization existing without its many volunteers. The same goes for the South Carolina Aquarium in Charleston. "Volunteers are essential to what we do," says Svenja Xeller, education programs instructor at the South Carolina Aquarium. She started as a volunteer six years ago, and has held her paid position as an educator for almost two years. She still volunteers on Saturdays.

For Xeller, being a volunteer has a major perk—she can dive with the sharks. She is able to get up-close with the sharks as well as teach the public about them. She also feeds the sharks and cleans the tank.

 Fact

Most people think of the movie *Jaws* when they think of sharks. Actually, sharks attack fewer than 70 people each year, according to the International Shark Attack File. Of those attacks, between eight and twelve are fatal. Shark attacks get a lot of attention, even though more people are struck by lightning every year.

As the education program instructor, Xeller works full-time teaching students from kindergarten to high school about marine life. She and the education staff give talks to visitors to the aquarium. She also sets the schedules of five full-time educators and one part-timer. "I work with schools to create lesson plans," she says.

Throughout the aquarium, she and the other educators impart their knowledge about the numerous exhibits. The aquarium also has an Amazon-themed exhibit, so Xeller works with boa constrictors, anteaters, opossums, macaws, and other animals from that part of the world.

Xeller earned her degree in psychology and education. She credits getting her job to volunteering. "The last two openings we had brought in over 100 applications from all over the country," she says. "That number was narrowed down to a handful. I applied and got the job because I already had my foot in the door as a volunteer. They knew me here. Many of us got our start that way."

Moser Gurrola agrees that volunteering definitely puts you ahead of the pile of resumes. She suggests getting a master's degree in education with an emphasis in the sciences, and interning or volunteering at a place you want to work.

Salaries vary greatly. In South Carolina, educators can earn between $23,000 and $28,000 to start. The salaries in California are higher, and reflect the cost of living.

Oceanographer

An oceanographer studies oceans and the plants and animals they contain. The field of oceanography has four distinct branches; there are biological oceanographers, physical oceanographers, geological oceanographers, and marine scientists. Even though each branch of oceanography differs, there are some similarities. All work in a variety of settings—from indoors in aquariums and laboratories to outdoors in the ocean. They can work both daytime and nighttime hours. Some work solo, and others work in teams.

Most oceanographers stay in their jobs for the duration. They enjoy what they do, and turnover doesn't happen very often. However, that should not discourage anyone from pursuing a dream career. Openings do occur. People who enjoy science and math courses have an edge. If you want to become an oceanographer, you should take courses in chemistry, physics, calculus, and statistics. Having a doctorate in marine science, oceanography, earth science, or marine science is recommended.

Oceanographers earn between $50,000 and $80,000 a year. Salaries vary according to the experience and qualifications of the oceanographer.

Biological Oceanographer

Biological oceanographers study marine animals and plants. Their main interest is in how marine organisms develop and relate to one another. They also study how these organisms interact and adapt to their environment. This is one of the most popular fields in oceanography. Biological oceanographers spend a few months outdoors in the ocean and an equal amount of time entering data into their computers.

Physical Oceanographer

Physical oceanographers study the movement of oceans and the causes of that motion, such as wind, waves, and tides. They use satellite technology to study the interaction between the ocean and its surroundings—the land, sea floor, and atmosphere. They closely look at the effects of weather and climate change on the ocean. Again, due to global warming, there is an increased demand for physical oceanographers. Physical oceanographers are part of a team. They work closely with biological oceanographers, geological oceanographers, and marine scientists.

Geological Oceanographer

If you are fascinated by mountains, plains, valleys, volcanoes, islands, and canyons on land, imagine how you will feel about discovering them under the ocean. That is what geological oceanographers do. Geological oceanographers, also called marine geologists, use sonar and acoustic devices to look for underwater volcanoes. They find volcanoes by bouncing sound waves off rock formations. The devices also locate valleys and mountains.

 Question

> **What is earth's largest continuous mountain range?**
> It is the Mid-Ocean Ridge, which stretches for more than 40,000 miles. It rises above the water's surface in Iceland and just a few other places. Most of it is underwater. In the Pacific Ocean, the Mariana Trench is a mile deeper than Mount Everest is high. There is a lot to explore under the sea.

Not long ago, it was impossible for geological oceanographers to study many of these rock formations. Because of their locations, most were impossible to get to. In just ten years, technological advances have allowed geological oceanographers to locate and explore many more of these undersea places. Some of the technology includes using piloted submersibles, remotely operated vehicles, and programmable acoustic instruments attached to boats. These new machines have allowed geological oceanographers to study life on the ocean floor, creating more opportunities in this field.

Marine Scientist/Biologist

The titles "marine scientist" and "marine biologist" are interchangeable. Marine biologists are scientists who study sea animals and plants as well as underwater ecosystems. They look at the relationship that the environment plays on various bodies of water. They also study the sealife in these waters. Some marine scientists or biologists will specialize in a handful of areas, such as the study of whales or the effect of noise pollution on dolphins.

Steve Heath, chief marine biologist at the Marine Resources Division of the Alabama Department of Conservation and Natural Resources, concentrates on marine fisheries management. He collects data on marine resources. "Currently we are collecting data on the sizes and distribution on numerous fish and invertebrates like shrimp, crabs, and oysters," he explains.

Because he works for a state agency, Heath often is embroiled in battles between commercial fishermen and environmentalists. "At times I feel like we are standing on a pitcher's mound," he says. "We try to call the right shots while remaining neutral to each side's cause."

By making recommendations to his state-run agency, Heath can allow or limit the number of fish that are caught by commercial fishermen. Not everyone is pleased with the decisions that are reached. "The commercial fishermen want to catch as much fish [as they need] for their livelihood," he says. "Others want us to stop sport fishing. We get opinions from all sides, and each one has a point."

Fisheries managers, like Heath, can work for either a state or federal agency. Every state has its own Fish and Wildlife Service. Under the direction of the nationally run U.S. Fish and Wildlife Service are state-run agencies that work to manage and preserve wildlife. Heath was drawn to his profession at an early age. "Like many people in my profession, Jacques Cousteau was my hero," he says. "I decided I wanted to be a marine biologist or oceanographer at an early age."

He got his bachelor's degree in zoology and his master's in marine science. He says that people need at least a master's degree to get a job as a marine biologist. "At the federal level or in academia, many go for their PhD," he says. "After I finished my master's in marine science, I applied for many different jobs. This one in fisheries management came along. At the time, I didn't know much about fisheries management. I did a lot of learning on the job." He's been working at the Marine Resources Division in Alabama for more than thirty years.

Since moving up the ladder to become the chief marine biologist, Heath does a good deal of office work managing a small staff. In the beginning he spent a bit more time outdoors. Hours tend to be between 8 A.M. and 5 P.M., with longer hours in the summer. "Daylight is longer in the summer, so we take advantage of that by being out on the waters," he says. "It's routine to work more than forty hours a week. I would say that is the same trend with most jobs today.

"When I first started, I would spend at least two days a week out on a boat and the other three in the lab and attending meetings," he says. "That has changed. As chief, I spend 95 percent of the time doing administrative work and attending meetings." What drew him to the upper management position was the ability to affect policy. "With authority comes responsibility," he says. "That can be a two-edged sword. I do love being outdoors—that's why most people go into this profession. But I can also make changes in policy."

For example, fishermen were using nets to catch a particular kind of fish. "We adjusted the mesh on the nets so other fish couldn't be caught," he says. "We can manage what fish can and can't be caught, and how much fish can be caught for commercial purposes."

Heath also spends time talking to students who are interested in marine science careers. Students need a lot of science and math courses. "They also need to know how to write and communicate clearly," he says. "Many people in the scientific community overlook the writing and communications aspects of the job. It helps if you can write and have scientific data published. You should also know how to write for the general public. If you want to keep this field alive, you have to promote it—and that means writing articles and occasionally giving talks."

 Fact

Thanks to technological developments in the area of submersibles, marine science has greatly evolved. These small mobile machines come in a variety of shapes and sizes, and contain power sources and sensors. They are equipped with photo and video cameras, instruments for measuring environmental parameters, and sonic equipment. Some use mechanical arms to collect samples. Others have compartments for a manned crew.

He tells everyone who wants to work in this field to either volunteer or get an internship. Master's degree programs have hands-on internships, but it is wise to have as much experience as possible. "I have taken some high school students out in January," he says. "Usually our internships are during the summer months when the waters are much calmer. It's rougher in the winter, and it's just plain cold. The three or four summer interns get to shadow us on various projects. They do a lot of grunt work too. An internship really lets you know if this is the job for you."

Heath says that within the next five to ten years many people in the profession will be retiring. "The baby boomers who went into this profession will soon retire," he explains, "thus creating a good number of openings."

Marine biologists start out earning $30,000 a year and move up to $80,000 over the course of several years on the job. Most of these jobs include full health benefits.

Sensory Biophysicist

How do sea creatures communicate? Sensory biophysicists study the sounds of certain sea mammals to see how they communicate with one another and how they behave. Certain sounds can evoke feelings of happiness or distress. Some marine mammals use sound to locate food. Others can imitate human sounds.

 Fact

At the New England Aquarium, a harbor seal was taught to say a few words. What makes him even more special is that he acquired a New England accent! At the Vancouver Aquarium, a beluga whale was able to say his name, which was Logosi.

Sensory biophysicists also study the sensory systems of aquatic animals. They are behaviorists of sorts. They study the animal's senses to see how it survives and functions in its environment. There are a lot of opportunities in this highly specialized field for sensory biophysicists who have a doctoral degree in physics and oceanography as well as hands-on experience, which one gets in school. Many sensory biophysicists must write and apply for grants. They can work as teachers in universities or in the field for drug, bio-tech, and robotics companies.

Marine Biotechnologist

Marine biotechnologists study marine microbiology—basically, bacteria found in water sources that can be used for antibiotics. They spend a few weeks each year gathering samples to bring back to their labs for research. They supervise students who are working to become marine biotechnologists, and write grants and papers to support their work. They spend some time diving and gathering specimens for research. If you talk to any marine biotechnologists, they will tell you that being on the water and diving are their favorite aspects of the job. They also enjoy bringing back those specimens and studying them in the labs. What most don't like is spending a lot of time writing grants and managing budgets. However, grant writing is necessary to secure funding for one's work.

 Question

Which fields of marine biotechnology are growing?
Marine biotechnologists are needed in the areas of drug discovery, aquaculture, and monitoring for pathogens in the marine environment. That means working for a pharmaceutical company is a good option. Also, because this field is so specialized, jobs are opening up in the academic world.

Marine biotechnologists must have a background in molecular biology and marine science. Schooling should consist of a master's degree and doctorate. Internships are essential. Many schools have summer internships, and those interns who do well are often offered jobs upon graduation. Salaries range between $80,000 and $100,000 for marine biotechnologists with ten or more years of experience.

CHAPTER 15

Working with Insects

Bugs are everywhere. In fact, there are more insects on this planet than there are animals and people combined. They exist in cities, towns, and rural areas. They have been found on mountaintops, in deep caves, in deserts and ice fields, puddles and oceans, and forests and plains. Bugs also live in our backyards and houses. Even the cleanest home has insects. You might not see them, but they do exist. Some are even microscopic. Entomologists have identified about one million insect species, and most believe that there are many more—anywhere between 10 million and 30 million.

Understanding Bugs

Cornell University has a course called "Alien Empire: Bizarre Biology of Bugs." Despite the fact that bugs are everywhere, they are alien to most people. However, they serve a valuable role. Honeybees are responsible for approximately 80 percent of all pollination in the United States. Pollination is a big business, producing crops worth about $20 billion each year.

Some cultures use insects as a food source. They are also used for clothing—as is the case with the silkworm—and other household products. Beeswax is used in cosmetics and as a base for ointments and lotions. Because of their short lifespan (usually ten days), fruit flies are used in genetic testing. Some species of insects are used to control parasites. On the negative side, some insects spread disease (for instance, the tsetse fly spreads malaria), and some can damage crops.

Question

How do museum technicians clean the skeletons of mammals on display?
They use carpet beetles because these insects will feed on almost anything. Carpet beetles are tiny bugs that eat most organic matter. The museum technicians store tiny colonies of these bugs to keep mammal skeletons clean.

Insects play an important role in human lives. Many are used to study behavior. Those living in colonies can help us understand cooperation. Ask a beekeeper or someone who studies ants and they will give an awe-inspiring account of how insects work for the good of the colony. It's pretty amazing to think that between 20,000 and 60,000 bees can live in one hive, or that there are 8,800 species of ants known to scientists. A typical colony can hold over 2,000 ants. That's close quarters.

Entomologists love the diversity and challenges they come across when studying insects. "It is unlike any other area of science," says Ronda Hamm, a graduate student and teaching assistant at Cornell University. Hamm was planning on becoming a veterinarian. She first came into contact with other entomologists in high school. "I didn't think I wanted to touch a bug every day," she says. "I was working with the Future Farmers of America while I was in high school. There I studied ants. Watching ant colonies is fascinating. You can learn a lot just by observing."

In high school, Hamm entered and won a few science fairs. She got some scholarship money and applied to Cornell. "What fascinates me is how adaptable insects are. They can adapt to changes in our environment."

As soon as Hamm gets her doctorate, she will go into teaching. She is currently working as a teaching assistant at Cornell. "Entomology is so much broader than people expect. Entomologists travel to exotic places—like Costa Rica—to study bugs that live on the edges of waterfalls. Since there are so many insects to study, the possibilities are broad. By studying insects we can learn so much about behavior, health, and the environment."

 Fact

More and more zoos and wildlife centers throughout the country are introducing bug exhibits. One good reason is because of their tiny size. Insects don't take up a lot of room. Setting up insect exhibits requires small aquarium tanks and often little maintenance. The budget for feeding insects is so minimal, too. Entomologists are often called in to set up the exhibits and care for the bugs. These exhibitions are a great way to teach visitors about insects.

Insects and the Environment

When most people see a yellow jacket, wasp, or cockroach, their instinct is to swat it or flee the area. Entomologists, however, are keenly aware that most insects have useful purposes. Cornell University's John Losey and Mace Vaughan are entomologists with the Xerces Society for Invertebrate Conservation, an international non-profit that works to protect biological diversity through invertebrate conservation. Losey and Vaughan created a spreadsheet that lists the economic benefits of native insects in the United States. They discovered that native insects offer services that otherwise could cost up to $57 billion a year.

Predator insects eat prey insects that host on crops, saving farmers billions of dollars in crop losses. The dung beetle, which feasts upon cow patties, keeps flies and parasites away from cow waste. They work to fertilize the pasture by decomposing bovine waste. Losey and Vaughan calculated a savings of $380 million to American ranchers and farmers.

Insects also serve wildlife. Without insects, birds wouldn't exist. Most birds feed upon a variety of bugs. Without birds, bird watching and other outdoor recreation would end. Outdoor recreation, which includes fishing and watching other wildlife in addition to birds, is a $50 billion industry.

E ssential

Approximately 8,000 men and women work as entomologists in the United States. They work in a wide variety of jobs including teaching, farming, raising bees, enforcing quarantines, doing insect survey work, providing pest management, and conducting scientific studies to end disease. The majority of entomologists do research and work to control harmful insects.

In Lincoln, Nebraska, insects were destroying prairie grasses alongside the highways. Earle Raun, an entomological veterinarian who was educated at Buena Vista College, University of Iowa, and Iowa State University, has been working on how to identify the insects and how to save prairie grass, which is a hardy plant. In order to save the prairie grass, he looked at different insecticides and other insects that would eat the pests without destroying the grass. "Being an entomologist is kind of like being a detective," he says. "I'm always looking for insects, many that you can't see unless you have a microscope."

Raun was all set to become a medical doctor just like his grandfather. "He was a horse-and-buggy doctor—traveling the countryside in a horse and buggy helping people," he says. "I thought I would become an MD. I passed my medical exams and started medical training. My roommate was a junior medic. Listening to his stories about being in hospital wards and experiencing some myself, I decided to go back to college and study zoology and entomology."

 Fact

Entomologists work closely with customs officers on all international flights. In 2006, at Newark Liberty International Airport in New Jersey, customs officers found eight insect species that had not been previously seen in the United States. Often, these pests are brought in on a single piece of fruit carried by a hungry passenger. When bugs are detected, the confiscated items are placed in quarantine until entomologists can determine whether they pose a threat.

Growing up in Lincoln, Nebraska, he was surrounded by farms, and knew that by working as a veterinary entomologist, he could help his friends and neighbors. Farmers would call on him when their animals got sick. The first place he would look is in the food supply. "Some feed is brought in from overseas, and others produced right here in the states can contain parasites," he says. "I look at the product and trace the steps backward to see where the problem is coming from."

In one case a farmer called him in because his hogs were dying. "I found dead grasshoppers in the feed," he says. "The feed had parasites in it that were making the hogs sick.

"I also look at the coats of horses and cows," he continues. "If an animal has mange, I know it is caused by mites." Controlling the spread of disease by managing insect populations is just one branch of entomology.

Raun says that if you are interested in becoming a veterinary entomologist, vet school is mandatory, followed by study specializing in entomology. "Before you do that, it is a good idea to take an 'introduction to insects' course in school, just to be sure you are comfortable around bugs," he suggests.

Veterinary entomologists are paid well because their type of service is so specialized. Salaries depend on experience and geographic location. Experienced veterinary entomologists can expect to earn between $60,000 and $85,000 a year.

Stopping the Spread of Disease

In sub-Saharan areas of Africa, and parts of Yemen, southern Mexico, Guatemala, Ecuador, Colombia, Venezuela, and along the Amazon in Brazil, nearly 18 million people are infected with river blindness. The technical term for this disease is "onchocerciasis," and it is spread though the bite of female black flies. These flies breed in swiftly flowing streams. Tourists to these areas usually do not get river blindness because many bites are needed for a person to become infected. To avoid getting river blindness, people need to stay away from areas with rushing streams. However, many villagers need water to grow crops. It is part of their livelihood.

Entomologists at pharmaceutical companies such as Merck & Co., Inc., are working to end the spread of river blindness. Scientists at Merck have developed drugs for this purpose, specifically one called Mectizan, that the company is distributing to the affected areas of the world.

Another American company is working in Africa, this one to stop the spread of malaria, which is transmitted by the bite of the tsetse fly. Buzz Off Insect Shield has created several different clothing lines that incorporate insect repellents in its products. The North Carolina–based company is working with MENTOR, an NGO (nongovernmental organization) based in the United Kingdom, to provide disease control and technical and operational support in emergencies and recovery crises.

E ssential

It was veterinary entomologists who proved that insects can transmit disease. Their discoveries launched research to control typhus, malaria, bubonic plague, and yellow fever. Their work has helped many animals and people.

Laura Hendrix, Buzz Off Insect Shield director of global health initiatives, is currently working with MENTOR's malaria-control project on-site in the Busia District in Africa. As director, she will promote community awareness of malaria prevention and treatment methods. She will also assist other workers in incorporating Buzz Off Insect Shield in the local native dress, *khangas*, which are colorful wraps worn by African women. They are also used to carry babies and as sleeping covers. These khangas will be distributed free. While in the Busia District, Hendrix will also conduct weekly surveys to gather information about the protection provided by these garments and the feasibility of the program.

Medical entomologists can work for private pharmaceutical companies as well as federal, state, and local health departments. Raun worked as a consultant for his local and state health departments. He would often inspect livestock and food supplies that come from other states or countries. Some days he could be found at his local airport inspecting large shipments of grain that were stored there before being allowed into the state or country. If he deemed these products safe, he would give the okay.

Other entomologists, such as the ones who work for Merck and Buzz Off, can divide their time between an office at a research laboratory in their home state and in foreign countries distributing medications, taking samples and surveys for research, and educating local populations on pest control.

 Fact

According to the Mayo Clinic, many germs rely on insect carriers. The common insect carriers are mosquitoes, fleas, lice, and ticks. These insects move from host to host, usually living in close quarters. Mosquitoes can carry the West Nile virus. Deer ticks can cause Lyme disease. These insect carriers are called vectors. The disease is spread when an infected vector bites or stings you.

Raising Bees

Beekeeping is possibly the one career that allows you to have alone time. "Almost never when I go outside and release my bees, do I get a crowd of people," says Kim Flottum, a beekeeper and the editor of *Bee Culture: The Magazine of American BeeKeeping*. "People tend to stay away when the bees are flying overhead, but there is nothing like it—being outdoors. It is just you and the bees. It's almost intoxicating to watch."

According to Flottum, you don't need a lot of space to own bees. "There are even a few beekeepers who have their hives on Manhattan [New York] rooftops," he says. "You don't need a lot of land. The bees will travel about a mile or two to find food."

Flottum lives in a small northern Ohio town with about 25,000 people and a local beekeeping association. He says that many towns have beekeepers. Most of them keep bees as a hobby—because they love bees and the honey. Flottum, who is a part-time beekeeper, has five hives in his two-acre backyard. He sells the honey locally at farmers markets and a few shops. Many beekeepers use the wax from the hives to make candles, and they sell those too.

He says his neighbors don't mind being close by, "because when you have bees, your garden does much better," he says. Despite the fact that many people love honey and understand that we need honeybees to pollinate plants, not many people are going into this profession.

 Fact

The number of managed honeybee colonies is less than half of what it was twenty-five years ago. In 2006, across the United States, honeybee colonies started to die. The problem is called colony collapse disorder (CCD). Scientists who are studying CCD don't know why it is occurring. They do have theories; some include attacks by parasites, increasing urbanization of the land, use of pesticides, and environmental factors.

According to Flottum, there are approximately 100,000 beekeepers in the United States. Of that number, most are hobbyists. He believes that about 1,000 are full-time commercial beekeepers, and about 5,000 are serious sideliners. "You can make a good living as a sideliner," he says. These are people who work full-time in other jobs, have a small number of hives, and sell honey and wax at flea markets and local stores.

To do this full-time you need a lot of land, and Flottum suggests that you have land in different parts of the country. That way, if there is a drought in one area of the country where you have your hives, you can count on the other areas where you have your hives to produce enough honey and wax for a profit. Large commercial companies own about 100,000 hives, and they need about 1,000 acres.

To become a beekeeper you will need to purchase hives. Flottum and other beekeepers make their own. You will also need a thorough understanding of bees and beekeeping. Flottum suggests contacting the National Honey Board (*www.honey.com*) or local beekeeping association in your town to attend classes. "Before you invest in equipment and your time, it is a good idea to take a beginner's course in beekeeping just to make sure this is something you really want to do," he explains.

Alert

Beekeeping is legal in most states. Before you begin, you should check with your local town or government office to see if it is allowed. Some towns have ordinances about beekeeping and may not want hives too close to schools. If you really want to go into this profession full-time or part-time, you might consider keeping bees at a nearby farm.

In addition to checking with the National Honey Board, check out the American Beekeeping Federation (*www.abfnet.org*) and the American Honey Producers Association (*www.americanhoney producers.org*). "Talk to beekeepers," says Flottum. "We are a friendly bunch of people and are eager to share information about the profession."

Entomology Teaching Careers

Everyone has an opinion about bugs. Entomologists are fascinated by them. Yes, they know many people are scared of certain bugs. They know that bugs can destroy plants and that some carry harmful diseases. They also know that many bugs are beneficial to the planet. That awe that fuels an entomologist's curiosity has helped many of people.

"We can learn so much from insects," says Ronda Hamm. "It's great observing bugs and observing students. Everyone reacts to bugs in a different way. Entomologists tend to be ambassadors of sorts to the world of bugs. We are so fascinated by them that we want our students to be equally enthused."

Question

What is the most endangered insect?
Butterflies are in danger of extinction due to habitat destruction. Collecting butterflies also contributes to their reduced numbers.

It's true that most entomologists want to share that enthusiasm. They want others to know that by studying the behavior of insects, we can better understand our own behaviors. Entomologists also study insects to learn about the environment. They are conservationists of sorts. By studying the habitats of insects, entomologists can teach us a lot about the broader environmental picture.

While most teachers of entomology work in a classroom, many spend a good deal of their time out in the field. Entomologists can be found at a local nature center teaching young children about bugs. There are many hands-on, catch-and-release programs that allow children to learn about grasshoppers, fireflies, ants, and other insects. Being out in the field is often more exciting than being in a classroom.

Back in the classroom, most teachers will bring in bugs to entice their students into learning. These hands-on lessons are anything but boring. When a tarantula is shown crawling on a teacher's hand or on the hand of a volunteer student, everyone in the class pays attention—even the squeamish.

The great thing about bugs is that they require a lot less care than does a classroom gerbil or hamster. Bugs can be kept in plastic containers or Mason jars. (However, there are a few requirements to keep in mind: the lids must be ventilated; some bugs require a humid environment; most eat only one kind of food; and all need adequate amounts of water.) Bugs are also easy to find. They can be purchased online, in some pet stores, or can simply be found in a backyard.

"It's one thing sharing information about an insect," says Hamm. "It's another when you bring in a sample for the class to observe."

 Fact

According to the U.S. Census Bureau, there are more than six million teachers in the United States. The majority of teachers— a whopping 71 percent—are women. The demand for good teachers is always high—especially people to teach the sciences. Jobs are available in every state. Those with advanced degrees have a better chance of getting a good job.

Most teachers of entomology work at the college or graduate level. They do research in addition to teaching. To become an entomology teacher, you will need to major in science and math in college, get a masters' degree in education with a specialty in the sciences or entomology, and also get a PhD. "High school science teachers can teach without a doctorate," says Hamm. "You need the doctorate for higher education and for research—it really helps.

"In addition to teaching students, and doing research, a good part of the job is spent writing grants for your research, and writing papers," says Hamm. "Writing grants and being published in journals are essential for college- and grad-level work."

The national average annual salary for a public elementary and secondary school teacher is $44,700. Plus, most teachers get excellent health benefits. Professors at private colleges earn approximately $101,200 per year; those at public colleges earn about $84,100.

Forensic Entomologist

Did you know that forensic entomologists, also called medicocriminal entomologists, can determine the time of death at a crime scene by studying insect evidence? Police and lawyers are calling on forensic entomologists to help them solve crimes. While weapons, gunpowder, and other evidence has been carefully collected and studied by crime scene investigators for years, calling in entomologists is relatively new. In the last ten years, entomology has been recognized as a major component in crime-solving.

While the need for forensic entomologists is growing, there are fewer than 100 forensic entomologists in the country. Of that total, most teach at universities, colleges, and high schools. The majority of forensic entomologists work as consultants for the police and legal systems.

 **Alert**

Being a forensic entomologist is not for the faint of heart. The job entails working around corpses—just like the majority of crime scene investigations. The plots seen on the popular CSI TV show don't show you the total picture. That program presents a sanitized version. If you are considering going into this profession, talk to an expert and see if you can shadow him for a day.

Many forensic entomologists work on a freelance basis training crime scene investigators to recognize, collect, and preserve entomological evidence. Forensic entomologists are often called on to testify as expert witnesses in trials. They usually are paid for their testimony.

Working full-time as a forensic entomologist is rare. Those interested in teaching entomology can supplement their income by becoming a forensic entomologist. However, those in the field are not in it for the money. They love working with insects and solving crimes.

To become a forensic entomologist, you must have a background in the biological sciences and entomology. You will need a doctorate in entomology, with a minor in criminal justice. While an education in criminal justice is looked upon as a major plus, you must have a degree in entomology to work in this field.

Robot Bugs

Though the idea might seem to come out of the pages of a sci-fi novel, a handful of U.S. government and private agencies are growing live insects with computer chips in them. The goal is to use these bugs as spyware. These robot insects are being used to guide missiles to targets and to locate survivors in collapsed buildings. Bees can sniff out explosives, and cockroaches can detect anthrax.

In an article from the *Washington Post*, it was reported that researchers funded by the Defense Advanced Research Projects Agency (DARPA) are inserting computer chips into moth pupae. It is during the pupal stage that caterpillars transform into moths. When the moths emerge from their cocoons, they can be used as a type of cyborg. They are used as cameras, and defense personnel can monitor their whereabouts. Researchers at DARPA are manufacturing cyborg beetles, too. These robot insects are being used for surveillance purposes.

The Department of Defense and Department of Homeland Security aren't talking about these projects. However, several universities and a few private companies are developing robot-like bugs. To find out more, check out the Robot Insects at *www.cis.plym.ac.uk/cis/projects/InsectRobotics/Homepage.htm* or Future for All's website at *www.futureforall.org/robotics/robot_fly.htm*.

Agricultural Entomologist

Agricultural entomology seems to go hand-in-hand with pest management. When insects invade and destroy crops, agricultural entomologists are called in to eradicate the problem. They can use pesticides, introduce predator insects that won't harm crops and plants, and plant crops that keep pests at bay. Farmers work with agricultural entomologists on a regular basis. They rely on them to keep their crops free from pesticides. The damage to crops from insect pests can approach a 25 percent loss of yield.

Some insects attack crops, while others destroy trees and ornamental plants. By feeding on the roots, foliage, or fruit, insects can wipe out an entire crop or do enough economic damage that farmers will call on entomologists for help. Agricultural entomologists research insects of economic importance and work to prevent the introduction of exotic insects that may harm crops, trees, and other beneficial plants.

 Fact

Agricultural entomologists teach an integrated pest management (IPM) system when presenting pest-control and environmental information to the public. Their goal is to use the most effective form of pest control with the least amount of harm to the public and the environment.

Agricultural entomologists work out in the field and in universities, as well as in private industry. In addition to their agricultural work, they educate the public about insect pests, pesticides, and pest management.

Although agricultural entomologists spend a good deal of time outdoors, they also spend a lot of time doing research and filling out paperwork. If you are interested in becoming an agricultural entomologist, you should have a background in math and science. Of course, you will need a degree in entomology. A master's degree gives you an edge in gaining employment on the state or federal level or in private corporations. The average annual salary for agricultural entomologists is $62,000.

Opportunities are on the rise, since highly trained agricultural entomologists are needed to combat pests that have adapted to chemically based fertilizers and insecticides. They are needed to practice sustainable agriculture, which balances crop output with preservation and protection of various ecosystems. For a complete listing of universities that offer entomology programs in agriculture and other areas, go to *www.entsoc.org/resources/education/colleges.htm*.

CHAPTER 16

Where You Can Work

From the great outdoors to a high-tech lab to a stylishly decorated private office, there are many places you can work if you have a career with animals. The locations and settings are as diverse as the occupations. One certainty is that you can work in almost any state, because opportunities are quite broad.

Animal Shelters

According to the Humane Society of the United States, thousands of puppies and kittens are born each day as a result of uncontrolled breeding of pets. Each year between six million and eight million dogs and cats are brought to shelters. About half of those animals are euthanized because there aren't enough homes for them. Approximately three million shelter animals are adopted each year. Animal shelters are located in large cities and small towns throughout the United States, and working in them can be both rewarding and hard.

On the positive side, many shelter workers do their best to educate the public about spaying and neutering their pets. Some shelters offer programs to school groups with the intent to educate the children about responsible pet ownership. The Northeast Animal Shelter, located in Salem, Massachusetts, brings shelter animals that are comfortable being around children into the classrooms. The Animal Mission of the Midlands, in Columbia, South Carolina, conducts shelter tours for school children. The Animal

Mission is home to farm animals, exotic animals, and cats and dogs. The workers here teach school children, and other visitors, about responsible pet care and the importance of taking care of all animals.

E ssential

Many shelters have information on hand to educate the public about the benefits of spaying and neutering. Spaying and neutering allows dogs and cats to live longer and healthier lives. The workers also teach the public that spaying and neutering dogs and cats makes the best economic sense. Many communities spend millions of dollars to control unwanted animals.

Shelter workers spend a lot of time on the telephone. When the workers enter a shelter in the morning, they usually see the red light on the answering machine flashing, alerting them that a few calls came in during the night. People call to say they found a stray dog or cat. Others call because they want to adopt a kitten or puppy. Then there are the calls that come in from people telling the shelter that they no longer want to keep their pet.

The shelter worker often counsels these callers about behavior training for the dog or cat, which often helps change a pet owner's mind. The shelter worker also explains the shelter's policies regarding adoption and euthanasia. All shelter workers hope for the best. They want to convince callers that they should keep their pets.

The Humane Society of America estimates that there are between 4,000 and 6,000 shelters in the country. A growing number of people are working to eliminate euthanasia in shelters. People are getting involved with their local shelters. Many shelters organize volunteers to walk and play with the in-house dogs and cats. Shelter workers spend a lot of time with the public—they don't just work with animals.

 **Alert**

Out of all of the animal careers, shelter workers have the highest burnout factor. That is because most dogs and cats that enter a shelter do not get adopted. Most people prefer cute and cuddly puppies and kittens over older dogs and cats. However, the environment at shelters is slowly changing for the better. There are several no-kill shelters, where dogs and cats are not euthanized. The workers at these facilities try their best to get these dogs and cats placed in good homes.

When an animal is adopted, the shelter worker feels rewarded knowing that the dog or cat is going to a good home. Unfortunately, when animals are returned, abandoned, or brought into the shelter because an owner no longer wants to care for it, it does take a toll on the emotions of the shelter worker. Long hours, limited resources, and low wages are other reasons why so many people who work at shelters burn out and leave.

The need for shelters in small towns, large cities, and rural areas throughout America is large. People who are drawn to working in shelters do it because they care about animals. Many are in this business because they want to rescue stray dogs and cats. It takes someone with a thick skin to work in a shelter, and shelter jobs are plentiful. If you are looking for job opportunities in this area, contact your local shelter or log onto *www.AnimalSheltering.org*.

Humane Societies

Under the heading of humane societies, there are animal rescue organizations, dog shelters, cat shelters, and shelters for exotic and farm animals. The Humane Society of the United States (HSUS), American Humane, and the American Society for the Prevention of Cruelty to Animals (ASPCA) are national groups. Many shelters and other nonprofits that have similar names or call themselves SPCA or Humane Society are not related to the national organizations. These humane societies run independently, and many were founded before the national groups.

Humane societies are located in every state in the country, and in large and small towns and cities. Several humane societies, not animal shelters, work on national animal welfare issues. Organizations including the Humane Society of the United States, American Humane, Defenders of Wildlife, International Fund for Animal Welfare, and many others all have offices in the Washington, D.C., area in order to handle state and federal legislation. Entry-level workers in these departments provide assistance on key projects. Some jobs, which are usually filled by law students, political science students, and anyone interested in working to improve the lives of animals, consist of maintaining and updating Capitol Hill contact lists, delivering documents to Congressional offices, and assisting staff in research.

Working for nonprofit animal welfare agencies in Washington, D.C, as well as other areas around the country, often means working long hours.

 Question

Some animal welfare agencies, such as the International Fund for Animal Welfare, employ legal and political experts and scientists working from offices in fifteen countries around the world. Many workers at these agencies, from public relations writer to economist, travel a great deal. A scientist based at the company's headquarters may travel 25 to 50 percent of the time. To find out more about jobs at humane societies, go to the Career Toolbox section of the Humane Society of the United States website, *www.HumaneCareer Toolbox.org.*

Private Practice

Many animal care workers work either from their own homes or are otherwise self-employed, working out of an office that is close to their home. If you are self-employed, you call the shots regarding where you can work. The good news is that in the animal care world, opportunities are everywhere. Most veterinarians go into private practice. Animal trainers, animal behaviorists, pet sitters, owners of doggie daycare centers, and pet groomers are just a few of the self-employed animal workers.

E ssential

Many people in the corporate world dream about owning their own business. The truth is that creating a successful business doesn't happen overnight. Building a profitable business takes time, money, and good business acumen. Even if you graduate at the top of your class, it is essential to take a few business courses. You might be the best vet or dog groomer, but knowing how to run an office and get clients are necessary skills for setting up a business.

Veterinarians can choose to live anywhere in the United States. The ones who set up shop in a rural part of the country often have more work than they can handle. Pet sitters, dog trainers, pet groomers, and owners of doggie daycare centers can have more lucrative careers by working in major metropolitan areas. They need to serve clients who work long hours, make good money, and dote on their pets. These clients often are employed by large corporations.

While dog trainers can work almost anywhere, it's true that they get more work in large cities. They may work either out of their own home or at a client's home. The same goes for animal behaviorists and some pet groomers. Pet groomers can work at retail pet shops, in their own homes, or they can take all of their grooming equipment with them to a client's home. One common denominator is that all self-employed people need a home office with a good computer to keep clients' records and billing handy.

Animal Hospitals

Veterinary hospitals operate in large and small cities throughout the country. The majority—especially the larger hospitals—are based in big cities. Many have twenty-four-hour pet care services. It is estimated that there are between 20,000 and 24,000 veterinary hospitals in the United States; that figure also includes small private practices. Most veterinary hospitals care for dogs, cats, birds, reptiles, and rodents.

The majority of the patients at veterinary hospitals are dogs and cats. However, those that treat the more unusual pets, such as boa constrictors, ferrets, gerbils, and cockatoos, are constantly on the lookout for veterinarians, vet techs, and vet assistants with experience caring for these less traditional pets. Opportunities and salaries are often fair to high at most veterinary hospitals.

 Fact

While all animal hospitals treat dogs and cats, almost all of the larger animal hospitals treat the nontraditional pet. Many veterinary hospitals have special services that include anesthesiology, behavioral medicine, cardiology, dentistry, dermatology, emergency medicine and critical care, intensive care, internal medicine, medical imaging, oncology, ophthalmology, soft-tissue surgery, orthopedic surgery, and wildlife and exotic animal medicine.

Veterinary hospitals are great places to work if you enjoy being around a large staff and working with an assortment of animals. Hours can be long, but flexible. Some professionals choose to work night shifts. Others prefer daytime hours. If you are interested in getting your foot in the door, you should be open to working evening or nighttime hours.

National Parks, Zoos, and Wildlife Centers

The great outdoors seems like a wonderful place to work. You can spend your days outside leading rugged nature hikes, operating a boat filled with tourists who want to spot a dolphin or whale, or taking water samples back to a laboratory. Mother Nature can be quite seductive, except on those snowy, wet days. Many marine biologists, who are charmed by the treasures of the sea, know that Mother Nature can be fickle. The just-out-of-college entry-level worker can be in for a major shock. Those calm, cool waters of the summer months are totally bone-chilling in February in most parts of the country.

Working at a national park means spending a good deal of time outdoors. The same goes for having a career at a zoo or wildlife center. Some of the time can be spent inside; however, you will spend the majority of the time outside. At Six Flags Great Adventure & Wild Safari, most of the animal wardens (zookeepers) spend a good portion of their days outdoors, caring for the animals.

 **Alert**

It seems that while all workers at national parks, zoos, and wildlife centers commune with Mother Nature during a good part of their workday, upper management spends more time inside at meetings, creating policy.

People who study animals in their natural environments must love traveling and camping. Chris Morgan, a bear expert who is working on a documentary called *BearTrek* about all of the bear species in the world, works from a home base in Washington State. However, he spends many nights on the road traveling from one country to another. He may be in the jungles in Borneo studying the sun bear or in Alaska observing black bears, brown or grizzly bears, Kodiak bears, and polar bears. Sleeping in tents and traveling with the bare essentials are part of the job.

Many animal workers at national parks and wildlife centers do get to go home at night, which can be especially welcome on rainy, cold days. However, those who work at national parks—such as the park rangers at the White Mountains in New Hampshire—can be seen walking the trails dressed in rain gear on those wet days. At the height of camping season they are outdoors in all kinds of weather.

The romance of the great outdoors can be quickly washed away in a blizzard or thunderstorm. However, most of these workers will tell you that they love their jobs, and that most of them knew what they were getting into. For all of the bad weather, there are many more sunny days on the job. A common mantra you will hear from department heads at these outdoor parks is "if you are having a bad day, go outside." It's true; being around the mountains, trees, ponds, lakes, and oceans—and spotting an animal—makes it all worthwhile.

To get a job at a national park, zoo, or wildlife center, you must be willing to relocate. You have to go where the jobs are. The good news is that there are zoos and wildlife centers in almost every state in the country.

Aquariums

Most people think that aquariums are only located in Florida or on the West Coast. While most people know that Sea World has locations in Florida and California, they get a puzzled look on their faces when they learn that Sea World also has an aquarium in Texas. (The company recently sold the one it had in Ohio.) There are aquariums in almost every state in the country—from SeaLife Center in Alaska to Adventure Aquarium in New Jersey.

Animal trainers, veterinarians, and animal caretakers who work at aquariums often put in long hours and tend to work when visitors are present. While clerical workers at aquariums may work from 8:00 A.M. to 4:30 P.M., Monday through Friday, there is a definite possibility for animal trainers, veterinarians, and animal caretakers to work overtime and on holidays. In other words, you work when the aquarium is open, and you also can be on call in the middle of the night if there is an emergency.

E ssential

Many aquariums have indoor exhibits. Even so, if you work as a marine biologist, educator, animal trainer, or part of the veterinary staff, you will have to spend time swimming with the fish. This can be a very hands-on job, so expect to get wet. Professionals who go into this line of work love the water as much as the sea creatures they encounter do.

Finding a job at an aquarium takes initiative. You must be willing to relocate, even though jobs do exist in almost every state. More good news is that even some zoos have aquariums or exhibits that feature aquatic animals. For instance, the Central Park Zoo in New York City has a wonderful penguin exhibit. Opportunities do exist for marine biologists, scientists, educators, oceanographers, veterinarians, and others who wish to work at an aquarium. As long as you have the degree, experience (even as an intern), and the willingness to work with sea animals, you can work almost anywhere in the country.

For an up-to-date listing of jobs, log onto the Association of Zoos and Aquariums' website at *www.aza.org* and click on job listings.

Retail Pet Shops

A good number of people who own pet shops started working in them when they were in high school or college. It makes sense to see if this is the type of job for you. Owning a business or a franchise is a major step. According to the U.S. Small Business Administration, 50 percent of all new businesses fail within the first year, and 95 percent of small businesses fail within the first five years. For your business to be successful, there has to be a need in your community and you must know how to market your business.

If you really want to own and run a pet shop, consider where you live. If it is a small town without a lot of pedestrian and automobile traffic, you might want to consider relocating. No matter what type of business you are operating, you must be in a prime location (that means a place with a lot of traffic), and there must be a need for the business.

 Fact

You might not want to go it alone. Owning a franchise can have benefits. In addition to offering name recognition (such as PETCO and PetSmart), owning a franchise means you are not alone. Companies that sell franchises want you to succeed. They offer training for you and your employees and have defined employee policies, a well-established pet supply line, and lots of business and marketing support.

If you don't want to own a pet shop, there are other job opportunities. You can be a manager, clerk, stockroom supplier, or buyer. You can work as a groomer on the premises of someone else's shop. You would just have to rent space and bring all of your own supplies.

The opportunities are plentiful, and you can work locally if there is a store near your home. Pet shops exist in most small towns and large cities. Most sell pet supplies, tropical fish, small rodents, and reptiles. All sell pet food and other items, ranging from pet clothing to bedding. Many these days do not sell dogs or cats. Often they make arrangements for the local shelter to bring in cats and dogs for sale, and it is the shelter that takes the donations for these animals—not the pet shop. This is done as a goodwill gesture that endears customers to the store.

CHAPTER 17

Running a Private Practice

M any people dream about being their own boss. The thought of self-employment conjures up images of making your own hours, working when you want, and not answering to upper management. These are major misconceptions. True, it is you who will call the shots. But when you work for yourself you often work long hours, and while you are the boss, you will have to answer to each and every one of your clients.

Getting Established

Before you even graduate from veterinary or business school, you should start looking for a job. Ideally, you will have interned at a business that is similar to the one you want to start. If not, you can still volunteer and gain some part-time experience. While you are an intern, volunteer, or part-timer, you should make and hold on to those contacts. Even if you don't plan to work for these employers when you graduate, they can offer you a lot of valuable business advice.

The next best thing after interning or volunteering is to go on an informational interview. "An informational interview gets you and your name in front of the particular business before you apply for a specific job," says Donna Gerhauser, a success coach based in New Jersey (*www.coachdonna.com*). "Most people want to talk about what they do because they have a lot of passion for their jobs. Before an opening comes up, pick up the phone to find out as much information as possible about the job you want. You might even learn about other opportunities. Spend a few minutes on the phone; or if you live close by, ask if you can come in for an interview."

This may seem like common sense to some, but not everyone knows that they must dress the part for the interview. Even if you are applying for a job as a zookeeper, biologist, or shelter worker and may wear a uniform once you get the job, you need to dress in business attire for the interview. The outfit can be a little artsy, but must be professional looking.

What's wonderful about this process is that there is nothing to lose. The person you are interviewing with doesn't feel pressured because you both know there is no job at the current time. "Being curious is a good thing," says Gerhauser. "It serves you well in the whole process of networking and getting contacts. And if you do want to work for this company, the hiring managers will already know you."

Setting Up Shop

Many small business owners failed the first or second time and made it on the third. Steve McCann, a business consultant, author, and owner of McCann Research Corporation, an organization dedicated to training businesspeople to reach their maximum potential, speaks from experience. He became a successful businessman on his third try. "I learned a lot from my mistakes," he says. "I had good business knowledge. What I needed was help setting up the business. What I did differently this time was get help from the Industry Council for Small Business Development (*www.icsbd.org*), Small Business

Administration (*www.sba.gov*), Small Business Resource Network (*www.sbrn.org*), and SCORE (*www.score.org*). All of these companies are nonprofit or government-sponsored organizations that help executives. All of the advice I received was free. Everyone who is setting up shop should take advantage of this help."

What these organizations do is offer free business advice in the form of articles and workshops. All of these organizations host workshops and hand out free information about business essentials, from bookkeeping to publicity. These small business associations, as well as companies like McCann's, work to assist future business owners on how to set up an office.

Another avenue to take advantage of is your school's job placement office. In addition to posting entry-level jobs, most job placement offices are staffed with professionals who will advise you about everything from setting up shop to licensing (if you need them). This service is free to graduates and current students, so take advantage of it.

 Fact

Government agencies such as the Small Business Administration, as well as school guidance counselors, job counseling centers, and private human resources firms, all share information about financing. You will have to pay a fee to a private company, but you will get a one-on-one service that is tailor-made for you. The counselors and government offices offer similar services, but you will have to do a lot more research on your own.

Whether you are going to work as a consultant or as a shop owner or owner of a veterinary practice, you will need capital. If you have a nest egg that you saved for this venture, you are quite lucky. Most graduates, however, come out of grad school in debt. Their top priority is to get established and pay back those student loans.

Here are other ways to raise funds for your business:

- Before you approach anyone for money, create a strong business plan that you can show to potential funders.
- Sit down with a staff member at a local Small Business Administration office to discuss the types of loans available and how much you will need to start and maintain your business.
- Borrow from family and friends.
- Get a loan from your bank. If you don't have a good credit history, and have lots of debt (college loans), it is likely that banks will turn you down. If you own a home, you might be able to get a second mortgage.
- Look up Small Business Investment Companies in your local phone book, and make an appointment to talk to one of their advisers. Before signing anything, get references from others who used these agencies. It's a good idea to speak to an accountant, business lawyer, and financial adviser if you are unsure about the company.

When borrowing money, look for the lowest interest rates, and work out a reasonable payment schedule—one that won't put you in further debt. You might also consider working for someone first before going it alone. This way you can gain on-the-job experience and start to pay back your student loans.

Running an Office

Whether you own a pet relocation service or large veterinary pet hospital, work out of a plush private office in your home, oversee an office at a veterinary clinic, or manage an office of workers at your local shelter or doggie daycare center, many of the same office management skills apply. Your office is the place where you contact clients and take business calls, schedule projects, hire employees, host meetings, and handle loads and loads of paperwork.

Having a well-managed office means being able to generate profits and take on any unexpected problems that may pop up. In some cases, you might want to hire an office manager. Veterinarians, for example, who want to go into private practice might not want to spend too much time running an office. "That is one issue many people in business face," says Donna Gerhauser. "Veterinarians become vets because they want to work with animals. They might not want to spend too much time running an office—even though it is their office.

They might want to hire an office manager and staff to schedule clients, do bookkeeping, handle billing, and oversee the daily chores that come with running an office. This way they can focus on their first love—taking care of animals."

E ssential

You just opened shop and have your own office. Before you invite the public in to use your services, spend a day or two among your workers. Walk around the office to ensure that the atmosphere is inviting and comfortable for your clients and your workers. Make sure everything that is needed is within easy reach, there is no clutter, and everything is logically placed.

Most business owners have some aspect of the job that they don't like doing. It often comes down to managing paperwork. If you are just starting out and don't have a large staff, or you are a one-person company, you will have to tackle the paperwork. If left unattended, it will just pile up and your other work will suffer. So, either hire someone to take on this job, or set a few hours aside each week to get this work accomplished.

In addition to paperwork, development of new business strategies often falls by the wayside. Many accomplished people who love what they are doing will focus on their top priority—in this case, taking care of animals. However, it is important both to keep fresh ideas on hand to stimulate staff and clients and to set goals to grow your business.

Hiring Associates and Workers

A business is only as good as the people it employs. True, you might be an exceptional veterinarian or an amazingly sharp pet shop owner. However, clients often see the office or store help first. The staff you hire represents your business. The people answering the phone or sitting behind the front desk in the reception area make the first impression. They are the ones who have contact with your clients. The assistant or staff you hire can make or break your business.

E ssential

For each job that needs to be filled, write a thorough job description. List all of the duties and qualifications for each position. Include job requirements such as prior experience or degrees. A written job description will help you make better choices when hiring. You can also share these descriptions with colleagues who know you are seeking office help.

No one wants to do business with people who lack enthusiasm. That doesn't mean your staff has to be overly friendly. Just think about the person who is bringing in their pet to be treated for an illness or boarded at your daycare center. These pet owners want to know that their pets are in caring hands. They also want to do business with an organization that has helpful, caring people at the helm.

Before you hire an assistant or staff, the first thing you should do is determine what type of jobs you need filled. Conduct salary surveys by asking colleagues and friends who work in similar businesses in your area. This way you can determine what type of salary you will have to pay your office manager, receptionist, bookkeeper, and so on. To get the best help, try to offer a little more than minimum wage if possible.

Advertise job openings in local papers and websites, or in trade papers if the position is specialized. You can also advertise a job with a membership organization such as the Association of Zoos and Aquariums if you are a member.

When hiring associates and workers, it is a wise idea to take your time. "Hire folks that accentuate your brand," says Travis Sheridan, member services director of the Central Valley Business Incubator based in Fresno, California. "It's better to have a vacant position than the wrong person in that position. Hiring the wrong person to represent your company will do more damage than good. You need to hire people who have the same attributes that your company stands for."

Publicizing Your Work

Every business owner understands the power of publicity. You might have a great product or service to sell, but without customers, you might as well as close up shop. Finding customers can be a challenge. Most successful business owners turn to publicists. For a few hundred dollars a month, you can buy a publicist's expertise. A lot of business owners look at having publicity and marketing as smart investments.

"The best form of publicity is to be a local expert," says Wayne Schaffel, president of Public Relations for Less, a private public relations company in White Plains, New York. "To become known as the local expert, start off by writing a column in your local newspaper about pet care or dog training. See if you can line up an interview on a local radio or cable show. You can even teach a class on pet care at a local pet store."

Volunteering can also bring in customers. "If you train dogs for a living, you might want to bring a few dogs to the local hospital or nursing home," says Schaffel. "While you are volunteering, make sure to hand out cards to people. You can also have the store, hospital, or school where you volunteer post flyers about you and your talks. Make sure all literature has your contact name, numbers, and address prominently displayed."

When you write a local newspaper or magazine column, give talks at pet shops, or demonstrate pet training at neighborhood centers, you are usually not making money. What you are doing is getting noticed. Make sure a tag line with your name, company name, and contact information follows each article. It can be one or two brief sentences. Hand out business cards, flyers, and articles you wrote when you make appearances. All of your handouts must have your company's contact information on them.

E ssential

If you volunteer at a hospital or pet shop, alert the local papers to get your company's name publicized. People like reading feel-good stories, which will make them want to seek out your services when they need them. Likewise, if you are giving talks on pet care at the local shelter, call the press. People who attend your presentation and like you will be inclined to hire you to take care of their animals.

These voluntary appearances and time spent writing a short (600-word) column will bring clients to you. These are key ways to get you noticed. "What you are doing is developing a platform—a key word in the publishing world today," says Schaffel. "Having a platform—an area of expertise—and growing a following is a sure way to have a successful business."

Building a following takes time. While you are gaining expertise, it's important to develop a publicity plan. "In a forty-hour work week, I figure that ten hours of that should be for promotion," says Rebecca K. O'Connor, a falconer, animal behaviorist, and animal trainer based in California. "This could be writing an article for a magazine, blogging, working on my website (*www.rebeccakoconnor.com*), sending out promotional materials, or making an appearance somewhere that may not pay, but gets me exposure to new people."

 Fact

A newspaper article about your company carries more weight among readers than does an advertisement about your business. Readers especially like human interest stories about people who volunteer. Talk to the editor or publisher of your local newspaper to see if you can get coverage of your next volunteer gig.

O'Connor has worked at zoos and wildlife centers in various parts of the country. She most recently worked as a consultant at the Guadalajara Zoo in Mexico. One of her first big jobs was training animals at Disney's Animal Kingdom. She had some prior experience training falcons before working at Disney. From there, getting work got easier.

"Word of mouth makes a huge difference," she says. "I have the experience, but the more people who know about you and hear that you do great work, the higher the likelihood of getting more work. So, I am a firm believer in networking."

Keeping Clients Coming Back

Developing a good client relationship is mandatory. It's essential to keep clients happy, to show that you care about them and their pets, and to go that extra inning. Showing thoughtfulness comes naturally to almost all animal care workers. That is why you are in this business. Taking that extra step can ensure a strong client/worker relationship. One of those first steps to take is to operate your business on a weekend day or have late hours a few nights a week to accommodate your clients.

Another way to win the respect of your clients is to follow up. "That means dropping an e-mail to a client who just had an in-home consult to see how they and their pets are doing," says O'Connor.

O'Connor also sends out holiday cards and thank-you notes. "I treat them like I care about them and their animals, which I do," she says.

Happy clients will often refer you to other customers, so building a positive client relationship is essential to the growth of your business. Following are a few tips on how to keep clients happy:

- Set up a client information database. In addition to contact names and the history of pets' visits, include some personal data such as birthdays and anniversaries. You may want to send birthday cards to your clients.
- Show them you appreciate their business. Keep a pot of fresh coffee along with hot water and plenty of tea bags in the waiting room. You might want to put out cookies too.
- If you have any literature about the latest pet care or if you write your own pet newsletter, have a stack available for clients to read or take with them.
- Be available to answer their questions about their pets.
- Never take customers for granted, and always show them respect.

By listening to your clients, showing them you care about them and their animals, and being able to answer their questions and concerns, you will keep them coming back. Try your best to always keep appointments on time, and always be courteous. A simple "thank you" really goes a long way.

CHAPTER 18

Joining a Practice or Other Organization

Joining a group practice is a great way to learn from others. You will find that everyone in a company practice has a role. It may take a few weeks or even two or three months to fit in, but most employers understand that there is a learning curve. At some group practices there is a hierarchy; those with more experience are at the top of the ladder. It's ideal to establish working relationships with everyone at your new job and to show everyone that you are eager to be a part of the team.

The Job Search

A good number of jobs are found by networking, and one of the best ways to get a job working with animals is to contact everyone you know in your field—from former professors to people you worked with when you volunteered. The next step is to tell everyone that you are looking for a job—even if they are not in your field. You never know if your neighbor has a friend who works in a similar profession.

Be open to all opportunities when looking for a job, whether you want to be a veterinarian, an animal trainer, or an entomologist. If you want to work with primates as a veterinary technician and can only find jobs working with dogs and cats, keep an open mind. Most people who work with exotic animals started as volunteers training dogs or assisting veterinarians at a private office or shelter.

It's important to show a can-do attitude and to take a job as close to your profession as possible. "One of my favorite quotes when it comes to summing up the animal profession is 'My quality of care is their quality of life,'" says Jodi Carrigan, who works as a zookeeper in the Primate Department at Zoo Atlanta. Carrigan suggests that it is important to be open to all possibilities, and that each position leads to the next.

 Fact

While you should always look for job listings on member association websites, in association newsletters, and at your school's job center, the best place to find work is by asking people with whom you've volunteered or interned at a zoo, shelter, or vet's office. Those part-time internships and volunteer positions often lead to long-term jobs.

It also is a good idea to be flexible. The job that you want might not be in your neighborhood. You might have to relocate. It all depends on the job market and the position. While there are lots of jobs at shelters taking care of animals, and a good number of jobs at pet retail shops, working as a zoo director at a leading zoological center will be harder to find. You might have to start as a zookeeper at a local zoo and work your way up.

Searching for a job can be stressful. It's important to know that in time you will find the right opportunity. In the meantime, try to relax and treat yourself to dinner, talk to friends, and take care of yourself while looking for work.

Finding Your First Job

The one issue that comes up over and over again when you are look-ing for your first job is that you must show potential employers you have experience. Okay, how can you get experience if you are a full-time student? Everyone who works with animals got their start vol-unteering. They eagerly cleaned cages. No job was beneath them. Happiness came from being around animals. Learning came from keenly observing those with jobs. Over time, even as a volunteer, experience happened.

So to make finding your first job easier, think of it as the sec-ond job you will have. The first will be volunteering while you are in high school, college, grad school, or trade school. Each volunteer job should be considered a real job—one with full responsibilities. Volunteers have been fired if they don't do the work. Volunteers have also been promoted to paying jobs when they open up.

 **Alert**

You just heard about a job opening at a place you really want to work. Apply, of course, but don't stop there and wait for the phone to ring. Apply to as many places as possible, even if that means you will have to relocate or take a part-time job to start. The more places you contact about work, the better your chances of finding full-time employment.

You can also think of your first full-time job as a stepping stone to your next career. Even if you just plan on working at a particular place for a year or two, make a good impression. Pitch in and ask to take on more responsibility. You will be an asset to the institution, and more important, you will become a valued worker—one who will be considered if a higher position opens up.

Even if you are lucky enough to think of your first job as perfect, chances are that a few years on the job may bring new needs and desires. You might consider moving up or moving to another company, or you might relocate to another state. As you move from one job to another, be sure to hold on to important contacts. Those contacts can be great references.

Resumes and Cover Letters

Many people don't think they have a lot to put on their resumes. Of course, you must include schooling, clubs you participated in, and all part-time, volunteer, and summer positions you have held. Every internship and part-time job counts as experience. Holding a position in a school club or local chapter of an association also makes a great impression. Your resume and cover letter are your first introductions to potential employers, and those first impressions do count.

It is a good idea to send resumes with cover letters to places you want to work before they post a job. True, they might not have an opening yet. However, when one comes along there is a good chance that if your resume makes a good impression, you will be remembered when a job opens up.

E ssential

Have more than one version of your resume ready to go. When you see a job advertisement, read it carefully and tailor your resume to fit the job qualifications. For example, if the employer is looking for someone who has worked with reptiles, and you have done that, highlight it in your resume. If the ad asks for someone with public speaking abilities, put that up front on your resume.

When a job is posted, the employer often gets more than 100 responses. How can you make your resume stand out in a crowded field? Lead with the most important information, and keep everything brief. Bullet points and short, clear sentences are easy to read. Use a lot of white space, and make sure your font size is at least 10 point; 12 point is better.

"You should also include a website if you have one," says Rebecca K. O'Connor, an animal behaviorist and trainer who works with birds of prey and other animals. "When I send out a letter to a potential client, I always mention my website and references. Your website should be professional looking."

Along with her cover letter and resume, O'Connor sends color copies of her published articles about animal training. The more ammunition you have about yourself and your qualifications, the better. Let potential employers know you have what it takes to do the job.

E ssential

Think of your resume as a public relations and marketing tool. You are the product, and you have to get your message across in an easy-to-understand, clear manner. Include information that lets the potential employer know a good deal about your work, school, and extracurricular activities.

The Internet has several job sites that can show you how to write and construct an attention-getting resume. One important bit of advice is that once you put your resume together, show it to a colleague, professor, or other professional for feedback. Listen to that feedback and make any necessary adjustments.

Don't overlook the cover letter. Even if the job you are applying for doesn't require writing skills, someone with a well-written cover letter will be chosen over someone with a poorly written one. Whether you enjoy writing or find it to be a chore, the best rule to follow when constructing a cover letter is to keep it short and to the point.

Employers don't have time to read through every cover letter and resume. They just want to see the pertinent information, so it is okay to keep the cover letter brief. If someone the employer knows has recommended you for the position, state that in the first sentence of your cover letter. In some cases, a cover letter just has to indicate that you are applying for a specific job. You can include on the cover letter a note explaining that your resume, application (if there is one), and any other backup materials are included.

E ssential

Proofread and spell-check your cover letter and resume. Your computer has spell check, so use it. However, spell check isn't perfect. You might accidentally use a word that is wrong in the context, even if it is spelled correctly. For example, instead of writing the word "behaviorist," you might write "behavior." Typos really do make a poor first impression. Be sure to read over your cover letter and resume before you send them out. It is also essential to have another person proofread your cover letter and resume to catch any errors you may have missed.

Networking

People like helping others, especially when it comes to finding jobs. According to a study by the U.S. Department of Labor, 60 percent of people get jobs by networking. It's good to have connections, and it is equally important to be well rounded and have the skills that are needed for the job. Many people who work with animals hear about jobs through their member organizations, or through friends, colleagues, professors, and people they worked for—even if they volunteered or worked part-time.

It also is wise to expand your network, which means asking everyone you know if they have a connection. A friend of a friend may work at a place where you want to work. The trick is to not be shy about asking. Remember, too, that when someone helps you out, you will in effect owe a debt to someone else. In the future, when you have job security and a newbie comes along asking for advice, you will be in the position to pay it back.

E ssential

When your membership organization hosts a lecture, holiday party, or workshop, go. Take along your business cards (you can print out a handful of them on your computer) and strike up conversations with people you want to meet. You can talk about the event, and let the others know that you are new to the field and are looking for work. Remember that people enjoy helping others find work.

Treat each networking opportunity like a job interview. It is important to be prepared. If you are meeting a friend of a friend, quiz your friend about the person you will be meeting. If you are going to an event or networking party, ask the host who will be attending and then learn about their organizations. A lot of company information can be found on the Internet.

People like knowing that you take an interest in them and their profession. Having done some research will make you a better conversationalist. Being prepared also can ease any tension. Be sure to ask questions and exchange business cards.

After the event, follow up with a note thanking your new contacts for any helpful advice they shared. Then don't leave it at that—keep in touch with them. By staying in touch, they will remember you when a job opens up.

When you do continue to follow up via phone, e-mail, mail, or in person, ask your contact if he knows anyone in your field or at a specific organization who could help you with your job search. If he does, ask if he could share those names and numbers with you. Then ask if you can use his name when you introduce yourself to the new contact. Chances are he will say yes.

Keep track of all of your networking contacts. You can start a database listing their names, company names, titles, contact information, and how you met them. When you do get your next job, remember to notify your networking contacts and stay in touch. You never know when you can repay the favor or when you will need another one.

The Interview

Congratulations! You landed an interview. Now you can make a good first impression in person. Arrive on time and dress the part. Even if you are going to be cleaning litter boxes or wearing a white lab coat when you get the job, dress in a professional manner. Before the interview, do your research. Showing the interviewer that you know a bit about the company goes a long way. It will make a positive impression.

Do a dress rehearsal. Ask a friend to quiz you about past positions, your job-related strengths and weaknesses, and why you are a good fit for this position. Do a bit of role-playing and talk about why you want this position. This way, when questions come up at the interview, you will be prepared and will answer with confidence.

Being prepared allows you to be confident and at ease. The last thing you want is to be nervous. If you are, you can be honest and briefly state that this job is quite important to you and that you are a bit nervous. Then go back to the interview. Once you are talking and learning about the job, your jitters will most likely disappear.

Take four or five copies of your resume with you—even if you know that the person interviewing you has one. You may be asked to interview with a second or third person. Also take samples of your work with you if it pertains to the job. These can be letters from clients who have used your services, or copies of articles you have written. Also take a list of references. This list should include the names, titles, company names, and contact information of three to five references.

Show that you are a good listener, and if you don't understand something, ask. Have a positive attitude and show your enthusiasm. Conclude the interview by stating that you are interested in the job. Thank the interviewer for his time, and ask him when you can expect to hear back. Always follow up with a thank-you note. Thank-you notes can be e-mailed or mailed, but keep in mind that most employers are wowed by a mailed thank-you note. These days, nearly all of us are quick to send e-mails. Sending a note through the postal service will make you stand out among the crowd.

Negotiating Salaries

Everyone in the animal world says the same thing: "We're in it for the passion, not the money." It's true that people who work with animals do so because they love their jobs. However, you do need to eat, have a roof overhead, and pay bills. You have to know what you will be comfortable earning. The bottom line is to ask yourself if you can live comfortably—without going into debt—on the salary that is offered to you.

Many entry-level jobs have set salary ranges. It is your job to try to get the upper end of that range. You can do so by showing your talents and asking for more. Some companies—many nonprofits—just don't have the funds to pay high salaries.

Your best defense is to come to the negotiating table prepared. If someone offers you a job—your dream job—and the salary is less than you desired, you can walk away, ask for more, or accept the offer. Before you ask for more money, talk to people in your field. Ask what starting salaries are like. Chances are you are in the right ballpark.

 Fact

Pay rates vary, depending on where you live. If you manage a pet shop in a small town, chances are your income will be less than that of someone who manages a similar business in New York City or San Francisco. You will also have fewer expenses. Likewise, a veterinary technician in Iowa may earn less than one in New Jersey. When asking for more money, consider cost-of-living expenses.

If money is tight in the company, find out—after you have been offered a job but before you accept it—whether you can ask your boss for a performance review/raise within the next three to six months. You also may be able to request better benefits or more vacation time. In addition, check to see if the company has any employee incentives such as paying for you to attend workshops or take classes that are related to your work.

CHAPTER 19

A Look Ahead

Jobs that didn't exist several years ago are on the rise today. Just thirty years ago, most veterinarians worked without the assistance of a veterinary technician. Upscale daycare centers for dogs and cats were unheard of twenty years ago. Using flies to locate people trapped in collapsed buildings sounds like something out of a science-fiction novel. Two decades ago you wouldn't have thought of hiring relocation workers to transport pets across the country or overseas to be with you in your new home. The pet and exotic animal industry is rapidly changing, bringing with it many new and expanded job opportunities.

The Future of Careers with Animals

All around the news is good. Many new jobs have been created, and tried and true careers continue to have plenty of growth potential. "The field of veterinary medicine is changing rapidly," says Kimberly May, DVM, MS, DACVS (Diplomate of American College of Veterinary Surgeons), and assistant director of the Communications Division of the American Veterinary Medical Association. "The human-animal bond continues to strengthen as people realize the social, mental, and physical benefits of having animals in their lives. Almost half (49.7 percent) of U.S. pet owners consider their pets members of the family. People value their pets and animals and, therefore, demand the highest quality diagnostics, treatments, and care for their animals. Advancements in veterinary medicine have largely been driven by this demand. Examples include major strides in chemotherapy and cancer research, orthopedic research (including prosthetics), alternative therapies (chiropractic, acupuncture, homeopathy, herbal medicine, and massage), and hospice care. People are expecting the veterinarian to provide all the same services their physicians provide for them."

Dr. May cites numerous highly publicized cases, such as Barbaro, the Kentucky Derby winner who injured his leg, and after unsuccessful treatments was euthanized. "Barbaro's injury has highlighted the progress in veterinary medicine and underscored the need for more research in many areas. Public support for laminitis research [laminitis is the inflammation of the innermost layer of the hoof wall found in horses, ponies, and donkeys] will likely generate great progress in that area."

 Fact

Veterinary medicine is becoming more specialized. Like physicians, veterinarians can specialize in numerous areas, such as various forms of surgery, internal medicine, radiology, ophthalmology, dentistry, nutrition, and many others. For more information about specific fields of veterinary medicine, go to the American Veterinary Medical Association's website at *www .avma.org/education/abvs/specialty_orgs/default.asp.*

Some of the most promising career opportunities in veterinary medicine are in the fields of biomedical research, food supply veterinary medicine, and veterinary practices in rural America. "We're very concerned about a worsening shortage of veterinarians in rural practice, biomedical research, and food supply veterinary medicine," says Dr. May. "By food supply, we mean veterinarians who work with food animals as well as those who work in the government to ensure the safety of our nation's food supply. As more veterinary students come from urban and suburban backgrounds with little or no exposure to food animals prior to veterinary school, we have less and less veterinarians entering the rural practice and food supply areas."

 Fact

> The need for veterinarians in rural parts of the country and in the area of food supply continues to multiply. To learn more about these opportunities, log onto the AVMA website at *www.avma.org/fsvm/default.asp* or the National Academies of Sciences website at *www.nap.edu/catalog.php?record_id=11366* and *www.nap.edu/catalog.php?record_id=11365*. The information on these web pages can be easily downloaded and is free.

While veterinary medicine is constantly evolving, so are a number of other fields. There are great career opportunities in animal cruelty investigation and enforcement. On a local government level, legislators are getting involved in developing and passing anti-animal-cruelty laws. If Assembly Bill A2773 in New Jersey is passed, chaining dogs on short tethers will be a crime. In New Jersey and other states, lawmakers are working hard to pass legislation prohibiting dogfighting.

Law enforcement fields are broadening opportunities as well. Police forces are adding more K-9 units, and the mounted police are training recruits to work on horseback. Crime scene investigators are working with entomologists to find clues as to the time a death occurs and with K-9 workers to locate missing persons.

According to entomology student Ronda Hamm, "There will always be a need for individuals to work with animals. We will need to care for not only our pets, but those that need human assistance to survive as a species, from the large cats to the smallest beetle. The emphasis might change in what species of animal to work with, but not the need for individuals to work with them."

Another reason the industry is growing is to help animals in need. "Threats to animals, from pollution to illegal hunting to mass extinction, are increasing worldwide," says Christopher Cutter, communications manager with International Fund for Animal Welfare (IFAW). "We seem intent, as human beings, to destroy the ecosystems on which we rely. There is already more than we can do right now, and the problems are trending the wrong way for animals. So, the opportunities to address and fight against those problems are growing as well."

How the Industry Is Changing

What's sparking the increase in jobs and change in the industry is the public's interest in animal welfare. When a large majority of people treat a pet as a member of their family, when they care about the environment, and when they have a deep concern for their food supply, change occurs. People who work with animals in every capacity are changing the way they do business. Animal welfare is a top priority, and so is human health.

"People who normally wouldn't think twice about where they get their eggs are suddenly buying cage-free eggs and organically raised eggs," says Dr. May. "There seems to be a trend toward 'city folk' buying 'hobby farms' in rural areas, increasing opportunities for animal interactions."

Many farmers are turning a part of their farms into bed-and-breakfasts with the goal of luring city folk to their properties for a farm experience. It's true that visiting a farm is not the same as working on a farm. However, many families who live in the city are bringing their children to these farms so they can get a small taste of farm life.

On the scientific front, researchers are continuing to find ways to improve both human and animal life. "Scientific discoveries are being made all the time, and finding ways to use the new techniques will provide lots of opportunities," says Ronda Hamm. "For example, you can learn a lot about an animal based on genetics. It might be something in the genetics that can be used to help a species or eliminate a problem they face. Think about using genetic resistance to a disease that might be driving populations to extinction."

The lines between helping people, animals, and the environment are blurring and bringing change to this industry. While different organizations address different niches, all work to improve the lives of animals and people. "For instance," says Christopher Cutter, "NRDC (National Resource Defense Council) is primarily an organization that tackles legal issues and so the best way into that organization might be as an attorney. On the other hand, a group like HSUS (Humane Society of the United States) is much more into policy and public advocacy. Greenpeace is more direct action, hands-on. So in that way, the overall industry/community serves different roles."

On a positive note, Cutter sees a willingness among NGOs (nongovernmental organizations) to collaborate to work on behalf of a cause. He also sees trends emerging regarding guiding philosophies of NGOs. "For example, some groups are trying to look at entire ecosystems rather than focusing on a single endangered species or a single population of animals," he says. "Similarly, there is a greater amount of experimenting with creative ways to address entrenched problems. For instance, IFAW has successfully reduced human/elephant conflict in China by offering microloans to local people to address the issue. In general, there is a better understanding of the networks and interrelatedness of species and even populations of a single species. The more we understand, the more we realize we need to continue to learn."

Rebecca K. O'Connor, animal behaviorist and trainer, also sees change as a way to improve the welfare of animals and people, and as a way to grow her business, which she operates out of a home-based office. She believes that everyone who works with animals (and other fields as well) should never stop learning. "The industry is becoming savvier, looking to science and psychology for solutions to behavioral problems, enriching environments, and other challenges," she says. "This means that education, and especially continued education, is going to count."

How You Can Change with the Times

One of the best aspects of working with animals is that you are constantly learning. Whether you are a veterinarian, vet tech, owner of a pet shop, or animal trainer, it is important to continue your education. Scientists are constantly learning how to eradicate diseases. Veterinarians must keep abreast of the latest technologies to improve the lives of the animals they treat. Pet shop owners need to keep clients coming back and spending money. Yes, you got the job. However, your education is never complete. Working in this field is a form of continuing education.

Question

What can I do if I can't find the time in my busy schedule to go back to school?
Learning has gotten easier thanks to distance-learning (online) courses. You also may be able to take a classroom course at night, or in some cases on a weekend.

For some who have completed college, veterinary school, and possibly additional courses specializing in dentistry or surgery, the idea of going back to school is daunting. After all, you are not even finished paying back student loans.

If you are working for a large company, chances are good that your company will pay for you to take continuing education classes—especially if the knowledge you gain can be applied to your current job. Many member organizations host workshops about changes and new technologies within your profession. Member organizations also hold annual conventions for their members. At these conventions, workshops are held so you can learn about new techniques and brush up on old ones. Continuing education takes many forms.

You don't always have to learn in a classroom. There is on-the-job learning from your supervisors, peers, and colleagues. If you belong to a member organization, chances are you are receiving its monthly or bimonthly newsletters, which are filled with information about your profession.

It's also a good idea to take courses that can enhance business practices. You might want to take an adult education class on how to publicize and market your business. Every learning opportunity broadens your horizons and introduces you to new contacts. Garnering more knowledge makes you a better worker and a more adaptable one.

Should You Join a Professional Organization?

If you want to meet people in your profession, people with connections, people you can bounce ideas off of about your profession, you should join a professional organization. Professional membership organizations are great places to network. Many national professional organizations have local chapters where you can meet with others in your industry. Often the local chapters host lectures and events that are directly related to your profession.

"I belong to the Association of Avian Trainers and Educators," says Rebecca K. O'Connor. "I will write the occasional article for their newsletter. I also belong to World Parrot Trust and the American Federation of Aviculture. Speaking at various events and blogging for World Parrot Trust allows me to meet people and interact with folks that might hire me to come out to their zoo, or more frequently to come speak or do a workshop at their parrot club."

Professional organizations such as the Association of Zoos and Aquariums offer their members a bounty of services, from continuing education workshops to networking events and annual conferences. One of the best reasons to join a professional organization is to meet people who can help you advance in your career. Another benefit is the online chat rooms. Online membership boards are great ways to get answers to questions. People in this, and other industries, like helping their peers. If you have a question about treating an animal, you can post it online. Answers and discussions are often immediate.

This is an especially good service for people who are self-employed. If you run a veterinary clinic or work as a consultant out of a home office, chances are you work alone. In that case especially, having a network of experts is a definite business boon.

E ssential

Some professional organizations have student memberships. Annual fees for students are a bit less than those paid by working members. The advantage to being a student member is that you can learn about numerous programs, and you can meet people in your profession. You can also participate in workshops and conferences. A few of these organizations also have mentoring programs.

To get the most out of your professional organization, it pays to get involved. Joining a committee, writing for the organization's newsletter, or running for office puts you in the spotlight. It's important to be an active member. Yes, you can join and just read the newsletter, but you won't meet colleagues that way.

By actively participating, even if it is only one day a month or a few hours each week, you will get noticed. By drawing positive attention to yourself, you will build credibility for yourself and for your business. By making yourself visible in your field, you will open yourself up to new opportunities to learn about your industry, and when job opportunities arise, your name will be in people's minds.

The Growing Need for Information Technology

Information about veterinary medical breakthroughs, important research, environmental concerns, and issues that affect animals and humans is disseminated on an almost daily basis thanks to the Internet. While it's hard to keep on top of all of this information, chances are good that if you are a farmer, a veterinarian, a dog trainer, or any other professional who works with animals, you have a computer in your office.

In fact, there are several computer applications that can make work a lot easier. Some software programs can help you create and print professional-looking business documents such as invoicing and billing statements; client records for vaccination history and certificates; detailed clinical records; and letters, appointment reminder postcards, and promotional materials. Others help with inventory control and can create accounting and management reports as well as calendars to schedule client appointments. In addition, you can store patients' photos and other digital images on your computer.

 Fact

Most jobs today rely on people who have strong computer skills. As more information and services are transmitted online, the computer illiterate are left behind. It pays to keep abreast of the latest technology in your field.

Having a keen understanding of computer systems will boost your business. As your business grows, good communication among your employees is essential. You can improve communication by linking your employees' computers to one common network. Often in mid-to-large firms, communication can break down. By sending out memos to your entire staff, everyone will be informed of important issues.

If computer technology seems daunting, remember that continuing education is the best way to stay on top of the latest breakthroughs in your field. By staying informed you will run a more successful business, and you will be an asset to your patients and clients.

While computer technology has improved the way businesses are run, new technologies are changing the ways jobs are being done. "Right now we are doing some CSI-type things with a scientist who is making a DNA map of African ivory," says Christopher Cutter. "When illegal ivory is seized by authorities, for instance, we can use DNA testing to tell where in Africa that elephant was killed. A technological advance becomes a legal tool and ultimately a political one as well. Other new technologies, as they are adopted, including those in the new media, provide new opportunities to help animals around the world."

CHAPTER 20

Taking Care of Business

Succeeding in the business world is more than just working hard. You need to be a well-rounded person. While you should give 100 percent to your job, you should also pursue outside interests. Devoting every spare minute to work quickly leads to burnout. To succeed in the animal care world you need to have basic business skills and a knowledge of what types of business situations you will encounter. This chapter will explore those issues further.

Animal Care Is Not a Nine-to-Five Job

While the normal hours for some businesses are 9 A.M. to 5 P.M., that is not the case in the animal industry. Many people in this industry are self-employed or contracted workers. Pet store owners, veterinarians, dog walkers, pet sitters, even lobbyists work day, evening, and early-morning hours. The staff at an emergency all-night veterinary clinic works the night shift. The farmer and on-call veterinarian delivering a baby calf in the middle of the night might be working after already putting in a full day.

The traditional nine-to-five schedule exists in some places, but it is becoming rare. Zookeepers arrive at most zoos at 7 or 8 A.M., before the zoo opens to the public. They can also stay as late as 7 or 8 P.M. after visitors leave. Tourists who visit zoos don't get to see the behind-the-scenes activities that are involved.

People who work in animal rescue have worked around the clock when a disaster strikes. Fundraisers not only plan special events, but are on hand when the event takes place—and that can be on a week-end or evening.

E ssential

There are times in this industry when you will have to pull an all-nighter. If an animal is sick, injured, or giving birth, you may have to be on hand. Even animal behaviorists—those who have developed relationships with the animals they work with—can be on call when an animal is in need. The veterinarian on call finds that having a familiar face nearby—one the animal knows and is comfortable being around—can make procedures go more smoothly.

"Most people in this business don't close the door at 5 P.M. and go home," says Susan Smith, development director at Palisades Inter-state Park Commission. "It depends on the day. I also find that wherever I go, I am always picking up ideas."

When she took a few days off to attend a friend's wedding in another state, she visited a zoo. "I had some free time and went to the local zoo," she says. "While I was there I observed how things were done, made mental notes, and shared those ideas with our zoo director. In one sense, I'm thinking about work a lot, but I'm not always working when I travel. I can relax and take time off. Plus, we are not expected to work seven days a week. But most people who work in this industry are always on the lookout for new and better ways to run their business. It can even be culling ideas from a newspaper article. Or when I'm watching a newscast about a group that got funding, I immediately make notes about contacting the donor for my organization."

Fact

Did you know that there is a museum devoted to veterinary medicine? It is the American Museum of Veterinary Medicine, located in Birdsboro, Pennsylvania. The museum's mission is to educate the public about the history of veterinary medicine. For more information about the museum, call 610-489-1229 or log onto *www.amvm.org.*

Flex time is a good option for many in this business. At the Animal Care Center of Plainfield in Illinois, veterinarians, vet techs, assistants, and others work a flexible schedule. Chrissy Zarony, a veterinary technician, works 7 A.M. to 2 P.M. which she says is perfect for people with families. At times, such as when someone misses a shift and the Center is short-staffed, she will have to put in overtime. "But we make up the time," she says. "I like the flexibility of the job."

Offering flexible hours is actually a necessity in this day and age of multiple-income households, kids, schools, daycare, and the juggling that comes with it all for parents. The good news is that people who work with animals often don't mind putting in the extra hours. They know that it is part of the job, and they take time off when needed.

Do You Need Medical Malpractice Insurance?

"Veterinarians carry medical malpractice insurance, but technicians generally do not need it because the veterinarians are ultimately responsible for overseeing the technician's work as well as their own," says Dr. Kimberly May, assistant director of the Communications Division of the American Veterinary Medical Association.

People who own farms and horse farms, riding academies, doggie daycare centers, and other animal-related professions where there is interaction between animals and visitors can get liability insurance, which covers sums judged against you in the case of negligence on your part or the part of an employee. It also covers the cost of your legal defense.

E ssential

Most professionals who work with animals provide workers' compensation for their employees. Workers' compensation is a form of insurance that covers payment for any on-the-job injuries. In all states, employers are required to have workers' compensation for most of their employees.

The American Veterinary Medical Association (AVMA) Professional Liability Insurance Trust (PLIT) is the largest provider of medical malpractice insurance. This one-stop shopping site for liability insurance also offers students preceptorship coverage, which in a nutshell is a liability malpractice insurance for medical interns. This insurance covers hospitals and its contents, insurance for your mobile practice, workers' compensation, business interruption insurance, embryo and semen storage insurance, employment practices liability insurance, commercial automobile, commercial umbrella, personal automobile, homeowners and renters insurance, and personal umbrella. To download an application or find out more information, click on *www.avmaplit.com*.

AVMA is just one organization that offers insurance coverage, including group health and life insurance, for its members. To find out about other companies, ask colleagues for references. You can also find companies online, but again, it is best to get a recommendation from a colleague or someone at a membership organization.

Should You Accept Pet Health Insurance Policies?

Health insurance policies for pets didn't exist a few decades ago. Today, however, some pet owners are purchasing them. As a result, a large number of veterinary practices accept pet health insurance. Veterinary Pet Insurance, the nation's largest pet insurer, has seen its corporate accounts go from a mere 15 to 1,600 in the past six years. Approximately 15 percent of Veterinary Pet Insurance's policies come from its corporate accounts. A handful of corporations are covering pet healthcare as a perk to their executives.

 Fact

Only about 2 percent of pets in the United States are covered by health insurance. PetHealth Inc., another leading pet insurer, sees the industry accepting more health insurance policies. The company expects a 10 percent increase in the purchase of pet health insurance by pet owners. Noninvasive procedures such as MRIs and CAT scans have become quite common for pets. Some health insurance policies will even cover organ transplants and pacemakers for cats and dogs.

With pets being considered a part of the family, some individual pet owners also are purchasing health insurance for their animals. Still, it's a small percentage. "It's really up to an owner to decide if pet insurance is right for them," says Dr. May. "There are people who were very glad they had a pet health insurance plan when their animal got sick and they had a $5,000 bill to pay. On the other hand, an owner might pay the premiums and never need them—after all, it's insurance."

While Dr. May states that the AVMA cannot recommend one provider over another, she does warn people to find out what the policy does and does not cover. She says, "Some policies will exclude coverage for breed-specific problems. For example, if a certain breed is predisposed to a condition, they won't cover it if it occurs."

She also advises veterinarians looking into accepting health insurance policies to read the fine print. "A wellness plan is not an insurance plan," she says. "A wellness plan is sort of a package plan that includes the visits, exams, and routine care for the year at a discounted fee. If the animal becomes ill, the wellness plan will not cover treatment of that illness."

Bookkeeping

Your eye is on the big picture. You are focused on the job, not the mundane activities that are needed to run a successful business. Animal trainers don't usually learn about bookkeeping at school. Instead the focus is on animal care and behaviors. That makes a lot of sense. However, if you are a consultant or a small business owner, knowing about the day-to-day operations of running a business is vital to the success of your company.

You might say to yourself, "but I'm not a business owner." If you run a veterinary clinic or a doggie daycare center, you are a business owner. Consultants who work out of a home office also must keep on top of paperwork, bills, and invoices. If the terms "balance sheets" and "income statements" make your eyes glaze over, it's time to turn to an accountant for help.

It's a wise idea to take a basic business course. It may seem obvious that clients won't pay if you don't send out invoices. That's where bookkeeping comes in. It's important to keep track of the money that comes in, goes out, and is billed to clients. You really have to play an active role in keeping track of all financial transactions.

It's also essential to keep on top of getting paid for your services. Send out invoices as soon as you can—preferably within twenty-four hours of services rendered. On the invoice, include a due date, which is usually thirty days. If a check isn't sent within that time frame, it is important to send out a reminder invoice with a polite note stating that interest will be charged if the bill isn't paid by a specified date. You can also follow up with a phone call.

E *ssential*

To guarantee that you get paid on time, have people pay you by credit card as soon as the work is complete. Accepting credit cards will cost you a few percentage points, but you will be paid promptly. Also ask clients for the dates of their bill-paying cycles. If they send out payments on the fifteenth of the month, and your invoice gets to them on the sixteenth, you will have to wait a month to get paid. It's best to send out invoices as soon as the job is done.

Types of Licenses and Exams You Will Need

Some animal-related careers require you to have a license to practice. Licenses are different for each profession. Veterinarian and veterinary technicians both need licenses to work. Veterinarians who work in food inspection and agriculture are required to get a license different from that of a vet who runs a small clinic treating cats and dogs. You apply for your license, for which you must pass an exam, after completing your degree program.

To become a board-certified equine surgeon, an animal dentist, or other specialist, you will have to satisfy additional residency training requirements and pass another exam. Exams vary from state to state. If you are licensed to practice in New York State and move to Vermont, you will have to pass an exam to run your veterinary clinic in Vermont. Each state licenses veterinarians and veterinary technicians separately.

Question

What is the difference between a DVM (Doctor of Veterinary Medicine) and a VMD (Veterinary Medical Doctor)?
Basically there is no difference between the two. They are equivalent degrees. A VMD is someone who graduated from the University of Pennsylvania, and a DVM is someone who graduated from another accredited school in the United States or Canada.

The North American Veterinary Licensing Exam is an eight-hour test that consists of 360 multiple-choice questions. Since licenses vary from state to state, so do the exam questions. The questions found on these examinations cover all aspects of veterinary medicine. These exams also have a section that tests one's diagnostic skills. For more information about veterinary and veterinary specialty licenses, contact the AVMA at *www.avma.org*.

If you work for a government-sponsored agency on the state or federal level, you may be asked to take and pass a civil service exam that is specific to your job. Mounted police officers and K-9 police trainers also must pass civil service exams. Not every agency requires these exams, but some do.

In the state of New York, as well as in other states, some civil service exams are scheduled on an annual basis. Other examinations are held on a continual basis if a position needs to be filled. Most civil service exams are multiple-choice questions that relate directly to specific jobs. In addition to the multiple-choice test, other parts of the exam includes an essay, an oral test, a performance test, a computer-administered test, and an evaluation of training and experience.

Acting as a True Professional

The way you interact with people can make or break a career. Everyone in this business knows that even though you are dealing with animals on a day-to-day basis, you are also working with people. Showing respect to others and listening to their opinions—even though those viewpoints differ from yours—demonstrates a willingness to get along with others. Professional conduct comes down to treating others the way you want to be treated.

Learning how to be a professional should start before you get your job. If you are immersed in studies, you should also become aware of people in your profession. Is there anyone you admire? Take your cues from a mentor or by observing others in the field you want to enter. If people in your desired profession wear suits, dress the part.

Remember your manners. This seems like such a simple thought. A kind greeting or a sincere thank-you really goes a long way. Addressing colleagues and clients by their names shows respect.

A professional attitude and good manners go hand in hand. In addition to looking and acting the part, professionals should use good manners in every situation—from writing polite e-mails to being on time for meetings. You shouldn't substitute e-mails for interaction. If you have a question or an idea, talk to your coworkers, boss, or employees. The same goes for interacting with clients. Sure, e-mail is fast, but it is a good idea to pick up the phone every once in a while to keep the business relationship friendly.

Stick with a professional attitude after-hours, too. Treat others with respect even when you are away from the office. Poor business etiquette puts you in a bad light. When people don't respect you, they won't look up to you as a leader, and in turn your business will suffer. Good business etiquette is about being comfortable and making others feel comfortable around you.

CHAPTER 21

Taking Good Care of Yourself

Everyone—even people who have found their dream jobs—must take good care of themselves. The majority of people who work with animals tend to work long hours. Sometimes they forget about eating lunch or taking a much-needed break. Work that you love should not make you ill. It is necessary to be proactive about your health so you can take excellent care of the animals you work with, help your coworkers, and run a successful business.

Expect to Get Sick Sometimes

No one wants to be ill. However, you start your day early, you skip lunch, you stay late, and you don't take any breaks. The work will always be there, but when it comes to healing sick animals, delivering a newborn, or completing a grant application before the deadline, you know you have to get the work done—even if that means not taking a break. Everyone does it, but you should know that your health is at stake. Breaks are necessary in order to complete a task—and complete it well.

"After a break you come back refreshed and ready to do the work," says Ulla Anneli, RN. "Take a walk. Do something to prevent stress buildup and mental fatigue. A break can just be a few minutes. You can sit at your desk and do short meditations, a visualization, or neck roll. Or get up and stretch. These brief breaks always provide immediate relief."

"It's also important to eat well," Anneli adds. "Watch your diet. Have some herbal tea or water at your desk. Snacks can include fresh fruit, a yogurt, or nut mix with dried fruit. These are quick pick-me-ups. When we are overworked, we tend to grab the wrong things to eat. Cut out the fat and sugary foods."

Many people don't want to take breaks because they fear they will break the routine and it will be harder to return to work. That's a common myth. If you are worried about taking too much time, set a timer for five or ten minutes. After a quick walk or stretch, you will be refreshed and better able to take on the work that is ahead of you.

Know that sometimes it is necessary to take time off. If you are sick, stay home. Your colleagues will appreciate your concern for their health as well. No one wants to work around a contagious, sneezing, coughing person. When you don't feel well, you won't be able to give 100 percent of yourself to the job. By pushing yourself, you will only extend your poor health. A day or two of rest goes a long way. When your body gets sick with a common cold or flu, it is telling you to slow down. Listen to it. After taking sick leave, you will return eager and better able to tackle the job.

Managing Stress and Burnout

The work you have always enjoyed can soon become a burden if you do too much or take on more than you can handle. Positive stress can turn into negative stress. "Positive stress motivates you," says Anneli. "However, if you are not getting enough sleep or rest or if you are not eating well and doing too much, you will soon burn out. That is why we have vacation days and work hours. True, sometimes you will have to work overtime. But when you do, you must take another day or even a half a day off to recharge."

The good news is that most people who work with animals are happy. However, even those who love their jobs can feel overwhelmed at times. When a veterinarian is called in at 2 A.M. to assist with the delivery of a foal or calf, it is both exciting and exhausting. The veterinarian might have to work regular hours later that day. Maybe there is an important meeting that he must attend.

The trick is not only to have scheduled time off, but to actually take the time. It's easy to save vacation days. Maybe you will even get paid for working on those days. In the long run, though, it is wiser to take an occasional day off.

 Fact

According to a study from Expedia.com, Americans don't take enough vacations. They often accumulate unclaimed vacation days each year. When they do take vacations, they are more able and inclined to take work with them thanks to hotel computer hookups, laptops, and cell phones.

Did you know that vacations promote creativity? When you are relaxed and happy, you can easily reconnect with your creative side. Those who take regular vacations don't experience burnout, and they are more productive than those who never take time off.

In addition to taking regular vacations, try to take a few minutes each day to do something that makes you feel happy. Practicing yoga, tai chi, or exercising at the gym are great stress busters. You have to find what works for you. It could be singing or playing a musical instrument. Walking, running, or playing a team sport also reduces tension.

If you are working overtime all of the time, talk to your supervisor before burnout sets in. If you are self-employed, you can say no to clients. Don't take on more than you can handle. It's better to have three or four clients that you will work hard for than seven or eight. Three or four clients are manageable. You can devote enough time to each client and come up with results that will please everyone. With more clients than you can handle, the work will undoubtedly suffer. Aim to have a good work/life balance. This way you will enjoy both your work and your life.

Be Proactive about Your Own Health

The best way to take care of your health is to be a well-rounded person. That means taking good care of your body. That is so simply said, but with all of the temptations around in life, it is not always easy advice to follow. The downward cycle is to work long hours, grab anything to fill you up, and skip exercise. Many Americans follow that pattern.

Making changes requires taking one step at a time. Start by taking breaks at work and going home promptly at the end of the day. Try to limit overtime when possible. Bring in a bagged lunch. If you do eat out, choose healthy foods over high-fat, sugary treats. Allow yourself to indulge every once in a while. Drink plenty of water, and get a full eight hours of sleep each night.

E ssential

Fight tunnel vision. Being a vet or an animal trainer or a dog walker is great. Just remember, that is only one part of who you are. Develop other interests. Find a hobby, read a good book, or cook an elegant meal. The idea is to broaden your tastes. You will be a much more interesting person, and a better worker.

On the job, ask for help if you need it. People will respect you for it, and in time you will be able to master the job on your own. Asking for help is better than botching a job. If you are on overload, create a schedule. Set aside an hour each day to do the busy work, such as filing or writing reports. This way, these projects won't accumulate.

When you are away from work, schedule time to relax and reconnect with friends and family. Go to a museum or take in a movie. Do something that makes you happy. The body/mind connection is quite real. Aim for a balanced lifestyle at work and at home.

Saying No to Work

How can you say no to more work if you are self-employed? More work equals more money. Saying no can also be difficult for those employed by a company. After all, you want to move up in the ranks. It's true that showing initiative and taking on more challenging projects will get you noticed by those who are in a position to boost your career. However, there are times when you have to say no, and you can do so without feeling guilty.

Is your plate piled too high with deadlines, meetings, and reports? Are you doing the job of two or maybe three people? Do you sometimes think you should bring a cot to the office, because you feel like you are there around the clock? Before it gets to that level, learn to say no both at work and at home.

This, once again, comes down to juggling and balance. First you have to prioritize. Start by making a list of what needs to get done. Yes, it is important to volunteer outside of work at your child's school. However, don't volunteer to create all of the costumes for the school play unless you actually have the time to do it. Instead, volunteer to do something that takes less time. Maybe you can offer to bake something for your child's class party.

On the job, do you have to attend each and every meeting when deadlines are looming? Talk to your supervisor to see if you can skip one or two of these meetings. Maybe he can fill you in with a summation at a later time.

The problem most people have with saying no is that they feel selfish and guilty. Saying no is not a selfish act. In fact, it's quite liberating when done correctly. You have to remember that saying no doesn't mean you are not helping out. In fact, saying no will guarantee that you will do a better job on the projects you have said yes to. By not taking on additional projects, you can focus all of your attention to what's on your plate—thereby doing a better job.

There will be times, of course, when you will feel that you should say yes to taking on a project. Just be sure to ask yourself if you can do the job quickly and without it taking too much time away from more important projects.

E ssential

Managers and business owners must also learn to say no. If you are heading up a company or a department, you have people who are working for the team. That means you can delegate. It's true that not everyone will do the job in the exact fashion that you want. Everyone is unique. Your team, with your guidance, will be able to do the best job possible.

When saying no to a project, follow through by adding a solid reason why you can't take on additional work. Just tell the truth. If your current workload will suffer, be honest. Most employers are reasonable and will understand.

Leave the Job at Work

People who excel in their jobs often have hobbies and other interests outside the work setting. Even if you adore your job, you will like it more when you develop other interests. Just think of the phrase "absence makes the heart grow fonder." When you miss something you love, you will appreciate it more when you return to it. That sentiment holds true for work, coworkers, and friends.

Whether you had a great day or a tough one at work, it's important to leave the job at the office. It's okay to share work stories with spouses and friends. You might have an interesting story to tell about a bear you spotted in the wild while leading a nature walk. Maybe you were able to train a dog that was jumping up on everyone it greeted. It's great talking about the work you love, but it's important to give it a rest at times.

Following are a few tips on how to leave work at the office:

- Turn off cell phones and don't answer the landline at night.
- Make plans to meet friends after work.
- Before you go home, spend an hour at the gym to unwind. When you enter your home, you will be focused on your family.
- Hire a babysitter to watch the kids. This way you can go out for a nice meal or even do your grocery shopping in the evening. The store won't be as crowded, and you won't waste part of your weekend shopping.
- Treat your commute home as your personal time. If you are in the car, turn to your favorite music station. Listen to a book on tape. If you take public transportation, read a book or favorite magazine.
- If you need to rant, do it on the drive home in the privacy of your own car. This way, you won't take it home to your family. If you take public transportation, write down your frustrations. Let it go before you walk in the front door and greet your family.

Learn to manage your time. At the end of your work day, write a list of things that have to be done the next day. Prioritize from most important to the least significant. If a major project is presented to you the next morning, hold on to the list for the following day. Talk to your supervisor and ask him if this new project has to be done now or if it can be passed on to someone else. You can even show him the list of duties that you have to get done. By putting your projects in order, you can tackle them one by one—and it feels good to cross things off your list.

If you work out of a home office, be sure to turn off the computer at the end of the day. This way you won't be tempted to look at e-mails. If possible, close the office door, and don't go in until the next morning. Try to separate work from home.

Express Your Emotions

Everyone experiences emotions at work. You can show enthusiasm and even anger. If a pet is in distress, you will feel upset. If a coworker isn't pulling his weight, you can get annoyed. When you have too much to do, you feel overwhelmed. When things are going smoothly and you just accomplished a major task, you most likely will talk about it and pat yourself on the back. The key is to express your emotions, let the angry ones go, and move on.

If it is possible to change a problem at work, talk to a coworker or supervisor. Remember that you are a valued employee, and if you are part of a team it is in the best interest of your supervisor to make sure everyone on the team is content. If you are a boss who is unhappy with an employee's job performance, gently explain why you are less than pleased. Work out a plan to rectify the situation. Self-employed workers can use the same advice. If your client is asking you to do more than you originally agreed, or if that client is late in paying you, talk to him.

 Fact

The "count to ten" rule works most of the time. If you are frustrated on the job by a coworker or problem that arose, count to ten before speaking. This quick method allows you time to calm down, think, and approach the situation in a less than combative manner. You will be more focused and better able to handle the situation.

If things are getting out of hand, find a quiet place to vent. You don't want to blow your professional image by having others see you ranting and raving. Set a time limit on your rant; it shouldn't be more than five minutes. By the end of the five-minute rant, you will have a better handle on your emotions and will be ready to move on to more important jobs.

You can also express yourself in writing. Jot down your feelings. If you are planning to write an angry letter, wait a full day before sending it. You will probably want to destroy the letter once you've had time to cool off and review the situation. Hit the delete button on your computer, or tear up a written note.

While you are putting your feelings down on paper, also write about the positives. Look at the entire situation to see what's working. By focusing on the constructive aspects of the job as well as the negative, you can come up with better solutions.

Don't forget to express affirmative feelings. Let coworkers and employees know that you are proud of the work they turned in. Tell a supervisor that you really admire the way he handled a project or difficult customer. Just be honest and sincere.

CHAPTER 22

Keeping Your Dream Job Fresh

Getting a dream job is a little like falling in love. When you first fall, your heart does somersaults. Being around animals, just like the stages of a new romance, is exciting. Your energy level is high. Plus, you are full of enthusiasm. Your new job is perfect. The pay is decent. The hours are okay. You are helping animals, and learning so much about their habits and behaviors. Even your coworkers are helpful and nice. You have a lot in common. What more could you ask for?

When Reality Sets In

The second stage of a relationship is reality. Sometimes what at first seems charming can become annoying. How did it get like this? This is the perfect job for you. You might find that you don't have enough time to complete certain tasks. You might be bogged down with rules and paperwork. True, being around the animals makes it all worthwhile, but disillusionment is starting to occur. As corny as this may seem, a job is a lot like a relationship. You get exactly what you put into it, and it takes work to come as close to perfection as possible.

It's quite possible to rekindle the flame. If you hate writing reports, do them in the morning to get them out of the way. Then make your rounds with the animals. Constantly challenge yourself to learn new things about the animals and your clients. Ask your boss if you can take on a new project if it interests you. Maybe you can assist someone in another department with a project that you can work on part-time—just as long as it doesn't interfere with your current job duties. New ideas are always a good motivator for keeping work fresh.

E ssential

Redecorate your office or cubicle. Rearranging the furniture, hanging up a favorite photo, or getting rid of the clutter can brighten up a tired-looking space. Also, bring in a potted plant. Plants soak up CO_2, freshen the air, and make people feel better.

Become a speaker or mentor to someone. By staying on top of your career and helping others, you will bring back the excitement of falling in love with your career all over again. It's great to see a career through the eyes of someone who is new to it. You know that excitement. Combining that with your experience will help others. When you take on a role as a speaker or mentor, you will have to brush up on the things you know and learn even more about your profession. Now, that's exciting!

Teach and Learn from Others

Good teachers learn from their students. Whether you are teaching a class or workshop or mentoring one person, you can gain a lot of expertise by listening to and observing your students. That same sentiment applies to directors, bosses, and business owners and their employees. By talking to clients and listening to their ideas, you can learn to look at your job in a different light. Being open to new ideas is a great way to keep your job from becoming stale.

Teaching can have such a positive impact on your work. Working as a part-time professor or instructor enables you to reconnect to your profession in a fresh manner. By teaching students, you get to keep on top of the latest cutting-edge technology in your field. Your students can challenge you with questions that will make you think differently about your job.

 Fact

The American Association of University Professors has found that the number of adjunct professors has more than doubled in the past twenty years. They cite economics as the main reason. Student enrollment at many universities and community colleges may be up, but these institutions are facing budget problems. Hiring people who work in the field to teach as adjunct professors is an affordable way to educate their students.

Adjunct professors tend to earn considerably less than full-time professors—usually $1,500 to $4,500 per course. Often there are no benefits. However, compensation isn't the impetus for people to teach on a part-time basis. According to the U.S. National Science Foundation, almost 41 percent of scientists with PhDs are teaching as adjuncts. These adjuncts already have full-time jobs. They are teaching because they enjoy it, and because they are constantly benefiting from new ideas gathered in the classroom. The situation is often positive for students, too, because many top-level students can learn about job leads from their part-time professors.

In most cases, a course runs for fourteen weeks, meeting once each week for two to three hours. That doesn't include prep time or the time required to read and grade papers and exams.

The research involved with preparing a class also takes time. However, most people who work as adjunct professors find that teaching makes them better scientists, veterinarians, behaviorists, and so on. Partly that is because you have to read everything—even materials that are slightly out of your niche.

It's great having an audience. Some teachers view teaching as being on a stage before an audience. Being an effective teacher gives you the tools to make a difference in your business and community. It keeps you in touch with all of the aspects of your job, and also boosts your ego.

To become an adjunct professor, you need a bachelor's degree, an updated resume, and reference letters. If you've written any books or articles or edited any newsletters specific to your profession, mention them when you contact the school. Apply to community colleges, trade schools, four-year colleges, and universities in your area.

Set Career Goals

From the time you knew you wanted to work with animals, you had goals. Some of your first goals were finishing and excelling in school. Your next goal, after graduation, was to obtain an entry-level job and then move on to your dream job. That too has been accomplished. Now that you are working in your ideal job, you should establish new goals. Even if your job is pure perfection, it is good to challenge yourself with new goals.

It is important to dream big. Most career counselors tell students and people who are changing jobs to have realistic goals. While there is a lot of truth to that, it is a good idea to introduce outrageous goals every once in a while. A goal that others see as impractical can have a positive effect. It's not about being practical. It's about pushing yourself beyond your limitations. You are learning along the way. If you don't try, you will always wonder. It's self-affirming to challenge yourself. Goals provide direction in work and in life. They also teach us a bit about ourselves. Each step toward your goal is an accomplishment, and you should reward yourself. Think of each step as an achievement bringing you closer to your final goal.

The first step in setting goals is to define them. Write down your goals and the steps you need to take along the way to make your goals happen. When you write down your goals, you have a clear guide to follow. If you only keep these goals in your head, you will constantly change them. A good written plan helps identify the course of action that you will need to take to make your goals a reality. Be as clear and specific as possible. Keep a timeline, and write down dates for accomplishing some of these goals.

Along the way, you may face some setbacks. Don't let them discourage you. Keep on track and stay focused. When things go awry, figure out why and implement new strategies to get you back on track. You might want to partner with someone to help you with your goals. For example, if you want to expand your veterinary clinic or retail pet shop, you might want to find a business partner.

E ssential

It's a good idea to involve others to help you with your goals. It's okay to ask for assistance and support from friends, family, and business colleagues—especially if they have experience in your field. Just realize that everyone needs help along the way and that many people are eager to share their expertise.

Be positive when planning and working toward your goals. Draw on your past achievements, and carefully regard each step along the way. You might find that you are being pulled in one direction toward another opportunity. Be open to all options, and know that each step brings you closer to achieving success.

Provide New Services

The key to keeping clients happy and coming back is to offer new programs, flexible hours, the latest technology, and, of course, exemplary service. Providing exceptional service is the most important part of running a business. It sounds obvious, but if you don't do it, clients will take their business elsewhere. Offering services that your competitors don't have also gives you an edge. The animal care industry is always changing. You need to be aware of those changes and to utilize them when needed.

If you run a doggie daycare center or a pet shop, make special offers to your customers.

You can offer a two-for-one service to your clients who have two pets. Instead of charging them $80 to board each dog per day, charge them $140 to board two dogs. You can also hold special sales in your store, and host special events for which you bring in experts to talk about pet care. Once your customers are in your store or business, there is a good likelihood that they will make purchases.

Veterinarians and veterinary technicians should be aware that many people are turning to alternative medicine for themselves and their pets. Many mainstream medical practices are incorporating acupuncture and other forms of alternative medicine because there is a demand for such treatments. The veterinary medical field is following that lead by offering pet massage, Reiki, pet acupuncture, and other alternative health procedures for dogs, cats, and horses.

 Fact

Did you know that every state has different guidelines and regulations regarding alternative medical practices? To find out what is allowed in your state, check with the International Association of Animal Massage & Bodywork (*www.iaamb.org*) or the International Association of Animal Massage Therapists (*www.iaamt.com*).

Many schools now offer certification programs in massage training, acupuncture, and other forms of alternative medicine for animals. The Northwest School of Animal Massage in the state of Washington is just one of many schools that offer classroom-based and distance-learning programs for people interested in massage therapy for dogs, cats, horses, and livestock. The distance-learning program includes a practical hands-on component.

Many veterinarians and massage therapists have been working with horses for ages. Massage therapy and other modalities are new for dogs and cats. Some veterinarians have witnessed the benefits of pet massage on a dog or cat. By having specialists on call, veterinarians have another option for bringing more services and benefits to their clients.

Learn from and Team Up with Corporations

It's quite possible for a small business to compete against a behemoth. However, instead of competing, try finding ways to gain the advantages that larger companies have. If you own a small pet shop, form an alliance with other small pet shops in your neighborhood. It's a great way to level the playing field. Larger companies have greater purchasing power. It is cheaper for them to buy the same supplies that you sell in your store because they are buying in bulk. By teaming up with other small pet shops in your neighborhood, you will increase your buying power and save money.

 Fact

To keep employees happy, more and more corporations are adding pet care services to their employee incentive packages. When a person who lives in another state is hired or when an employee is transferred to an affiliate branch overseas, a corporation may pay a pet relocation service to safely ship pets to be with their owners in their new homes.

If you are self-employed, you can team up with large corporations by offering them employee discounts. Some doggie daycare centers are teaming up with corporations that have offices in their neighborhoods to provide pet sitting and daycare services for the corporation's employees. It's not that different from corporate packages that offer childcare services, with the corporation paying a portion of the fees.

Kevin O'Brien, co-owner of PetRelocation.com, has linked his business to many leading corporations. "The cost of relocating you and your family to a new job across the country or overseas is often covered by large corporations," says O'Brien. "Since people consider their pets family members, many corporations are paying to safely relocate the family pet. So, it makes sense for a company like mine to hook up with a large corporation.">

Salary Guide

It has been discussed throughout this book that people in this industry are in it because they love animals. The money isn't a driving factor for becoming a veterinarian, vet tech, animal behaviorist, or any other type of animal care professional. Some people leave corporate jobs with high salaries for a better lifestyle and decent income because they want to work with animals. An economist formerly at a large corporation now earns considerably less at her current job as an economist at the Humane Society of the United States. A former banker is earning more as a dog trainer. Both are much happier.

Salaries for animal care professionals range from low to quite comfortable, depending on the job, experience, and geographic location. For an exact breakdown of salaries for first-year veterinarians, log onto *www.avma.org/reference/marketstats/1yremploy.asp*. There you will find the 2007 figures from the American Veterinary Medical Association. The figures range from low ($23,000) to mid ($55,000) to high (above $75,000).

The same salary logic of job, location, and experience also applies to marine biologists, biological scientists, ecologists, oceanographers, and zoologists. Among government workers, federal-level employees tend to make about $5,000 a year more than state workers. For example, a zoologist who works for the federal government can earn a median salary of $90,000, while a state-employed zoologist can earn $85,000 a year.

 Fact

Ask anyone who works with animals and they will tell you that job satisfaction is their number one concern. Being happy outweighs earning a high salary. Most people in an animal-related field live comfortable lives and know their priorities.

The truth of the old adage that money can't buy happiness depends on the person. People who work in this profession have passion and drive, a positive outlook on life, and a great quality of life. If you love animals, there is nothing better than having a career working with them.

Appendix A
Additional Resources

American Beekeeping Federation
P.O. Box 1337
Jessup, GA 31598-1038
912-427-4233
www.abfnet.org

American Board of Forensic Entomology
Sponsored by the
Office of Research
University of
Missouri–Columbia
www.research.missouri .edu/entomology

American Farrier's Association
4059 Iron Works Pkwy. Suite 1
Lexington, KY 40511
859-233-7411
www.americanfarriers.org

American Hippotherapy Association
P.O. Box 6230
Scottsdale, AZ 85261
602-992-1570
www.americanequestrian .com/hippotherapy.htm

American Honey Producers
www.americanhoney producers.org

American Pet Products Association
APPA, 255 Glenville Road
Greenwich, CT 06831
800-452-1225
www.americanpetproducts.org

Animal Behavior Society
Indiana University
2611 East 10th Street, #170
Bloomington, IN 47408-2603
www.animalbehavior.org

The College Board
45 Columbus Avenue
New York, NY 10023-6992
212-713-8000
www.collegeboard.com

Earthwatch Institute International Headquarters
3 Clock Tower Place, Suite 100
Box 75
Maynard, MA 01754
1-800-776-0188
www.earthwatch.org

The Entomological Foundation
9332 Annapolis Road, Suite 210
Lanham, MD 20706
301- 459-9082
www.entfdn.org

Entomological Society of America
10001 Derekwood Lane
Suite 100
Lanham, MD 20706-4876
301-731-4535
www.entsoc.org

Independent Pet and Animal Transportation Association
745 Winding Trail
Holly Lake Ranch
Texas 75755
903-769-2267
www.ipata.com

The International Ecotourism Society
1333 H St., NW
Suite 300, East Tower
Washington, DC 20005
202-347-9203
www.ecotourism.org

Jockeys' Guild, Inc.
103 Wind Haven Drive, Suite 200
Nicholasville, KY 40356
www.jockeysguild.com

National Association of County Agricultural Agents
252 N. Park Street,
Decatur, IL 62523
217- 424-5144
www.nacaa.com

National Geographic Society
1145 17th Street N.W.
Washington, DC 20036-4688
www.nationalgeographic.com

National Honey Board
11409 Business Park
Circle, Suite 210
Firestone, CO 80504
303-776-2337
www.honey.com

Pal-O-Mine Equestrian, Inc.
829 Old Nichols Road
Islandia, NY 11749
631-348-1389
www.pal-o-mine.org

Peterson's College Guides
Princeton Pike Corporate Center
2000 Lenox Drive
P.O. Box 67005
Lawrenceville, NJ 08648
609-896-1800
www.petersons.com

Six Flags Great Adventure & Wild Safari
P.O. Box 120, Route 537
Jackson, NJ 08527
732-928-1821
www.sixflags
.com/GreatAdventure

Thoroughbred Owners and Breeders Association
P.O. Box 910668
Lexington, KY 40591-0668
859-276-2291
www.toba.org

U.S. Department of Labor, Bureau of Labor Statistics
www.bls.gov

Other Helpful Websites

College Board
Information on SAT and ACT college entrance exams, links to financial aid, and information about other college entrance exams
www.collegeboard.com

Free Application for Federal Student Aid
Has an online financial aid application
www.fafsa.ed.gov

FinAid
A good website for financial aid information
www.finaid.org

Graduate Record Exam
For GRE information
www.gre.org

Appendix B
Veterinary Schools

The following schools are accredited by the American Veterinary Medical Association in the United States and Canada:

Alabama

Auburn University
College of Veterinary Medicine
104 J. E. Greene Hall
Auburn University,
AL 36849-5517
334-844-4546
Status: Full Accreditation
Last Evaluation: 2005
Next Evaluation: 2012
SAVMA Chapter: Yes
www.vetmed.auburn.edu

Tuskegee University
School of Veterinary Medicine
Tuskegee, AL 36088
334-727-8174
Status: Full Accreditation
Last Evaluation: 2006
Next Evaluation: 2012
SAVMA Chapter: Yes
www.tuskegee.edu

California

University of California
School of Veterinary Medicine
Davis, CA 95616-8734
530-752-1360
Status: Full Accreditation
Last Evaluation: 2004
Next Evaluation: 2011
SAVMA Chapter: Yes
www.vetmed.ucdavis.edu

Western University of Health Sciences
College of Veterinary Medicine
309 E. Second Street—
College Plaza
Pomona, CA 91766-1854
909-469-5628
Status: Provisional Accreditation
Last Evaluation: 2007
Next Evaluation: 2010
www.westernu.edu/veterinary

Colorado
Colorado State University
College of Veterinary Medicine
and Biomedical Sciences
Fort Collins, CO 80523-1601
970-491-7051
Status: Full Accreditation
Last Evaluation: 2008
Next Evaluation: 2014
SAVMA Chapter: Yes
www.cvmbs.colostate.edu

Illinois
University of Illinois
College of Veterinary Medicine
2001 South Lincoln Avenue
Urbana, IL 61802
217-333-2760
Status: Full Accreditation
Last Evaluation: 2006
Next Evaluation: 2013
SAVMA Chapter: Yes
www.cvm.uiuc.edu

Florida
University of Florida
College of Veterinary Medicine
PO Box 100125
Gainesville, FL 32610-0125
352-392-2213
Status: Full Accreditation
Last Evaluation: 2008
Next Evaluation: 2013
SAVMA Chapter: Yes
www.vetmed.ufl.edu

Indiana
Purdue University
School of Veterinary Medicine
1240 Lynn Hall
West Lafayette, IN 47907-1240
765-494-7607
Status: Full Accreditation
Last Evaluation: 2004
Next Evaluation: 2011
SAVMA Chapter: Yes
www.vet.purdue.edu

Georgia
University of Georgia
College of Veterinary Medicine
Athens, GA 30602
706-542-3461
Status: Full Accreditation
Last Evaluation: 2006
Next Evaluation: 2013
SAVMA Chapter: Yes
www.vet.uga.edu

Iowa
Iowa State University
College of Veterinary Medicine
Ames, IA 50011
515-294-1242
Status: Full Accreditation
Last Evaluation: 2006
Next Evaluation: 2010
SAVMA Chapter: Yes
www.vetmed.iastate.edu

Kansas

Kansas State University
College of Veterinary Medicine
Manhattan, KS 66506
785-532-5660
Status: Full Accreditation
Last Evaluation: 2003
Next Evaluation: 2010
SAVMA Chapter: Yes
www.vet.ksu.edu

Louisiana

Louisiana State University
School of Veterinary Medicine
Baton Rouge, LA 70803-8402
225-578-9900
Status: Full Accreditation
Last Evaluation: 2005
Next Evaluation: 2012
SAVMA Chapter: Yes
www.vetmed.lsu.edu

Massachusetts

Tufts University
Cummings School of Veterinary Medicine
200 Westboro Road
North Grafton, MA 01536
508-839-5302
Status: Full Accreditation
Last Evaluation: 2004
Next Evaluation: 2011
SAVMA Chapter: Yes
www.tufts.edu/vet

Michigan

Michigan State University
College of Veterinary Medicine
G-100 Veterinary Medical Center
East Lansing, MI 48824-1314
517-355-6509
Status: Full Accreditation
Last Evaluation: 2005
Next Evaluation: 2012
SAVMA Chapter: Yes
http://cvm.msu.edu

Minnesota

University of Minnesota
College of Veterinary Medicine
1365 Gortner Avenue
St. Paul, MN 55108
612-624-9227
Status: Full Accreditation
Last Evaluation: 2007
Next Evaluation: 2014
SAVMA Chapter: Yes
www.cvm.umn.edu

Mississippi

Mississippi State University
College of Veterinary Medicine
Mississippi State, MS 39762
662-325-3432
Status: Full Accreditation
Last Evaluation: 2007
Next Evaluation: 2012
SAVMA Chapter: Yes
www.cvm.msstate.edu

Missouri

University of Missouri–Columbia
College of Veterinary Medicine
Columbia, MO 65211
573-882-3877
Status: Full Accreditation
Last Evaluation: 2006
Next Evaluation: 2013
SAVMA Chapter: Yes
www.cvm.missouri.edu

New York

Cornell University
College of Veterinary Medicine
Ithaca, NY 14853-6401
607-253-3700
Status: Full Accreditation
Last Evaluation: 2003
Next Evaluation: 2010
SAVMA Chapter: Yes
www.vet.cornell.edu

North Carolina

North Carolina State University
College of Veterinary Medicine
4700 Hillsborough Street
Raleigh, NC 27606
919-513-6210
Status: Full Accreditation
Last Evaluation: 2007
Next Evaluation: 2014
SAVMA Chapter: Yes
www.cvm.ncsu.edu

Ohio

Ohio State University
College of Veterinary Medicine
1900 Coffey Road
Columbus, OH 43210-1092
614-292-1171
Status: Full Accreditation
Last Evaluation: 2006
Next Evaluation: 2012
SAVMA Chapter: Yes
www.vet.ohio-state.edu

Oklahoma

Oklahoma State University
Center for Veterinary
Health Sciences
Stillwater, OK 74078
405-744-6595
Status: Full Accreditation
Last Evaluation: 2003
Next Evaluation: 2010
SAVMA Chapter: Yes
www.cvm.okstate.edu

Oregon

Oregon State University
College of Veterinary Medicine
Corvallis, OR 97331
541-737-2098
Status: Full Accreditation
Last Evaluation: 2007
Next Evaluation: 2014
SAVMA Chapter: Yes
http://oregonstate.edu/vetmed

Pennsylvania

University of Pennsylvania
School of Veterinary Medicine
3800 Spruce Street
Philadelphia, PA 19104-6044
215-898-5438
Status: Full Accreditation
Last Evaluation: 2002
Next Evaluation: 2009
SAVMA Chapter: Yes
www.vet.upenn.edu

Tennessee

University of Tennessee
College of Veterinary Medicine
2407 River Drive
Knoxville, TN 37996
865-974-7262
Status: Full Accreditation
Last Evaluation: 2008
Next Evaluation: 2014
SAVMA Chapter: Yes
www.vet.utk.edu

Texas

Texas A&M University
College of Veterinary Medicine & Biomedical Sciences
College Station, TX 77843-4461
979-845-5051
Status: Full Accreditation
Last Evaluation: 2008
Next Evaluation: 2014
SAVMA Chapter: Yes
www.cvm.tamu.edu

Virginia/Maryland

Virginia Tech
Virginia-Maryland Regional College of Veterinary Medicine
Blacksburg, VA 24061-0442
540-231-7666
Status: Full Accreditation
Last Evaluation: 2007
Next Evaluation: 2014
SAVMA Chapter: Yes
www.vetmed.vt.edu

Washington

Washington State University
College of Veterinary Medicine
Pullman, WA 99164-7010
509-335-9515
Status: Full Accreditation
Last Evaluation: 2003
Next Evaluation: 2010
SAVMA Chapter: Yes
www.vetmed.wsu.edu

Wisconsin

University of Wisconsin–Madison
School of Veterinary Medicine
2015 Linden Drive West
Madison, WI 53706-1102
608-263-6716
Status: Full Accreditation
Last Evaluation: 2008
Next Evaluation: 2014
SAVMA Chapter: Yes
www.vetmed.wisc.edu

Canada

Calgary

University of Calgary
Faculty of Veterinary Medicine
Calgary, AB T2N 4N1
Canada
403-210-3961
Status: Letter of Reason-
able Assurance
Last Evaluation: 2007
Next Evaluation: to
be determined
www.vet.ucalgary.ca

Ontario

University of Guelph
Ontario Veterinary College
Guelph, ON N1G 2W1
Canada
519-824-4120
Status: Full Accreditation
Last Evaluation: 2002
Next Evaluation: 2009
SAVMA Chapter: No
www.ovc.uoguelph.ca

Prince Edward Island

University of Prince Edward Island
Atlantic Veterinary College
550 University Avenue
Charlottetown, PE C1A 4P3
Canada
902-566-0882
Status: Full Accreditation

Last Evaluation: 2004
Next Evaluation: 2011
SAVMA Chapter: Yes
www.upei.ca/~avc

Quebec

Université de Montréal
Faculté de médecine vétérinaire
C.P. 5000
Saint Hyacinthe, PQ J2S 7C6
Canada
450-773-8521
Status: Full Accreditation
Last Evaluation: 2006
Next Evaluation: 2012
SAVMA Chapter: No
www.medvet.umontreal.ca

Saskatchewan

University of Saskatchewan
Western College of Veterinary
Medicine
52 Campus Drive
Saskatoon, SK S7N 5B4
Canada
306-966-7447
Status: Full Accreditation
Last Evaluation: 2003
Next Evaluation: 2010
SAVMA Chapter: No
www.usask.ca/wcvm

Index

Tour guide, 161-63
Travel, 24
Typical day, 7-8

U
Universities, 39

V
Vermeeren, Doug, 34, 35-36, 40
Veterinarian, 21, 49-51
    board-certified surgeon, 55
    for large animals, 170-71
    for marine mammals, 179-81
    orthopedic veterinary
        medicine, 54-55
    research veterinarian, 53-54
    at zoological or wildlife
        park, 87-91
Veterinary
    assistant, 53
    farm technician, 171-72
    medicine careers, 49-57
    specialties, 22, 55-57
    technician, 51-53, 91-93
    technologists, 22
Vocational school, 38

W
Walton, Laura, 169-70
Wildlife
    biologist, 61-63
    center, 214-15
    conservation officer, 63-64
    rehabilitator, 68-69

Wood, Jonathan and
    Susan, 68-69
Working with other humans, 3
Work/life balance, 263-65
Writer. *See* Columnist/writer

X
Xeller, Svenja, 182-83

Z
Zarony, Chrissy, 52, 251
Zoo(s), 214-15
    designer, 101-4
    directors, 21
Zookeeper, 95-97
Zoological and wildlife parks
    careers, 87-107
    director, 21, 93-94
    educator, 97-99

The Everything® Career Guide Series

Trade Paperback, $14.95
ISBN 10: 1-59337-583-2
ISBN 13: 978-1-59337-583-6

Trade Paperback, $14.95
ISBN 10: 1-59869-227-5
ISBN 13: 978-1-59869-227-3

Trade Paperback, $14.95
ISBN 10: 1-59337-432-1
ISBN 13: 978-1-59337-432-7

Trade Paperback, $14.95
ISBN 10: 1-59337-657-X
ISBN 13: 978-1-59337-657-4

Trade Paperback, $14.95
ISBN 10: 1-59869-417-0
ISBN 13: 978-1-59869-417-8

Trade Paperback, $14.95
ISBN 10: 1-59337-725-8
ISBN 13: 978-1-59337-725-0

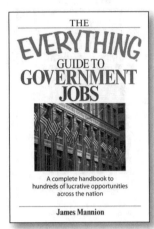